A REGIONAL HISTORY OF
THE RAILWAYS OF GREAT BRITAIN

General Editors: DAVID ST JOHN THOMAS and J. ALLAN PATMORE

VOLUME IX
THE EAST MIDLANDS

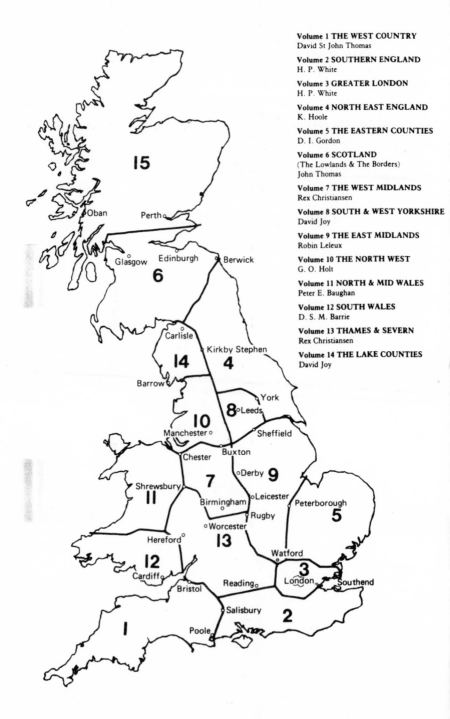

Volume 1 **THE WEST COUNTRY**
David St John Thomas

Volume 2 **SOUTHERN ENGLAND**
H. P. White

Volume 3 **GREATER LONDON**
H. P. White

Volume 4 **NORTH EAST ENGLAND**
K. Hoole

Volume 5 **THE EASTERN COUNTIES**
D. I. Gordon

Volume 6 **SCOTLAND**
(The Lowlands & The Borders)
John Thomas

Volume 7 **THE WEST MIDLANDS**
Rex Christiansen

Volume 8 **SOUTH & WEST YORKSHIRE**
David Joy

Volume 9 **THE EAST MIDLANDS**
Robin Leleux

Volume 10 **THE NORTH WEST**
G. O. Holt

Volume 11 **NORTH & MID WALES**
Peter E. Baughan

Volume 12 **SOUTH WALES**
D. S. M. Barrie

Volume 13 **THAMES & SEVERN**
Rex Christiansen

Volume 14 **THE LAKE COUNTIES**
David Joy

Frontis A veteran Midland Railway goods engine shunts the small but busy town goods yard at Basford on the outskirts of Nottingham in April 1922 when the railways were the most important carriers of general merchandise. Wagons from the Great Western and Glasgow & South Western Railways are among the different companies' vehicles in the yard showing how diverse traffic flows had become in the railway age, while in the background is the industry which was stimulated by the railway system. The Midland and Great Central Railways were responsible for much of the economic

A REGIONAL HISTORY OF
THE RAILWAYS OF GREAT BRITAIN

Volume IX
THE EAST MIDLANDS

by
Robin Leleux

WITH 31 PLATES
8 ILLUSTRATIONS IN TEXT
9 MAPS
AND FOLDING MAP

DAVID ST JOHN THOMAS
DAVID & CHARLES

British Library Cataloguing in Publication Data

Leleux, Robin
    The East Midlands—(A Regional history of
    the railways of Great Britain; v. 9)—
    2nd rev. ed.
    1. Railroads—Midlands (England)—History
    I. Title   II. Series
    385'.09424   HE3019.M/
    ISBN 0–946537–06–2

© Robin Leleux 1976, 1984

First edition published by David & Charles Limited 1976
This second, revised edition published by David St John Thomas
and distributed by David & Charles Limited

Printed by Redwood Burn Ltd, Trowbridge
Distributed in the United States of America
by David & Charles Inc
North Pomfret, Vermont, 05053, USA

Contents

CHAPTER I

Themes and Scope

Amid a fanfare of local publicity, the Mayor of Northampton flagged away the 07.46 train to London on Monday 6 May 1974, inaugurating a new express service in response to the demands of growing commuter traffic. Patrons of the other Northampton–Euston trains may wonder why the service is still of semi-fast suburban trains, rather than through expresses. Once on their way, observant passengers can enliven the journey by looking out for engineering works or the remains of branch lines. It is the purpose of this book both to chronicle these features and to discuss their significance.

History can be written in two distinct but equally valid ways, by narrative and by analysis. Railway history is no exception. The narrative approach, usually in the form of a company history, is the most common, but the impact of the railway on an area is difficult to assess unless the company virtually monopolised it. Moreover, the wider and richer the area, the greater is the probability of competing railways. Three major railways—the Midland, the Great Northern, and the Great Central—competed for traffic in the East Midlands, with a fourth, the London & North Western, active in certain areas. It is with these considerations in mind that social, economic and geographical studies, such as this series, have begun to appear in recent years.

The effects of the railways on Britain's economy, landscape and society are now better known than was the case only recently. The movement of coal was the stimulus for many lines, and other industries benefitted accordingly, stimulating further railway building. The widespread development of coal mining, iron ore quarrying, iron and steel production, and fishing was very dependent on the railways for the cheap movement of bulky goods or the fast movement of perishable goods. Light industries such as agriculture (principally grain, malt, potatoes and cattle), hosiery, boots, hats and engineering, could all reach wider markets than was possible even by the network of inland waterways. The physical growth of towns was made considerably easier by the railways, which could bring in locally-produced bricks and stone for building and street paving, window glass from Lancashire, roofing slates from Wales, timber from the Baltic ports, coal for heating and gas lighting, and food from all parts of the country. The Great Exhibition in London in 1851 was a great encouragement to railway excursion promoters, while the growing prosperity and improvements in working conditions from the 1850s enabled many to make trips to the seaside, impracticable without railways.

The aim of this book is to relate these general trends to the East Midlands, within the framework of a description of the growth and decline of this region's railways. Northampton, Leicester and Nottingham have a chapter each, while the other chapters deal separately with the areas approximately covered by Northamptonshire, Leicestershire, Derbyshire, Nottinghamshire and Lincolnshire respectively. In each chapter, opening comments on the town or county set the scene. The problems of building the early railways are then outlined. After that, the area is usually discussed by taking each line in turn, with its branches, with intermediate towns of importance being dealt with en route. The exception is the lengthy Chapter II, dealing with the northern Home Counties. Here the approach is more company-orientated, but serves as a comparison of the problems facing major railway promoters at different stages of the 'Railway Age'.

This approach necessarily leads to some repetition, as regions are no more watertight entities than are historical periods. Some readers may find this wearisome, but those who want information on a particular part of the East Midlands may read only a chapter, yet still need an introduction to relevant events already discussed. For example, the origins of the Midland Counties Railway are fully dealt with in the Leicester chapter, but as the line ran to Rugby, Derby and Nottingham, its origins are briefly referred to in the Leicestershire, Derbyshire and Nottingham chapters. Repetition has been cut to a minimum consistent with this aim. Similarly, there is some slight overlapping with other volumes in this series where it has been essential to complete the picture, as around Buxton.

What constitutes the East Midlands? Inevitably there will be dispute over the exact borders, and any division must involve anomalies. Leicestershire and Nottinghamshire are obvious, as is Derbyshire east of the Peak District. North West Derbyshire must be included from the railway point of view because of the connections between the East Midlands and the North West, although Buxton looks more to Manchester than it does to Derby. Lincolnshire must also be included as it has always looked westwards, and until the mid-twentieth century the Humber was always an effective boundary. The Doncaster–Sheffield area might be termed Midlands, but its complex railway system is part of the West Riding study. In the south, Northamptonshire has been included in government studies of both the East Midlands and the South East, while Independent Television regards part of it as East Anglia. Increasingly it is looking to London. That leaves the salient reaching south from Northamptonshire to outer London, and bounded by the Great Central on the west and the Midland on the east. It does not conveniently fit in to any region, but it can and will serve here as an introduction to the East Midlands.

There is little homogeneity about the East Midlands, especially as here delineated. Local feeling, where it persists, is parochial rather than regional, and there is no acknowledged regional 'capital'. Industry too is localised, and although there has been some industrial interdependence between parts of the region, as for example, the use of Northamptonshire iron ore in Derbyshire, markets have tended to be either local or national rather than regional.

The number of completely new towns in the East Midlands created by the railways is small, the best examples being Wolverton (railways), Coalville (coal), Skegness and Clee-thorpes (both seaside resorts). On the whole, railways followed existing lines of communications (roads or canals) between major old-established towns such as Leicester, Derby and Nottingham, and it was these which developed most. Unless a town at the end of a line had something special to offer, like the fishing port of Great Grimsby, the impact of a railway was less marked (as at Mansfield), than on towns on through lines, like Hinckley. Even so, the possession of industry was important, for Kettering was rescued from poverty by the Midland in 1857, with the consequent development of the iron industry, yet Market Harborough on the same line grew far more slowly as a market town. The same situation applied to the major towns, for Leicester and Derby grew at Nottingham's expense as they were on through routes until the Midland's new line in 1880, and undoubtedly Northampton would have grown more had it been on the main line from the beginning. Almost without exception, coaching towns were badly affected as railways took away through traffic. St Albans revived with the Midland after 1868, but Towcester and Caistor declined into obscurity.

These industrial and commercial changes involved an unprecedented movement of population. Expanding industries obviously needed increased labour, but so also did the expanding towns, in the 'service industries', while the railways were themselves great employers of skilled and unskilled manpower; as George Stephenson put it when stopped by a new ticket collector at Ambergate, 'Aa'm the man who made jobs for such as thou.'

Another side-effect of the railways was the growth of the police forces. Working-class discontent manifested itself after 1838 in the Chartist disturbances. The army was still the mainstay of public order, and in 1842 seven hundred men were sent from London to Manchester by the L & BR. The 1848 outbreak was the worst, three companies being kept on the alert at Weedon barracks ready to be rushed by rail wherever necessary. Liberal politicians felt that the extension of police forces, based on Sir Robert Peel's Metropolitan Police (1829) would be preferable, and the railways agreed, feeling that as troop carriers they were a likely target for rioters' sabotage. To prevent this in 1848 the LNWR had supported the drive for special constables, all the 478 personnel from the Wolverton works being sworn in under railway pressure.

What of the future? This book was begun as the railways were being drastically cut back following the Beeching Report (1963). Road traffic appeared invincible, and little was being done to attract back the general public. Some rationalisation of the excesses of nineteenth-century railway speculation was essential, despite railway enthusiasts bewailing the decline of the Great Central route to the Midlands. By the

1970s however, many felt that this had gone too far, and began to stress the dangers to the environment of unrestricted road transport. BR responded with greater attempts to win back patronage. Then came the 1973 oil crisis as the later stages of this book were written, followed by deepening economic recession. Immediately, road-building ceased to be seen as the panacea for all economic ills, and while the future was very uncertain, there was more hope that what was left of the East Midland's railways would have a major and continuing part to play in the region's economy.

Revision for the second edition came in 1983 in the wake of the government-inspired Serpell Report on Railway Finances. This has merely created further uncertainty over the future of the railway network, for BR's plans over the intervening decade to meet imposed government targets, for example further electrification, have been undermined by the fact that the government has responded by changing— 'revising'—the criteria. Meanwhile the system has remained virtually intact, for the post-Beeching decimation had occurred before the first edition was printed. Naturally changes have taken place, and as far as possible the text has been updated to accommodate them without extensive recasting of the whole. The full story of recent developments is told in Chapter XIV (Postscript: A High-Speed Future?), and in places readers of the main chapters are referred to it. The myopic nature of Serpell notwithstanding, the tone of the chapter prefers to support the outgoing Chairman of BR who has consistently insisted that the railways have a strong future if only government would encourage them to get on with it.

CHAPTER II

Three Main Lines

'Now an Inter-City express leaves London for Birmingham every half-hour,' proclaimed British Rail in 1972, '. . . and the 112 mile journey takes as little as 92 minutes.' This new time-table may be a far cry from the initial 1838 timetable of the London & Birmingham Railway of six trains each way, the fastest taking 5hr 37min, but it is a logical development, for in building the country's first trunk railway, Robert Stephenson produced a superbly-engineered route conspicuous by its absence of steep gradients and sharp curves. This was to ease the burden on the tiny locomotives then available, trundling along at 30mph, not for high-speed running, for surprisingly, unlike his friend Joseph Locke, Stephenson did not then adequately foresee the development of larger, faster loco-motives.

Second-class passengers now enjoy well-upholstered seats, toilet and refreshment facilities as a matter of course, with air conditioning increasingly available. In 1838 the official time-table described second-class coaches as 'open at the side, without linings, cushions or divisions in the compartments.' Fares too have changed, single fares from Euston to Rugby in 1838 being 24s 6d ($£1·22\frac{1}{2}$p) by First Class Mail, 15s (75p) Second Class. In 1972 they were $£3·05$p First and $£2·00$p Second Class, two-and-a-half times as much, but relatively much less when compared with the rise in the cost of living over the intervening 134 years.

The success of the L & BR encouraged the promotion of other railways. Competition between the companies was fierce, resulting by 1910 in five main lines between London and the Midlands: the Great Western, L & BR, Great Central, Mid-land, and Great Northern, the middle three being the subject of this chapter. However, the great success of the electrified main line has resulted in the rationalisation of traffic, involving the reduction in status of the GWR and Midland lines and the virtually complete closure of the Great Central north of Aylesbury.

The three routes were all designed primarily as trunk routes linking the industrial Midlands and North with London. As such, their promoters were prepared to by-pass smaller centres en route, so that their immediate effect on the Home Counties was less than elsewhere. Luton, for example, was a fast-expanding town yet it was not on a railway, and then only a branch line, until 1858. Only as London has expanded has the presence of railways had a wider effect on these localities, with the growth of commuter traffic; even this has been patchy.

PLANNING THE L & BR

The London & Birmingham Railway was the most ambitious and important of the railways proposed after the opening of the Liverpool & Manchester Railway in 1830. The initiative came from Birmingham, whose exports were suffering from increasingly successful Continental competition, on account of its dependence on long slow canal communications. Several prominent London bankers joined the Company, notably George Carr Glyn, later Chairman. Opposition was widespread in the intervening countryside, for here were the estates of some of the wealthiest of the nobility and gentry. Their parks, laid out by the great landscape gardeners of the eighteenth century, were now coming to full maturity. They could not see any reason why these should be cut up for the benefit of the rising commercial middle classes for whom they had scant sympathy, especially when at the same time their dominance in the House of Commons was being actively challenged by the same people in the furore over the Great Reform Bill (1831–2). Their fears were summed up by Sir Astley Cooper of Hemel Hempstead, knighted for minor surgery on George IV: '. . . if this sort of thing be permitted to go on, you will, in a very few years, destroy the *noblesse*.' It is ironical that when Robert Stephenson later entered Parliament as MP for Whitby, he was a high Tory, like many of his opponents of the early 1830s.

The building of the Grand Junction Canal in the 1790s,

whose route the L & BR substantially followed from Watford to Rugby, had also cut up parkland, but with less opposition as water blended in easily with its natural surroundings. In fact the railways ultimately did too, and contemporary opinion tended to regard the new earthworks with mingled awe and satisfaction. Even landed opposition was based as much on such practical reasons as the cutting-up of hunting and farming land, drying-up cows and burning hayricks, as on aesthetic reasons.

Great opposition also came from the road and canal interests who disliked the idea of a new competitor. The canals were enjoying their monopoly of handling heavy bulk cargoes and were developing a system of flyboats. Some twenty-six of these fast boats plied daily on the Grand Junction, carrying light and perishable goods which would inevitably be lost to a faster competitor, as the railways likewise were to find with the motor lorry after World War I.

On the roads, the work of Telford and MacAdam allowed the coaching industry to expand, increasing frequencies and cutting journey times with such efficiency that a change of horses could be accomplished within thirty seconds. Even so, fares were high—£1 1s od (£1·05) inside from Luton to London (1794)—and accidents were common as drivers raced each other. Goods traffic was heavy on the Watling Street, which also followed much of the route of the new railway. There were sixteen daily coaches between London and Birmingham as well as 8,000 head of sheep and cattle going weekly to London. The road industry depended on an army of innkeepers, ostlers, serving maids, blacksmiths and others, which in turn brought prosperity to towns like Stony Stratford, Towcester and Daventry. While redundant ostlers and servants could be re-employed on the railway, for the innkeepers change was less easy, while the posting towns away from the railway suffered sharp loss of trade and stagnating populations. Towcester's population remained just below 2,500 over the twenty years after 1831, whereas Watford's, on the railway, increased from about 2,800 to 6,500.

In spite of this weighty opposition, the Bill for the L & BR passed the House of Commons easily on 1 June 1832, only to fall before the Lords on 8 July. Stephenson then carried out a third survey to meet landowners' objections, and to buy off remaining opposition; the land for the L & BR cost

£750,000, three times its original valuation. The railway was finally authorised in May 1833.

BUILDING THE L & BR

Robert Stephenson and his father had originally been appointed through their powerful financial connections among Liverpool merchants and London bankers, like Overend, Gurney, against opposition from Francis Giles and Sir John Rennie, both older-generation canal engineers who were out of their depth on this project. Then in 1833 Robert was made engineer to the L & BR; before it was finished he reckoned he had walked its entire length fifteen times, together with journeys on horseback. His route, crystallised in 1831, differed from Giles's of 1830 in reaching the Tring Gap, in the Chilterns, by way of Harrow and Watford instead of Barnet and South Mimms. The Countess of Bridgwater also suggested the Watford route, rather than via Uxbridge and Aylesbury (through the Wendover Gap) as her land at Berkhamsted and Tring was 'already gashed by the canal'. However, the line was forced to pass Watford on the east owing to heavy local opposition from the Earl of Essex, necessitating the tunnel (1m 57yd) and a three-mile embankment up to 40ft high.

As the maximum gradient adopted north of Camden was no more than 1 in 330, heavy earthworks were inevitable. These included deep cuttings at Tring and Blisworth, an awkward embankment at Wolverton, and long tunnels at Primrose Hill, Watford and Kilsby. All work was done by hand with an army of navvies which never fell below 12,000, often rising to nearly 20,000. Each man could lift up to twenty tons of spoil daily over his head into a truck. Barrow runs were needed up cutting sides to remove spoil from the bottom. In the 40ft deep Tring Cutting there were over thirty of these narrow muddy planks up which the navvies would run with their loaded barrows, aided by a horse-drawn rope. Most navvies fell to the bottom several times, followed by their load, but only one man was killed. This was better than in the Watford Tunnel where one working shaft fell in, burying ten men so suddenly 'that one poor fellow was found, three weeks afterwards, standing perfectly upright with his trowel in his hand.'

Working in these conditions it is hardly surprising that the navvies, as at Kilsby, could drink barrels of beer on village greens, or occasionally roast whole cows for dinner, or need the militia to put down their rioting. The engineers also could celebrate, as on 23 December 1837, when they gathered at 'The Dun Cow', Dunchurch, the line being nearly completed. Robert Stephenson arrived late at 5.30pm and left the table at 2.00am. His father tottered away at 4.00am, Thomas Gooch at 6.00am, while a few stalwarts saw in the dawn at 8.00am.

Of the major earthworks, only Watford Tunnel was completed by the original contractor without the railway company having to intervene. This was because the tunnel was dug through chalk, not clay. At Tring the contractor was defeated by the sheer size of the work. The cutting runs for $2\frac{1}{2}$ miles through the Chilterns at an average depth of 40ft, but for a quarter of a mile it is 57ft deep. The Lords had thought that the cutting sides would be too steep, but Stephenson pointed out that the angle was the same as in Telford's road cutting nearby at Dunstable. One and a half million cubic yards of chalk were removed, some being used for the following six-mile embankment, which consumed 828,000 cubic yards of spoil.

The $1\frac{1}{2}$ mile embankment across the Ouse Valley at Wolverton, at 48ft the highest on the line, also caused difficulties as the ground yielded under the weight of half a million cubic yards of spoil. A temporary wooden bridge over the canal was necessary during building, but the canal company disputed the railway company's right to drive piles into the canal banks. Stephenson got round this by building it on Christmas Day 1834, aided by a large army of navvies. The canal company retaliated on 30 December with another large army of navvies who pulled it all down again. The issue was transferred to Chancery in January 1835, when the railway won. Part of the embankment then slipped at the southern end of the Ouse viaduct, while another section caught fire owing to the alum shale, containing sulphuret of iron, which ignited spontaneously. The work was not finished until June 1838, at a cost of £28,000. The excavations at Blisworth and Kilsby are narrated in the next chapter.

The first section of the line to be opened was from Euston to Boxmoor (for Hemel Hempstead) on 20 June 1837, with full

Plate 1 The Great Central Railway's London Extension epitomised the competitive spirit of Victorian railways. Its Nottingham (Victoria) station exhibited the cathedral-like qualities of the best of Victorian railway architecture. Here, a Stirling 2–4–0 from the Great Northern Railway (joint owners of the station) simmers quietly between duties. [Nottingham City Library.]

Plates 2 and 3 Building the railways: although mechanical excavators were available to help the navvies on the GCR London Extension *(above)*, earlier earthworks were entirely dug by hand, such as Roade Cutting *(below)* on the London & Birmingham Railway. Note the thick retaining walls and tunnel of girders over the Northampton Loop. *(see page 51)* [S. W. A. Newton collection, Leicester Museum; author.]

ceremony and great excitement. Beforehand, tó allay fears about railway travel among the local population, free rides had been given between Watford and Bushey. The sections from Boxmoor to Denbigh Hall, and from Rugby to Birmingham, were opened on 9 April 1838, causing an immediate rise in the number of passengers carried. This amounted to 158,838 between January and June 1838, of whom 122,814 were carried after 9 April. By July, weekly passenger and parcels receipts were reaching £7,000, and the line was running at a profit. Coaches took passengers from Denbigh Hall to Rugby until full opening on 17 September 1838, although works trains had been running through Kilsby Tunnel since June.

Contemporaries waxed eloquent on the benefits of the new railway. In 1838, Osborne declared in his *London & Birmingham Railway Guide*:

> . . . it has already begun to produce great and material changes in society. Many who, but a few years since, scarcely penetrated beyond the county in which they were born are now induced to visit places far more remote . . . and become acquainted with customs, manners and habits which previously were unknown to them.

He noted a better moral tone resulting from raii travel, for there was no opportunity to stop at inns smoking and drinking and 'no opportunity for spendthrifts . . . to show off by treating the coachman and guard.' Third class travel was made easier by Gladstone's Railway Act of 1844, but while the *noblesse* was not yet destroyed, Dr Arnold of Rugby School, watching the first train pass Rugby, could rejoice 'feudality is gone for ever'.

The initial service of six through trains each way plus one to and from Wolverton in each direction had increased by 1840 to nine plus three intermediate locals as traffic continued to rise. For the great Christmas cattle market of 1843, the L & BR in two days carried to London 1,085 oxen, 1,420 sheep and ninety-three pigs, in 263 wagons. In the same year, one of Lord Palmerston's horses could race at Newcastle on Wednesday and Winchester on Friday, travelling via the L & BR. As yet, passenger receipts were more important than goods, being in the ratio of £30,000 to £15,000 weekly in 1843.

The opening of the Midland Counties line from Leicester

to Rugby in 1840 and the Trent Valley line north from
Rugby in 1844 progressively funnelled more goods traffic as
well as passenger over the L & BR (LNWR from 1846). Train
working was still rudimentary, several trains being allowed
into a section at once, as at Wolverton in 1862 when an up
goods train was followed by a cattle train at caution, and
a coal train also at caution. The latter's driver was not
cautious enough, running into the rear of the cattle train;
but the cattle train driver was blamed—for not going fast
enough!

Heavy traffic brought the duplication of the up line from
Primrose Hill to Bletchley in 1859, the tracks being gaunt-
letted through Watford Tunnel. In 1874 Watford New Tunnel
was opened, taking the two slow lines, the fourth track being
extended to Bletchley in 1876. At Leighton Buzzard, Linslade
Tunnel was widened by digging a single bore to the east in
July 1859 and another to the west in April 1876, the tracks
being rearranged so that the down fast used the new tunnel,
the up fast and down slow the original double-track tunnel
and the up slow the 1859 tunnel. Quadrupling continued
towards Roade, the new lines then making the Northampton
loop to Rugby. The works, including diversions at Wolverton
and flying junctions at Rugby, were opened in 1882.

Robert Stephenson's aim was to link London with Birmingham as easily as possible. He therefore made scant reference
to possible traffic from intermediate towns; it was fortuitous
if the railway served them, like Watford, or by-passed them,
like Northampton. In spite of this, the coming of the railway
influenced economically the areas it passed through, by stimulating the growth of Watford, creating the railway towns of
Wolverton and Bletchley, and causing decline to Towcester
and other coaching towns. In more recent years the presence
of railways has encouraged commuter traffic, leading to the
growth of villages south of Bletchley. Some places on the line
were hardly affected: Roade lies right beside the railway,
with its own station, closed on 7 September 1964, yet its
population remained static at around 700 for over eighty years
after 1851.

WATFORD

Osborne described Watford as a market town whose inhabitants were mainly engaged in straw-plaiting or in the three

silk mills. It was, however, a declining town; the canal was too far away, silk spinning stagnated, tanning and candlemaking were dying out. Even so, property owners among the 2,960 inhabitants prevented the railway from crossing the fields adjacent to the High Street, thus keeping it half-a-mile from the town. The railway reversed the decline and by 1861 the population had reached 6,546, just topping the 10,000 mark twenty years later, when the town could boast an impressive list of general industries. By this time the LNWR was boosting Watford as a residential area for London office workers by offering free 21 year season tickets to buyers of houses above a certain price, the ticket to remain with the property. This feature was further developed prior to 1914 as demand for commuter services into Euston developed.

There was already a station at High Street in the heart of Watford, on the Rickmansworth branch, which was opened 1 October 1862, enjoying in 1910 an irregular service of fourteen down trains (twelve up) with two and three more on Saturdays. Now a new electrified line was to be built from Euston, parallel to the main line as far as Bushey, whence it deviated west in a loop to a junction at the rebuilt High Street station. A new branch was thrown off the Rickmansworth branch for Croxley Green, opened 15 June 1912. The new line services began on 10 February 1913, with posters exhorting Londoners to 'live in the country,' having the benefits of country life coupled with cheap season tickets to work. Bakerloo line underground trains ran to Watford over the new line from 16 April 1917, but ceased north of Stonebridge Park on 4 October 1982. LNWR electric trains began on 10 July 1922.

By 1931 Watford's population had risen more than fivefold to 56,799, with light industries such as engineering and brewing. Since then, while continually growing, its train services have been altered to suit changed needs. The Rickmansworth branch, electrified in 1927, closed on 3 March 1952, having been duplicated by a joint Metropolitan Railway—LNER branch from Moor Park opened on 2 November 1925. The Croxley Green branch, electrified in 1922, had by 1972 a shuttle service in peak hours only of fifteen trains each way to Watford Junction; at the time of writing its existence was threatened. On the new lines, four trains an hour left Watford for Euston in off-peak periods. In the peak periods these increased to six, some going to Broad Street; also, four

Bakerloo line trains were extended from Queen's Park. In addition, the hourly Bletchley locals and Rugby semi-fasts called, while most down morning expresses picked up passengers, and up evening expresses dropped them, giving connections with the direct coach service to London Airport. Finally the St Albans branch, opened on 5 May 1858, when the main line station moved south of the St Albans Road bridge, was carrying twenty-two diesel trains daily each way, compared with fourteen (steam) in 1910.

Between Watford and Bletchley the impact of the L & BR on this agricultural district was less marked. Initially, only the market towns of Hemel Hempstead, Berkhamsted, Tring and Leighton Buzzard were served, all having benefitted from the canal. At Berkhamsted there was a protest meeting in 1833 against the L & BR, which had razed the castle's main gateway and barbican to make way for its station. This mock-Elizabethan structure was replaced in connection with the 1875 widening. At King's Langley and along the Colne Valley, John Dickinson's paper mills had been established thirty years earlier, and although that company used the railway, it has long turned almost exclusively to lorries.

Tring was a growing town of 4,000 inhabitants engaged in canvas weaving, silk spinning and straw plaiting. Although they never looked healthy, they showed 'the most commendable public spirit' (Osborne) in paying the difference in the cost of the land for their station between the price the L & BR was willing to pay and what the profiteering landowner wanted to charge; but for this, the station would have been $3\frac{1}{2}$ miles away, at the north end of the cutting. The town also built the two-mile road to the station. With the opening of the new lines south of Watford in 1913, Tring became the effective outer suburban station, though between the wars Bletchley increasingly took over this role. In 1935, twenty-six up trains left Tring, six in the morning rush. By contrast, in 1955 there were only sixteen up trains, eight leaving between 07.13 and 08.45, two going to Broad Street. The rest of the day was erratically served, including a four-hour gap in the afternoon. From 18 April 1966 a new electric service was inaugurated, of an hourly service from Bletchley throughout the day, heavily supplemented during the rush hour. In 1972 these numbered ten up trains between 07.00 and 08.31, and ten down between 17.30 and 19.00. Leighton Buzzard,

Berkhamsted and Hemel Hempstead were also served hourly by the Rugby semi-fasts.

LEIGHTON BUZZARD

Commuting to London from beyond Watford was on the increase between the wars, but not until the 1960s did it expand rapidly, as the new housing estates along the line will testify. This encouraged the provision of a good train service, and this in turn encouraged further commuting, so that Northampton and even Rugby are now acceptable residential areas for London workers.

Leighton Buzzard was a market town of 3,330 in 1831, famous for its fairs, but it only grew slowly in the nineteenth century until the sand industry developed, with the cutting off of imported supplies (as ships' ballast) in 1914. Previously sand was taken by cart to the LNWR Dunstable branch but the extra wartime demand seriously damaged the inadequate roads. The result was a 2ft 0in gauge light railway $3\frac{1}{2}$ miles long, opened on 20 November 1919 'to retain for Leighton Buzzard the enormous sand traffic captured during the war by the cessation of foreign competition', as the *Leighton Buzzard Observer* put it. In fact the line was the culmination of several local schemes dating from 1892 for a standard gauge light railway linking Leighton with Hitchin. At its peak during the 1930s and early 1950s the line carried over 100,000 tons of sand annually, much carried away by the LMS and BR, but by the 1960s more traffic went to customers by lorry, while BR preferred block freight trains to wagon loads of sand. Closure of the western portion came at the end of 1969 along with the remnants of the BR branch to Dunstable, but the eastern section still carries heavy internal traffic. A preservation society now uses the western end (page 229).

Until 1965 the Dunstable branch also carried heavy chalk trains from Totternhoe quarries. As these trains often stalled on the steep gradient up to Leighton Buzzard station, the main Wing Road crossing gates were not opened until after the trains had cleared the summit.

Prior to the 1840s, Bletchley was a hamlet overshadowed by the busy market and fair town of Fenny Stratford, on Watling Street. In 1846 Bletchley became the junction for the Bedford Railway, and in 1850 for the Buckinghamshire

Railway. As a railway junction, Bletchley grew, while Fenny Stratford stagnated as Watling Street traffic fell away. However, the latter's proximity to Bletchley allowed it to share in Bletchley's rising prosperity while developing its own brush and timber industries. Now the two towns are joined under the name of Bletchley, although railway employment has fallen from about 500 to 140.

The locomotive shed here was mainly for freight and commuter turns in recent years, but would occasionally provide a substitute for failed express engines. One day a Royal Scot failed on a Liverpool express. The only locomotive available, an ex-LMS Class 5 4-6-0, was a notoriously rough rider. The train driver, a Liverpool man, saw his new charge, solemnly took out his false teeth, wrapped them in a handkerchief and handed them to the station inspector, commenting that they would be safer in his care.

North of Bletchley is Denbigh Hall bridge over Watling Street. Here from April to September 1838, while the major intervening earthworks were being completed, passengers detrained and joined coaches for Rugby. There was no hall, merely an inn on the site of a cottage where the Earl of Denbigh once found refuge when caught in a snowdrift.

WOLVERTON

Wolverton is a true railway town, but in 1831 it was only a hamlet of 417 inhabitants, overshadowed by the ancient market town of Stony Stratford (population c 1,500), where Watling Street crosses the Ouse. As Wolverton lay midway between London and Birmingham, with the canal adjacent (its influence hitherto was minimal) the L & BR chose the town as its locomotive centre, opening the works in 1838 with a labour force of 400, widely drawn from established skilled engineering areas. Housing was supplied, together with a church, schools and ultimately gas and water. As the local landowner refused to sell any more land to the railway, housing development after 1854 took place at Bradwell, to the east. From 1878 the LNWR let private builders take over, and the works drew labour from Stony Stratford and Newport Pagnell as well. By 1901 Wolverton and Bradwell numbered 9,200 inhabitants, rising to 15,000 by 1951; meanwhile Stony Stratford only climbed to some 2,000 and 4,000 respectively on these two dates. At its peak, (1886–1900) the works employed over 5,000 men, and covered thirty-five acres. Rationalisation has reduced these to about 2,000 men and twenty-four acres.

Apart from a large printing works in 1876, industrial diversification in the area is only recent, with the result that skilled labour for the works is harder to find. Between 1846 and 1861 Wolverton was the chief repair depot for the southern division of the LNWR, but then all locomotive work was concentrated at Crewe. From 1865 Wolverton concentrated on carriage and wagon building and repairs, with up to fifty wagons and six coaches being built weekly. From 1962 coach repairs only have been effected, at the rate of fifty a week.

Until the introduction of dining cars, express trains would stop at Wolverton for a ten-minute refreshment break. A female attendant was appointed to supervise a host of waitresses, chefs, housemaids and laundrymaids, plus a baker, garden boy and odd-job man, running the rooms like a country house but at great speed. Stout and Banbury Cakes were most popular. Third class passengers, however, enjoyed less palatial surroundings at Roade.

The present station was built in 1881 when the main line was realigned east of the works, which had expanded either side of the original main line. A branch had been planned in 1845 to link Wolverton and Newport Pagnell with the Bedford Railway at Ridgmont, but was dropped in favour of a line from Bletchley to Wellingborough via Newport Pagnell and Olney, thus presenting a shorter route to Peter-borough in the face of competition from the London & York Railway. Although authorised in 1847 the scheme was dropped and the London & York opened its line, over twenty miles shorter, in 1850. In 1863 the Newport Pagnell plan was revived with powers, subsequently abandoned, to extend to Olney (1865) and the LNWR and MR at Wellingborough (1866). On 2 September 1867 this short branch was opened to Newport Pagnell, a small market town and important bridging place over the Ouse. By 1910 it was carrying eleven down and twelve up trains, reduced to nine (twelve on Satur-days) by 1955. It closed on 7 September 1964.

The 3ft 6in gauge Wolverton & Stony Stratford steam tram-way was proposed in 1882, but not opened until 27 May

1887. By 1919 it had changed its name six times, had four termini in Stony Stratford and Deanshanger, been bankrupt twice and closed once (1887-9). The LNWR took it over to bring in workers from Stony Stratford as there was no bus, and of the 600 passengers carried daily on the fourteen return trips, 550 were season ticket holders. By 1926 there were twelve buses available and the line was closed by the General Strike on 4 May.

THE MIDLAND MAIN LINE

It was thirty years before the Midland could effectively challenge the monopoly of the LNWR and GNR for traffic into London from the Midlands and North, and in so doing greatly improved Bedfordshire's rail access. Delays over access to the LNWR at Rugby had led to the building of the Leicester–Hitchin line, opened with much celebration in 1857 (Chapter IV), but that only threw the Midland into the arms of the Great Northern for the final thirty-two miles into London. Congestion over traffic for the 1862 Exhibition brought matters to a head when 2,382 Midland freight trains, and 961 passenger trains were delayed south of Hitchin. There was insufficient room on either the LNWR or the GNR tracks for the fast-expanding Midland traffic, especially in coal which was currently reaching five million tons annually. Neither the Midland's demands for a permanent tenancy at King's Cross, nor the GNR offer of quadrupling their line in return for the Midland trebling its annual minimum toll to £60,000 was acceptable to the other, the upshot being the Midland's bill for a new line from Bedford to London, authorised in 1863.

The failure of the great banking house of Overend, Gurney & Co in 1866 delayed construction through financial restrictions, and made the Midland anxious to gain revenue from the line as soon as possible. Opening was on a piecemeal basis, with none of the fanfares of 1857. Goods traffic began on 8 September 1867, local passenger services (to Moorgate) on 13 July 1868, and main line services, when St Pancras station was opened, on 1 October 1868. Train services quickly developed, as the Midland had a flair for competition, reaching a peak at the turn of the century, but at the cost of heavy delays to freight traffic in spite of the progressive quadrupling of the line between 1875 and 1894. This was partly due to the company's small engine policy. Coal trains to Brent in 1917 numbered 22,348, seventy per cent more than in 1913.

In 1831 Bedforshire still depended on agriculture, but improving roads were increasing the importance of Bedford (population 6,959) and Dunstable (population 3,500) as market centres at the expense of towns like Ampthill and Harrold. Dunstable also prospered as a coaching town on Watling Street, Bedford had its agricultural engineering and Luton straw hat making, while all three had breweries. Over the next sixty years change was dramatic. Bedford's population with a railway grew by twenty per cent every decade until 1881, and then by fifty per cent, reaching 28,023 by 1891. Luton, without a railway until 1858, quadrupled its population by 1861 to 15,329, then doubled it by 1891 to 30,053, overtaking Bedford. Meanwhile Dunstable, having lost its coaching traffic to the L & BR, stagnated at around 4,500.

RAILWAYS AT BEDFORD

The struggle to provide adequate rail communications for Bedford was protracted. Heavy goods—coal, iron, grain—came by barge down the Ouse from King's Lynn, while under Mr Whitbread's patronage daily London coaches, non-existent in 1820, numbered ten by 1846. In 1836 there was a plan for a line from Cambridge to the L & BR via Bedford but nothing happened. In 1844 George Stephenson visited Bedford to discuss a branch, which resulted in a group of local businessmen, chaired by the mayor, a coal merchant, negotiating with the L & BR. So the Bedford Railway was born in 1845, to be built by the company and run by the L & BR. The opening took place on 17 November 1846 when 600 people left Bedford for Bletchley in thirty coaches, accompanied by brass bands, with church bells ringing and a vast crowd watching. The London coaches inevitably faded away.

The Bedford Railway soon became a part of the LNWR empire (it was finally absorbed in 1879) and formed the nucleus of the Oxford–Cambridge line, which was projected in 1846 but eventually built piecemeal. In 1847 Hudson promoted a Cambridge–Bedford branch to frustrate the GNR designs on Cambridge, but ultimately the Bedford & Cambridge Railway was locally promoted in 1860, incorporating the Sandy & Potton Railway. This four-mile line was opened for freight on 23 June 1857 (passengers in December 1857) as a hobby of Captain William Peel, son of the Prime Minister. The through line to Cambridge was opened for passengers on 7 July 1862, being worked by the LNWR and absorbed by it in 1865. There was a connection with the GNR at Sandy. Only Sandy and Potton really developed as a result, and of the three sections, traffic on this was the thinnest. In 1910 it boasted only seven trains each way throughout, compared with eight down (nine up) from Bletchley to Oxford (opened in 1851), and twelve from Bletchley to Bedford. Three return trains ran from Oxford to Cambridge. The service was similar in 1955, only with fewer through trains.

The BR Modernisation Plan (1955) called for an expansion of the line especially as a freight link from the East Coast ports to South Wales. An expensive flyover was built at Bletchley to avert traffic conflicting with the busy West Coast main line, and land was acquired at Swanbourne for a mechanised marshalling yard. Spurs were to be developed at Bedford and Sandy to aid northbound traffic on to the Midland and GN lines. Subsequently the plan was abandoned and in 1959 closure was proposed. This was opposed by local authorities and diesel trains were put on to reduce operating costs, to the extent that the Beeching Report (1963) only called for the closure of minor stations, whereas the lines from Peterborough to Northampton, Rugby and Leicester would go. However, in December 1963 BR proposed to close all four lines, thus leaving no cross-country link south of Nottingham–Grantham. At the same time Bedford's population of 72,000 was expanding, like other places en route, and the South East Study (1964) proposed the building of a new city for 250,000 people at Milton Keynes, by the line near Bletchley. Traffic on some trains was heavy; in one week in March 1964 Bedford (St Johns) handled 6,782 passengers and Woburn Sands 3,204. In spite of the possibilities, cross-country services such as Norwich–Bedford–South Wales, although proposed, were never developed. With expenses at £199,700 against a revenue of £102,200 in 1964, closure ultimately came, but not until 1 January 1968, as buses could not handle the extra traffic. The Bedford–Cambridge section lost everything; the Bletchley–Oxford section its passengers and local goods services, and the Bletchley–Bedford section its local goods. This latter section was given an hourly passenger service and is well used. Brickmaking at Stewartby, a model village built in the 1930s, began about 1900. The brickworks, the largest in Europe, sent out forty-five wagons daily in 1973 (page 249).

The Midland Railway reached Bedford from Leicester en route to Hitchin, as explained in Chapter IV. Some delay was caused by the choice of a station site, for the Midland wanted a joint station with the LNWR (St Johns from 1924) south of the Ouse, while the town council one to the north. This, Midland Road station, was not opened until 1 February 1859, trains meanwhile reversing into St Johns. When the London Extension was opened in 1868, the Hitchin line became a branch maintaining a service of four daily return trains until 1958. Then diesel railbuses were introduced and the service increased to seven in an attempt to win passengers, but the line lost these services on 1 January 1962, and goods traffic was progressively curtailed.

The Extension curved away sharply from the south end of Midland Road station, and two new higher platforms were made. Later part of the original trackbed was filled in to create two bays at either end, still retaining their low platforms. The Hitchin line crossed the LNWR on the level, and the London line was to diverge south of this point, but the plans were revised in 1864. The sharp station curve was a hindrance to express running so the avoiding curve was brought in to use in 1894. Meanwhile the sharply-curved branch to Northampton was opened in 1872, closing in 1962.

RAILWAYS AT LUTON

The prospectus for the Luton, Dunstable & Welwyn Junction Railway (1855) described Luton, with its population approaching 12,000 and its manufactured goods, especially hats, worth £2 million annually, as the largest town in the country without either railway or canal accommodation. Indeed Luton was desperate for a railway, although its intransigence earlier had cost it a branch. The coach took nine hours for the thirty miles to London, while the hatters took their goods by cart to the canal at Leighton, twelve miles away. Back in 1844 George Stephenson had met Luton officials to discuss a line from Leighton, through Luton, to London, but they favoured the rival Direct London & Manchester Railway, and were concerned with preserving the Great Moor, a large open space. Stephenson left angrily and the LNWR branch, opened to passengers on 1 June 1848, terminated five miles short, at Dunstable.

The LNWR was anxious to keep the GNR out of Luton and Dunstable. Its various plans of 1845–7 resulted in a line authorised from Watford to Dunstable via St Albans, where it would join a GNR branch, and Luton, whither the GNR would have running powers. As this never materialised, the GNR served Luton (Bute Street) and Dunstable with a branch from Welwyn, opened on 1 September 1860 and absorbed in 1861. Even so, when the Luton–Dunstable section had opened on 3 May 1858 it was worked for two years by the LNWR. The 1858 opening day was chaotic : the first train, of twenty-two coaches, had people hanging on to the roofs and sides, many not having bought the 6d (2½p) return tickets. LNWR trains from Leighton to Luton restarted on 1 March 1883 and continued until 2 July 1962. In 1955 there were two Leighton–Dunstable and two Leighton–Luton trains each way.

By 1880 the GNR was offering seven trains to London to the Midland's thirteen, most trains taking just over an hour, but three MR expresses took only fifty minutes. In 1955 ER ran eight trains to Welwyn Garden City (five originating at Dunstable) although only one reached King's Cross; all were withdrawn on 26 April 1965 (goods 1966–71). The first connection between the GNR and MR was made just south of the Luton stations on 3 January 1966, although authorised as long ago as 1863, mainly for block trains to Dunstable cement works (opened in the 1920s but since 1971 only a distribution point). Dunstable's goods yard closed in 1967.

The hat industry boomed with the main line, but Luton was still over-dependent on this trade, which was seasonal and female-dominated. However, good rail connections helped make Luton an attractive town for expanding engineering and chemicals industries. The first major engineering works came in 1871, followed among others by Vauxhall Motors in 1905, Commercial Cars 1906 and Skefko bearings in 1910, when the population had risen to 50,000. World War I killed the hat export trade and boosted the motor industry, since when Luton has become an important engineering town of over 164,000 people, although hats are still made. Trucks of

finished cars and crates of car parts have replaced the crates
of hats as the town's staple freight traffic.

By 1886, the Midland station, adjacent to the GNR's Bute
Street, and rebuilt 1937–40, enjoyed slip coaches, some
expresses calling on request, and six stopping trains each way.
Between the wars these had risen to twenty-nine each way,
in addition to expresses, with six out and back in the rush
hours. The introduction of diesel trains on 11 January 1960
was a great improvement as they gave hourly semi-fast and
stopping services to London from Bedford and from Luton,
but electrification was eagerly awaited in 1983. Hourly Inter-
City trains called from 1966 and HSTs from 1982.

As with the LNWR line these fast, regular-interval services
have generated considerable commuter traffic, with consequent housing development at many points south of Bedford, Ampthill being the only town to lose its station, on 4
May 1959. Harpenden is a good example; in the 1870s it was
a pretty village whose only claim to fame was its annual race
day which, said a contemporary, 'made travelling in a first
class railway carriage of the Midland Railway a danger to
men and an impossibility to Ladies'. However, in the 1920s
and 1930s hundreds of comfortable houses for well-to-do
Londoners were built. Harpenden boasted a branch opened
in 16 July 1877, to Hemel Hempstead, a market town of over
7,000 inhabitants. The line carried only three trains from
Luton in 1886, rising to eight from Harpenden in 1910, the
junction having been reversed in 1888. In spite of the building of Hemel Hempstead new town after World War II the
branch never prospered, as Boxmoor station on the LNWR
offered a better service, and it lost its passenger service on 16
June 1947. It lasted until 1979 as a six-mile private siding
for a concrete firm.

St Albans, a market town with silk and straw-plaiting
industries, was an important coaching centre on Watling
Street, handling seventy-two coaches daily in 1826 as well as
packhorse trains. Although the opening of the L & BR hit
this trade badly, it was not until the coming of the LNWR
branch from Watford on 5 May 1858 that many innkeepers
went bankrupt. Originally this branch had been authorised
in 1847, continuing to Luton and Dunstable. Another plan
in 1860 was to extend it to Shefford on the Midland's
Bedford–Hitchin line, while in 1863 the Midland's Act

allowed a connecting spur to the new main line at Napsbury; this was only used for contractors traffic. The GNR branch from Hatfield was opened on 16 October 1865 using the LNWR station ('Abbey' from 1924) from 1 November 1866. Finally the Midland arrived in 1868, and St Albans developed as a residential and light industrial city. Its population doubled over the next thirty years, to 16,000 in 1901, with expansion continuing, to 50,000 in 1961. The GNR branch was closed to passengers on 1 October 1951.

THE GREAT CENTRAL LINE

The Great Central, the last main line into London, was the creation of Edward Watkin, Chairman since 1864 of the Manchester, Sheffield & Lincolnshire Railway, and then of the Metropolitan and the South Eastern Railways, with interests in the proposed Channel Tunnel as well. His ambition was to run through trains from the North to Europe over his companies' tracks, while more immediate aims were an independent route to London, and access to South Wales and the South West via the GWR for the MS & L coal, steel, fish, and other traffics.

By its Act in 1893 the MS & L was authorised to build a line from Annesley, in Nottinghamshire, to a junction with the Metropolitan Railway at Quainton Road, in Buckinghamshire. The company adopted the name Great Central Railway in 1897, but by then it had quarrelled with the Metropolitan Railway over the proposal to build a separate GCR terminus at Marylebone, instead of using Baker Street. Other disputes followed over the next decade, encouraging a GCR–GWR alliance, and delayed the opening to coal traffic on 25 July 1898. The first coal train, deliberately sent early, was stopped short of Quainton Road by the Metropolitan, which insisted that the train return to Woodford, but without allowing it access to the next crossover to run round. Formal opening was on 9 March 1899, with passenger services beginning on 15 March, although only fourteen people travelled on the 9.15am express from Marylebone.

Lutterworth was the only town on the line hitherto without rail access. North of Rugby the line competed with the Midland for much of the way. At Rugby the proposed connection with the LNWR Peterborough branch never materialised. Southwards, Brackley (population 2,500) was the only town before reaching Aylesbury. In fact, that part of Northamptonshire was declining, and the railway did little to arrest this; Brackley's population fell to 2,131 by 1931. Woodford Halse was the exception. In 1891 a declining village of 527 persons, the GCR made it a junction with the E & WJR and erected a shed for thirty locomotives, wagon and sheet repairing shops, while thirty-five acres of sorting sidings were laid on a vast embankment formed by spoil from Catesby tunnel. Erected for the staff were 136 houses, and the 1901 census returned a population of 1,220, rising to 1,738 in 1931 and 1,775 in 1961. Here it remained, about 600 being railway employees, until new housing development took it past 1,900 by 1981, although many of the workers commute to Daventry or Coventry. When the yards closed in 1965 many of the staff had to go eight miles away to Daventry for work.

Woodford's status as a junction was enhanced from 1900 when the GCR's important spur to the GWR at Banbury was opened, having been built with GWR money. Freight traffic began on 1 June, of immediate importance, over 60,000 wagons passing through in the first six months. Passenger traffic began on 13 August with two daily GWR trains between Oxford and Leicester, soon supplemented by three connecting locals. Through trains began running from Marylebone to Stratford via Woodford (North Spur) and Byfield in 1902, lasting until 1936. The Woodford–Byfield locals were withdrawn on 31 May 1948; in the same year the station's name changed from Woodford & Hinton to Woodford Halse.

The GCR's alliance with the GWR produced the joint line between Grendon Underwood Junction and Northolt Junction, via Princes Risborough, opened for goods on 20 November 1905 and passengers 2 April 1906, to provide an alternative route to London than over the Metropolitan. Improving relations with the Metropolitan, and the opening of the GWR Ashendon Junction–Aynho section in 1910 (which provided an improved Paddington–Birmingham main line) caused GCR interest to decline, and the Woodford–Banbury line remained more important, especially for freight. Coal from Annesley Yard, fish from Grimsby and steel from Scunthorpe went west, while bananas from Avonmouth and returning empties came east. 232,000 wagons passed in 1914, over 490,000 in 1916 with another peak of 689,000 in 1940.

After nationalisation in 1948, this line was regarded as the main line, with the Marylebone line almost as a long branch from Woodford, the terminus for local trains. The expresses from the North East to Bournemouth or Swindon, begun in 1902 continued until closure. In 1960 the yards at Woodford handled eighty-six arrivals and ninety departures daily, only fifteen of each being on the London line. This included fish trains to Plymouth, Whitland and Banbury, and nine steel trains for South Wales, routed via Byfield, the SMJ having been strengthened in 1950.

Closure was protracted. Declining traffic in coal, steel and fish, and the improvement of the Midland route via Birmingham rendered the GCR/GWR route unnecessary; freight traffic ended on 5 April 1965. Expresses from Marylebone were withdrawn in 1960, Sunday and local passenger trains between Aylesbury and Rugby on 4 March 1963, leaving only three semi-fasts between Marylebone and Nottingham, supplemented by the useful cross-country expresses, and locals north of Rugby. All trains between Rugby, Banbury and Aylesbury were withdrawn on 5 September 1966, and the lines quickly lifted north of Calvert. Here a 1940 spur to the Oxford–Bletchley line, built to relieve wartime pressure on London for through traffic, still carries daily empty stock and parcels trains, and the brickworks receives rubbish containers.

RAILWAYS AT AYLESBURY

Aylesbury, a market and coaching town on Akeman Street, famous for its ducks and long the county town of Buckinghamshire, was unhappy at being missed by the L & BR. Local interests promoted a branch from Cheddington on the L & BR, authorised in 1836 and opened on 10 June 1839 with three daily return trains. The day was a public holiday, and many travelled on the numerous specials. An extension to Oxford, urged by Sir Harry Verney, was dropped because of a local bank failure. By 1910 there were eleven return trains, and for many years several ran through to Euston, but the development of the direct services from 1892 reduced the importance of this line; it lost its passenger service on 2 February 1953.

The GWR arrived next, with an extension of the Wycombe

Plates 4 and 5 Luton: *(above)* close competition between the Midland and Great Northern (Bute Street) stations; *(below)* hat boxes in Bute Street station yard in 1910 reveal Luton's staple trade before the coming of the motor car. [Home Counties Newspapers Ltd; Luton Museum.]

Plates 6 and 7 Railway byways: *(above)* a scene on the Wotton Tramway betrays its agricultural origins; *(below)* a quiet stop at Swanbourne station about 1900. [S. W. A. Newton collection, Leicester Museum; A. C. Heady collection.]

Railway from Princes Risborough, opened on 1 October 1863. This was joined by the Aylesbury & Buckingham Railway, worked by the GWR, on 23 September 1868, a single line which joined the LNWR at Verney Junction, named after the local landowner and deputy chairman. From 1891 the A & BR was taken over by the Metropolitan which doubled the tracks. The main Metropolitan line reached Aylesbury on 1 September 1892, but did not share the GWR station until 1894. Through running between Baker Street and Verney Junction began in 1897. Finally, the GCR arrived in 1898–9, via the A & BR from Quainton Road. After inter-company squabbles had been overcome, the station became the jointly leased property of the Metropolitan & GCR and GWR & GCR Joint Committees in 1907, GCR suburban services to Marylebone having begun the previous year. Thereafter the area along the line developed, particularly as 'Metro-land' in the inter-war years and after.

The A & BR was run by the Metropolitan & GCR Joint Committee from 1906. As the Metropolitan regarded itself as a main line company, it unsuccessfully opposed the formation in 1933 of London Transport, which felt in 1934 unable to run trains ultimately beyond Amersham. This marked the end of the long-declining branches from Quainton Road to Verney Junction and Brill, which closed on 6 July 1936 (goods 7 September 1947) and 2 December 1935 respectively.

The Brill branch had originated as a private line on the estate of the Duke of Buckingham and Chandos, opened on 1 April 1871 from Quainton Road to Wotton, using horses. By the summer 1872 passengers were being carried and the line extended to Brill. Traffic was mainly in hay, manure, ale and coal. The coming of the Metropolitan and GCR made the Wotton Tramway strategically important as a route on to Oxford. Accordingly the Oxford & Aylesbury Tramroad was promoted in 1888 to build a tramway between Brill and Oxford. This never materialised, but by 1894 the O & AT had rebuilt the Wotton Tramway, making a connection at Quainton Road, and was running the line, leasing it to the Metropolitan in 1899. That company ran four return trains daily, but these were losing around £4,000 annually by 1935.

South of Aylesbury the main development was in the market towns of Amersham, Chesham and Rickmansworth. Rickmansworth, with its brewery, watercress beds, papermills

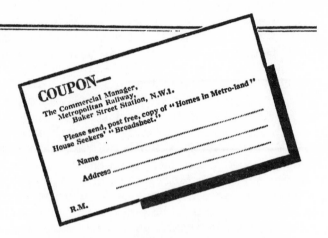

LIVE IN METRO-LAND

THE problem of where to live presents many difficulties, but there can be no doubt that with its glorious scenery; its helpful and bracing air and its wide and varied choice of site and situation, the delightful residential area served by the Metropolitan Railway claims the serious consideration of every House-Seeker.

The train service provided is unequalled for frequency and rapidity; the educational and shopping facilities are unlimited; the Season Ticket Rates are low and the local housing developments especially active. Residents in this district have also the added advantage of being able to travel to and from the City without change of carriage, whilst Baker Street is linked up by escalator with London's Tube system, thereby providing every facility for expeditiously reaching any part of the Metropolis.

As an aid to the House-Seekers, a particularly useful "broadsheet" has been prepared setting out in detail the various housing propositions obtaining in Metro-land, and a copy of this should be secured by every House-Seeker without delay—the coupon above will bring you a copy by return.

BAKER STREET STATION, N.W.1.   J. S. ANDERSON, GENERAL MANAGER.

'Live in Metro-land.' The Metropolitan Railway had a vested interest in encouraging residential development along its route to Aylesbury. (Railway Magazine) and 5,337 inhabitants in 1871 was first reached by a branch from Watford on 1 October 1862. This line, absorbed by the LNWR in 1881, was electrified in 1927, but as the Metropolitan provided a more direct service to London, passenger services ceased on 3 March 1952. The Metropolitan reached Rickmansworth on 1 September 1887 from Pinner, and with the GCR planned a branch to Watford, although World War I delayed the building; opening was on 2 November 1925, with electric trains from the beginning.

The Aylesbury & Rickmansworth was originally a separate company but soon came under the Metropolitan Railway. The main line to Chalfont Road, and thence single-track branch to Chesham, were opened on 8 July 1889. Chesham, a busy little market town, trebled its population during the nineteenth century as light industry supplemented the watercress beds. Expansion as a commuter town continued, the population reaching 9,000 by 1950. The section from Chalfont Road to Aylesbury was opened on 1 September 1892, serving the agricultural centre of Amersham, where the brewery now houses a perfumery. The station was away from the old town, but new villas quickly grew up nearby.

The Metropolitan was electrified out from Harrow to Rickmansworth in 1925, but the war prevented completion of quadrupling of this section and electrification to Amersham and Chesham, while the increasing number of suburban trains delayed the LNER ones. Work was resumed in 1958 and completed in 1962. Metropolitan line trains ran into Aylesbury for the last time on 9 September 1961. BR took over all services north of Amersham until 1984 (page 248).

THE BUCKINGHAMSHIRE AND SMJ RAILWAYS

The Buckinghamshire Railway of 1847 was a merger of two companies proposing lines from Bletchley to Oxford and Aylesbury to Banbury, as part of the LNWR attempt to foil GWR approaches to Birmingham. The Bletchley to Banbury line was opened on 1 May 1850, the Oxford line from Verney Junction following on 20 May 1851. While the Banbury line remained a branch, the Oxford line, as we have seen, became an important cross-country link until closure on 1 January 1968, though freight and empty stock services still continue. Except at Winslow, Bicester and Islip, the stations were distant from the communities they served. Nevertheless in its heyday Swanbourne served as the railhead for five coal merchants and farmers from ten local villages, with good traffic in livestock, hay, corn and wool, while butter was sent daily to Queen Victoria's table.

Neither Buckingham nor Brackley significantly profited from the railway, both remaining at under 2,500 inhabitants. Buckingham was declining badly following a disastrous fire in 1725 and the collapse of the wool trade. Banbury however was expanding, but was better served by the GWR when its Birmingham line was opened in 1852. In 1910 Buckingham enjoyed six trains from Bletchley, four going on to Banbury including a through coach from Euston, slipped at Bletchley. There were seven up trains, five from Banbury, one running to Euston. By 1955 these had dropped to three between Bletchley and Banbury with four return, but the following year BR chose the branch from Buckingham for a pilot scheme of introducing railcars to save branch lines. Despite an augmented service and the opening of two halts, running costs were reduced by a third. Revenue increased fourfold, cutting the annual deficit from £14,000 to £4,700. Although Bletchley and Banbury were growing, intermediate traffic was sparse except on market days, while the change of trains at Buckingham was unpopular. The Banbury line closed to passengers on 2 January 1961, the truncated Buckingham branch, with eight return trains, on 7 September 1964. Goods services to Banbury ended on 2 December 1963.

Whereas the Buckinghamshire Railway was always an LNWR creature, the SMJ was independent until 1923. Its history, like its finances, was complicated, beginning with the abortive Northampton, Banbury & Cheltenham Railway 1846. Similar schemes were canvassed before the Northampton & Banbury Junction Railway was authorised in 1863. It never reached either town on its own tracks, but ran from the LNWR yard at Blisworth via Towcester to join the LNWR (Buckinghamshire Railway) at Cockley Brake Junction, whence it had running powers over the five miles to Banbury. Running powers over the LNWR from Blisworth to Northampton were never exercised. The Blisworth–Towcester section opened in May 1866, and on to Cockley Brake on 1 June 1872, with four mixed return trains daily, the handbills announcing the line's opening referring to 'frequent trains'.

The local discovery of iron ore prompted grandiose N & BJR schemes for a new direct line to South Wales, but its finances were sufficiently stretched building towards Banbury.

Meanwhile the East & West Junction Railway had been authorised in 1864 from Towcester to Stratford-upon-Avon, an extension to Worcester having been abandoned, as was its plan in 1872 to link the N & BJR with the Bedford line in Northampton. In August 1864 Lady Palmerston, a local landowner, cut the first sod, the Prime Minister himself gracing this ceremony, which was attended with all the usual pomp, brass bands and flag-waving locals, while Lord Grafton had reversed his dislike of railways so far as to become a principal promoter. But within two years construction had ceased for lack of money. Extensions of time and credit allowed the final opening of the line throughout on 1 July 1873, with trains running over the N & BJR metals between Blisworth and Greens Norton Junction, beyond Towcester.

It was said that income never covered the cost of greasing the locomotives, and when the Sheriff's men with a writ for £250 had no satisfaction at the Towcester office, they seized the company's locomotive at Blisworth, padlocking it to the rails. The driver's language was choice; the company needed its locomotive to maintain services, and the padlock was broken. The receiver was appointed on 31 July 1877, passenger services ceasing for eight years.

The chimera of vast local iron ore deposits encouraged the E & WJR to float the Easton Neston Mineral & Towcester, Roade & Olney Junction Railway in 1879, together with an extension westwards to Broom. This line was ultimately opened on 13 April 1891 for goods as the Stratford-upon-Avon, Towcester & Midland Junction Railway, the Midland using running powers for through goods trains. The spur at Roade was rarely used. Passenger trains, hired from the Midland, ran between Olney and Towcester between 1 December 1892 and 30 March 1893, bringing revenue of £5 weekly at a total cost of £1,290. Some trains had no passengers. The ST & MJR appointed its receiver in 1898.

By 1901 legal tangles could only be solved by an Act authorising the sale of the E & WJR and ST & MJR (plus the Evesham, Redditch and Stratford-upon-Avon Railway) to either the GWR, LNWR, MR or GCR, but none was interested. In 1908 they amalgamated as the Stratford-upon-

Avon & Midland Junction Railway, with the N & BJR joining in 1910. Despite activity as the 'Shakespeare Line', World War II killed traffic—one compartment could hold all the passengers on any train. The N & BJR lost its passenger trains on 2 July 1951 and goods on 29 October 1951. Passenger trains from Blisworth to Stratford ended on 5 April 1952, but goods traffic west of Woodford Halse was heavy until closure of the GCR to freight in 1965.

In spite of being the junction of three railways, Towcester never regained the prosperity lost on opening the L & BR. Its population was static at around 2,500; its furnaces had a short life (1875–82); its iron ore was indifferent. In 1910 it enjoyed three trains to Stratford, three to Banbury and seven to Blisworth. But Easter Mondays saw the Grafton Hunt steeplechases at Towcester, when between 7,000 and 8,000 passengers would be handled, many arriving in North London Railway carriages labled 'Mansion House'. These specials lasted until 1939.

From 1873 until 1902 through trains ran over the E & W from Euston to Stratford (except 1877–85) and from Marylebone from 1902, until 1936. Freight traffic varied. During the 1880s the LNWR sent through freight via Blisworth and Stratford, but more important was the Midland's use of the line between 1891 and 1913 for London–Avonmouth traffic, saving twenty-five miles on its Birmingham route. The LMS revived this traffic after 1927 so that the Broom–Ravenstone Wood Junction (near Olney) line was continuously manned except at weekends. World War II saw heavy traffic, but iron ore traffic from Byfield and Charwelton mines to South Wales was spasmodic. The Ravenstone Wood–Towcester line finally closed on 28 June 1958; one driver regularly kept a shotgun in his cab, catching rabbits for supper en route.

CHAPTER III

Northampton—The Town that Missed the Railway

On Saturday 31 May 1845 the London & Birmingham Railway's branch from Blisworth was opened from Northampton to Peterborough, when a party of the directors, accompanied by the Mayor and Corporation and other inhabitants of Northampton journeyed in a train of fifteen first class carriages from Northampton to Peterborough. The *Northampton Mercury* reported:

> Every station along the line was crowded with gazers, and at frequent intervals in the vicinity of a village, the fence was clustered with old and young, gentle and simple, looking with wondering eyes upon the imposing novelty.

Public patronage since 2 June, continued the report, was:

> so unexpectedly heavy that considerable delays occurred. In the early part of the week it was utterly impossible to accommodate the hundreds who thronged the intermediate stations.

This branch line was the poor reward for fifteen years of effort to obtain a direct railway to London. Ever since, Northampton has been notorious as the town that did not want the railway. Recent attempts at vindication have not destroyed this unjustifiable legend, for it was Northampton's geographical situation rather than its attitude that hindered the development of railways through the town, as it had done with the building of canals forty years earlier.

Northampton's importance dates from the twelfth century when the Normans built the castle, where parliaments were held and where Henry II quarrelled with Becket. By 1806 Northampton was England's principal shoemaking centre, as the industry had been stimulated by war at home and abroad for the past 160 years. The coming of the Grand Junction Canal in 1815 made possible further great increases in production. In the eighteenth century Northampton was important, too, as a stopping place for travellers on one of the main roads from London to the North; indeed, the innkeeping industry was the town's largest employer. The town's population growth reflected this rising prosperity. From about 5,000 in the mid-eighteenth century, it had reached 7,000 by 1800. Then the rapid expansion of the shoe industry caused a population increase of well above the national average, to reach 15,000 in 1831 and over 21,000 by 1845.

THE PROBLEM AND EARLY RAILWAYS

Northampton was an obvious town to be connected to the growing canal and railway systems were it not for the comparative difficulties of getting these systems to it, for the town is situated on the north bank of the River Nene, where its northern and western tributaries join. The surrounding countryside is hilly on three sides as the Northamptonshire Uplands stretch away to meet the Oxfordshire Cotswolds. The only easy route out is down the broad valley of the Nene to the east towards Wellingborough, Peterborough and the Fens; otherwise road, canal or railway must somewhere climb steeply out of the valley, especially when going south.

These geographical features created difficulties for the Grand Junction Canal engineers in the 1790s, which foreshadowed those faced by the Stephensons and others when planning and building the London & Birmingham Railway in the 1830s. They also caused the building of Northamptonshire's first two railways, over Blisworth Hill in 1800, and into Northampton in 1805.

The Grand Junction Canal was promoted as a direct link between the Midlands and London, but the crossing of the Northamptonshire Uplands was a major obstacle necessitating long tunnels at Braunston and Blisworth. The former through the Kilsby ridge was dug with no difficulty, but tunnelling at Blisworth failed, so the company decided to finish the rest of the canal first; it was opened in September 1800. The previous year, William Jessop, the canal's consulting engineer, advised that a 'cast iron' railway be built over Blisworth Hill

to cope with the expected heavy traffic between the two parts
of the canal. This idea was not novel, as such railways—
properly called tramways—were commonly used then as canal
feeders. The company agreed, after visiting industrial tramways in use in Derbyshire and Nottinghamshire. The contract was let to Benjamin Outram, an experienced tramway
engineer, in October 1799 for £9,750.

The double-track line between Blisworth and Stoke
Bruerne, on the line of the tunnel, was completed by the end
of 1800, regulations for the line's day-to-day running being
approved by the company in February 1801. It had flanged
rails, each 3ft 0in long and weighing at least 37lb, fixed to
locally-quarried stone sleepers. The gauge was probably 4ft
2in.

The company ordered eighty waggons at a cost of £800,
each desgined to carry 30–40cwt, though from the start the
conveyance of goods was in the hands of contractors, with
their own waggons. Elaborate sidings were unnecessary at
the wharves as the waggon wheels were flangeless; waggons
could be turned off the track and parked where convenient.
Up the steeper parts of the hill the waggons would be hauled
in twos or threes, then coupled into trains of about a dozen
and hauled by two or three horses. The freight carried
between the two parts of the canal included coal, lime, salt,
pig iron, stone, bricks, slates and timber, as well as manufactured goods and agricultural produce.

The line was well used for over four years until the opening
of the canal tunnel on 25 March 1805 rendered it unnecessary.
The rolling stock was then sold and the rails probably lifted,
being too valuable to abandon, although the stone sleepers
were not, and some may still be seen *in situ*.

Meanwhile Northampton had publicly approved the idea
of a canal in 1792. There were to be a branch from the Grand
Junction, and a direct line from Leicester down the northern
Nene Valley (Leicestershire & Northamptonshire Union
Canal), both joining the Nene in Northampton. The Grand
Junction would not build its branch until it saw what the
Union was doing, but the impecunious Union had abandoned
in 1795 its proposed canal beyond Market Harborough
because of the engineering difficulties involved in cutting
through the Uplands. After prolonged agitation from North-
ampton, alarmed at the prospect of no canal, the Grand

Junction reluctantly built a double-track tramway from Gayton, at a cost of £12,000 and opened on 7 October 1805. Many
of the rails were probably from the Blisworth Hill railway
recently abandoned, and it seems most likely they were laid
on wooden sleepers, as no stone ones have been found on its
course. Rolling stock, too, probably came from Blisworth, only
a mile south of Gayton.

This tramway, however, being essentially a second-best
solution, failed to satisfy Northampton, which still wanted
a canal branch. A five-mile branch from Gayton, falling
through seventeen locks into the Nene Valley, was opened on
1 May 1815, and the tramway, now the canal towpath, was
closed and lifted. Northampton was thus joined to the canal
system, and the shoe trade was stimulated accordingly, but
the abandonment of the 1792 Union line, and the presence of
seventeen locks on the Gayton branch, emphasised the physical
problems facing contemporary engineers working towards
Northampton—hence the thirty years' delay before Northampton was again on a railway.

PLANNING THE LONDON & BIRMINGHAM RAILWAY

There is no obvious route between London and Birmingham,
as any line must cross both the Chilterns and the long ridge of
the Oxfordshire Cotswolds, merging with the Northamptonshire Uplands. Sir John Rennie proposed a route via Oxford
and Banbury while Francis Giles favoured one via Coventry.
George Stephenson was called in to decide, and preferred
the Coventry route which the company adopted. The Stephensons were then made joint engineers-in-chief, though in
practice Robert did the detailed practical work.

On 5 October 1830 the *Northampton Mercury* reported a
rumour that Northampton was recommended as the central
point on the line, but this was mistaken as on 23 October
Robert Stephenson recommended to the company that the
line bypass Northampton by $4\frac{1}{2}$ miles to the west. Opposition
to the railway was growing from the landed gentry and clergy,
both numerous in that part of Northamptonshire, and led by
the Duke of Grafton, Mr Thornton of Brockhall and Sir
William Wake of Courteenhall (an ardent Whig, *pro* the
Reform Bill but very anti-railway). Not unreasonably, they
feared damage to their estates and a threat to their hunting.

They summed up their fears at a meeting at the White Horse Inn, Towcester, on 30 December 1830: the railways would 'spoil our shires and ruin our squires.' They then passed three resolutions:

1. That the railway would do great harm to properties passed through.
2. More than adequate means of transport exist between London and Birmingham by the numerous daily coaches (at 10mph) and the canal.
3. There is no necessity for greater speed than that supplied by improvements always being made in point 2.

On their second point they were on shaky ground as coach fares were very high, being by post (the fastest way) 1s 6d (7½p) per mile and 3d per mile for the post boy, plus tolls and tips. Although improvements as mentioned in the third point were proposed to counter railway competition, as for example the attempt in 1833 by the Northamptonshire road trustees, backed by Telford, to get a Bill for widening their turnpikes to take steam carriages, the railway killed them.

Yet at the same time there was strong feeling in Northampton that the railway should come through the town. A committee was appointed to urge this on the railway company, and in reply Stephenson explained the company's plans and offered a branch to the town as 'best that could be offered to meet the wishes of the town' (L & B minutes). In these negotiations the town was acting unofficially, as the unreformed corporation, a self-perpetuating body of Anglican Tories, was unrepresentative of commercial feeling in the town, and even early in 1831 opposed the railway through fear of its effects on the corporation's estates at Bugbrook. This is the only evidence of official Northampton opposition to the railway; it lasted a mere eight months.

The railways company's answer was to increase its propaganda and to explore other possible routes. The Northampton Corporation quickly dropped its opposition when the company threatened to take the railway twenty-four miles from the town, and then joined the committee in its negotiations with the company for a railway. The rural opposition took longer to overcome. Meanwhile Richard Creed, the company secretary, spent several weeks in the saddle exploring alternative routes, to avoid both landed opposition and the Kilsby ridge, one of his suggestions being a line from the West India

Docks, London, via Baldock and Bedford, through North-ampton, to rejoin the original route near Rugby. But in neither was he successful, and he reported that the company could only expect 'a change of difficulties as a result of an attempt to move the line more to the eastwards' (ie nearer Northampton). Stephenson fully confirmed this when he reported to the directors in October 1831:

> We have examined other districts of country by several lines of levels, with a hope that some of the expensive works on the present line might be obviated such as are occasioned by the high tracts of country at Ivinghoe (Bucks), Blisworth and Kilsby, but the result has been that the line upon which we report [substantially his original one] is the best between London and Birmingham, keeping in mind economy in the execution; favourable levels for the operation of locomotive engines; and ultimate economy in the conveyance of passengers and heavy goods.

In February 1832 the company's Bill began its Parliamentary career, and after much inquiry passed to the House of Lords. Here, in committee, the utility of the line was expounded, based on the popularity of the canal, and to its proximity to the military depot at Weedon, but to no avail. Grafton and Wake succeeded in getting the Bill defeated by 19–12, on the grounds that there was no case for forcing the railway through the estates of so many opposing landowners. This was followed by a meeting of peers, MPs and others favouring the railway, who resolved that the Bill's failure was due to landowners' fears about the effect on their estates, which they believed were unfounded. The railway company then reopened negotiations with their opponents to gain their support; by January 1833 Wake and Grafton assented, while Thornton was neutral. All were suitably compensated, Mr Thornton to the extent of having the company's fences erected at the bottom of the railway cutting where the line ran through his estate, rather than at the top where they spoiled his view. The Bill received the Royal Assent in May 1833, the route being Stephenson's line of October 1831. The company had spent the enormous sum of over £72,000 on getting its Act, before ever a rail was laid, but wide opposition to a project of this magnitude was inevitable, especially from substantial conservative landowners whose estates were to be cut apart in the interests of a commercial class for which they had scant sympathy.

THE NORTHAMPTON LEGEND

Northampton would definitely not be on the main line, but why was it preferable to run the line four miles to the west? One suggestion has been that the Duke of Wellington, as Master-General of the Ordnance, put pressure on the company to run past the Ordnance depot at Weedon, which would be impossible if the line ran through Northampton. Wellington however was well out of power in 1831, and it was the company which gained the support of the military authorities.

Then there is the legend that the town's opposition lost it the railway, though the extent of that opposition has been shown. The origins of the legend are obscure, but it was certainly published in 1839 in Roscoe's little guidebook *The London and Birmingham Railway*. Ten years later it was given publicity in Sir Francis Head's semi-official history of the LNWR (successor to the L & B) *Stokers and Pokers*, especially as it maintained that Northampton's opposition to the railway necessitated the building of Kilsby Tunnel. Samuel Smiles repeated this in his biography of George Stephenson (1857). The then Mayor of Northampton protested, quoting the favourable resolution passed by the committee in 1830. Smiles wrote to Robert Stephenson for an explanation, and got this reply which he published in *Lives of the Engineers*:

> Meetings were held in almost every town on the line both for and against the railway, but Northampton distinguished itself by being rather more furious than other places in opposition to railways and begged that the line might be kept away from them. It is true that the low level of Northampton presented a very grave objection to the line approaching it nearer than it does; but I had a strong leaning for that direction because it would have admitted of the line approaching the Kilsby Ridge up the Althorp Valley in a favourable manner.

Stephenson had considerably changed his tune from his report of 23 October 1830 (before any local protest meeting) and in any case a line up the Althorp Valley would still have rejoined the 1830 line south of Kilsby, which was the obvious place to pierce the Uplands. Herein seems to lie the reason for Stephenson's strong support for the Northampton legend. The boring of Kilsby Tunnel with its disastrous sequence of events captured the imagination of the age, but the disasters were the result of vital surveying blunders which might well have ruined the reputation of a lesser man than Stephenson. He was expecting no difficulties as the boring of the Braunston canal tunnel three miles away had encountered none. If Kilsby was a distasteful episode for Stephenson, it would be convenient to lay the blame for having to build the tunnel on the obstinate opposition to the railway of the neighbouring big town. (This hypothesis is fully argued by a local historian, Mr Victor Hatley—see bibliography.)

There were sound political and geographical reasons for taking the line west of Northampton. Stephenson liked 'to avoid parks and pleasure grounds where possible' (sic) and a line through Northampton would be bound to pass close to Althorp, seat of Earl Spencer, whose son was then Chancellor of the Exchequer; their possible opposition might have been fatal. He also liked 'to select a line on which the difference between the highest and lowest levels is the best [ie least] which the character of the country will admit of', preferring no gradients steeper than 1 in 330. By avoiding Northampton he avoided a sharp drop into the Nene Valley as shown by the seventeen locks on the canal branch. His opinion was that it would be easy enough to get the trains into Northampton, but very difficult to get them out again. Bearing in mind the inadequate and barely reliable locomotive power available in 1830, he had a strong point, though it also shows lack of foresight regarding the development of railway locomotives that the new main line would stimulate. There is the other point, that Stephenson favoured the 'inter-city' idea, joining the largest towns by the shortest easy route available, unlike Hudson who would build his lines towards all centres of population en route. Stephenson would therefore have felt unconcerned about leaving Northampton to the east, so it was thus left off the new railway. The town may have been inconvenienced, but Stephenson produced a well-engineered railway eminently suitable later for high-speed running, as the present 100mph Inter-City expresses show.

MAJOR EARTHWORKS

Building of the L & B began in June 1834 and after four years the line was opened from London to Denbigh Hall

(Bletchley) and between Rugby and Birmingham, passengers being carried by coach over the intervening section. The delay in opening the line throughout was caused by the heavy earthworks needed at Roade and Kilsby. The Roade (or Blisworth) cutting, 1½ miles long and sixty-five feet deep at its lowest point, was dug through limestone on top of clay. One million cubic yards of spoil were removed by 800 men of various trades, using 3,000 barrels of gunpowder. Retaining walls over 2ft 0in thick in places were built to keep the clay from bulging. Even so the LNWR deepened the cutting in 1875 to take the new Northampton line, and lengthened the retaining walls. Nevertheless there was a bad slip after heavy rain in November 1891, followed by another of 2,000 tons the following January before the earlier slip had been cleared by 2,000 navvies. Iron girders were then placed across the Northampton line to keep back the retaining walls; each one (there are more than a hundred) had to be raised a few inches to accommodate the overhead wires when the line was electrified in 1966.

The contract estimate for Kilsby Tunnel was £98,988. Some trouble with water was expected, but not the quicksand which suddenly broke into the workings, causing the men to swim for their lives to the shaft. Drainage proved impossible, so for over eight months water was pumped out at an average rate of 2,000 gallons per minute. The contractor had gone bankrupt and died, leaving the company to finish the work. Later, seventy yards of brickwork collapsed. In all, over three million bricks were used in the 1½ mile tunnel; the cost was £291,030. But these troubles were not all, for in April 1837 the navvies rioted, and the militia had to be called in from Weedon to quell them. Drainage problems continued to plague the tunnel into the present century.

The London & Birmingham railway was opened throughout on 17 September 1838 with six trains each way, all except the Night Mail calling at Blisworth, for Northampton. Expresses took 3hr 11min from Euston to Blisworth, the two mixed trains, calling at all stations took twenty minutes longer. Single fares for this journey were 18s 6d (92½p) first class and 11s 6d (57½p) second class, no third class fare being quoted. Children under ten went half-fare, infants in arms, unable to walk, free. Smoking was strictly forbidden, even on station platforms with the consent of fellow passengers. A writer in 1838 could happily state that the Northampton to London journey, which recently took two days, with an overnight stop at Dunstable, now took three hours (he was optimistic as it was more like four!) Royal patronage came on 12 November 1844 when Queen Victoria and Prince Albert travelled from London to Weedon by train in 2hr 18min, including a water stop at Tring, en route for Burleigh House, Stamford.

THE PETERBOROUGH BRANCH

Northampton was itself at last reached by a railway when the L & B proposed a branch from Blisworth, through Northampton, and along the Nene Valley to Peterborough. Among the advantages cited were earlier postal deliveries in Peterborough, Wisbech and King's Lynn, and the carriage of cattle from the lush Nene pastures. The line, opened for passengers to Northampton on 13 May 1845, and on to Peterborough on 2 June 1845 was easy and cheap to build, the $47\frac{1}{2}$ miles of line taking only two years to lay, at a cost of £429,409, but it was prone to flooding, as was shown in 1847 and 1852 when parts of embankments and bridges were swept away. The stations, many in an attractive mock-Tudor style, were situated where the line crossed roads, and served more than one village lying a mile or more away up the valley sides. In recent years these inconveniently-sited stations were unable to compete with local buses running through the villages. Local traffic declined even between the towns (Northampton, Wellingborough, Thrapston, Oundle and Peterborough) while the many level crossings were expensive to man, so in spite of its utility as a through route, it was closed to passengers on 4 May 1964, and to goods in stages between 1964 and 1972.

The initial service was three slow and two fast trains each way, four coming from Euston. Journey times between Euston and Northampton were between $2\frac{1}{2}$ and three hours, with another good two hours on to Peterborough. By comparison, in 1963 there were four trains from Northampton to Peterborough, each taking just under $1\frac{1}{2}$ hours. There were two through buses after the line was closed, taking about $2\frac{1}{2}$ hours.

THE SOUTH MIDLAND RAILWAY

The most important of the several early but unsuccessful schemes concerning Northampton was the South Midland Railway of 1836, to join the Midland Counties Railway at Leicester with the L & B near Blisworth, with a branch from Market Harborough to Stamford. The Marquis of Northampton headed the list of patrons, showing how the attitude of the landed interest had changed over the last six years:

> It is not now the question whether the prinicipal lines of railways throughout the country will be formed or not. This is certain. The question is, Shall the important districts here referred to [ie the area covered by SMR] participate or not in the advantages that other parts of our country will inevitably be possessed of? (from a pamphlet supporting the SMR.)

Northampton had originally supported the MCR, assuming their line would come through the town, but when it discovered its mistake, it promoted the SMR to bring the MCR's goods traffic, especially coal from Derbyshire and Nottinghamshire, southwards through Northampton instead of through Rugby as the MCR planned. In the opinion of the meeting in Northampton to promote the SMR, it would give Northampton the coveted direct access to London whereby 'the trading and general interests of this town and neighbourhood would be greatly benefitted.'

Cogent arguments were put forward showing the advantages of the SMR line both *per se* and over the MCR's Rugby line. It would be shorter, have easier gradients and avoid Kilsby Tunnel (a great advantage to passengers in open coaches). Greater passenger traffic would be available, as shown by the twenty-eight daily coaches between Northampton and Leicester (three more than between Liverpool and Manchester before the railway) as opposed to one running four times a week between Rugby and Leicester. Northampton with its thriving markets was an entrepot for agricultural produce, sending corn to Leicester, and wool to the Leicester and Yorkshire textile industries, while cattle from the lush Northamptonshire pastures were popular at Smithfield. Annually sent from Market Harborough to Smithfield were 39,300 head of fat cattle and 135,000 fat sheep and lambs, but their condition deteriorated badly after the eighty- to ninety-mile walk, their value dropping by £1 18s 6d (£1·92½) per head of fat cattle. Lambs dropped 7s 6d (37½p) each. The railway charge would be £1 os 9d (£1·04) and 3s 6d (17½p) respectively bringing obvious profits to railway and farmer. Coal too would be cheaper in Northamptonshire by over 4s (20p) per ton compared with canal-borne coal, while Ketton stone and wine, timber, pitch, hemp and other Baltic goods imported via King's Lynn would reach a wide market in the south. Access to Birmingham and the west, which the Rugby line would allow, was only the MCR's second aim 'one of much less importance' (*sic*), and in any case could be given by the proposed Derby–Burton–Birmingham line.

These arguments sufficiently convinced parliament to introduce a clause into the MCR's Bill suspending powers for the Leicester–Rugby line until August 1837, and asking the MCR not to oppose the SMR. In spite of all this, the Rugby line was built; its utility was short-lived, for serious delays to passengers and coal traffic were evident by 1847, prompting the Midland Railway (as successor to the MCR) to build its own London line. These delays caused the SMR scheme to be revived during the Railway Mania in 1845, with additional branches to Bedford and Huntingdon, but the scheme lapsed.

When Northampton and Market Harborough were joined, it was by the LNWR, with a branch rather than a main line, and no lasting connection with Leicester via the Midland. The branch left the Peterborough line west of Northampton station (later Bridge Street) and passed through a new small station by the old castle and West Bridge, which the company rebuilt for the corporation, heading north up the Nene Valley. It was authorised in 1853 and opened on 16 February 1859. As with the Peterborough branch the stations were at road crossings serving villages more than a mile distant, so local passenger traffic fell an easy prey to increased road competition; passenger services ceased on 4 January 1960 except for occasional excursions and the overnight Glasgow–Leeds–London sleeper. Through traffic to Leicester had to be worked via Wellingborough until the LMS in 1924 laid a connection between ex-LNWR and MR metals north of Market Harborough station. This involved lowering the LNWR line by six inches. The *Northampton Independent* for 5 April commented 'the improvement cannot fail to be a boon to the ordinary travelling public, and will tend to accelerate business between Northampton and our neighbours at Leicester.' It was rarely used by passenger traffic, as Leicester trains still ran via Wellingborough, and Nottingham trains used the Joint Line (Chapter VI), whose opening in 1879 involved the doubling of the branch. The line finally closed in 1981.

OTHER SCHEMES AND LINES

Other local mania schemes involved railways from Northampton to Warwick and Worcester, Banbury and Cheltenham, Bedford and Cambridge, and Lincoln and Hull, this last to tap the traffic potential of North Lincolnshire and bring it south. A wider project was the Midland & Eastern Counties Railway linking Cambridge, Northampton and Worcester, joining several railways and opening up coalfields and agricultural districts alike. The long-term utility of the scheme was shown by its revival a century later as a part of the post-war reconstruction plan.

In 1847 Northampton was served by nine trains from Euston, day return fares being 14s 6d (72½p) and 10s 6d (52½p). Benefits Northampton received from the railway were not great. The shoe trade was already flourishing when the railway came, war and the canal having provided the stimulus, and no new major industries arrived until the twentieth century. All that can be said is that it prevented stagnation, and it enabled Northampton's goods to be carried away quicker than by canal. In 1852 the corporation complained to the LNWR directors that its freight and coal charges were excessive, to which the directors replied that traffic to Northampton was expensive as a result of the town's position away from the main line, '. . . a position which was caused by circumstances quite beyond their control' (sic).

In 1859 the town was complaining strongly at its lack of adequate railway facilities. A public meeting chaired by the mayor called for a new main line from Bletchley to Rugby through the town, '. . . if the line were . . . intended only for the local traffic we believe it would be an injury rather than a benefit to the town.' It wanted fast through trains to London, better connections at Blisworth, and more trip workings thence and to Wellingborough (MR) to connect with northbound expresses. (These sentiments were shared by many people a century later.) 'The present stations [ie Blisworth and Northampton] are a disgrace to the company' (*sic*). As there was no connection at Market Harborough, Midlands coal had to come via Rugby, which was unnecessarily expensive at $\frac{3}{4}$d per ton mile compared with a possible $\frac{1}{2}$d per ton mile from Swannington. The meeting resolved that if it got no satisfaction, the town would encourage a competing company.

Sixteen years later the LNWR obtained powers to quadruple the main line northwards from Bletchley, the two new tracks (the 'slow' lines) diverging at Roade to form a main line through Northampton, up the Althorp Valley to Rugby. The new line fell into the Nene Valley on a long gradient of 1 in 103, joining the Market Harborough branch sharply at Castle station, and leaving it at Kingsthorpe. Castle station was rebuilt, the river being diverted for $\frac{1}{4}$ mile, while the castle ruins were bought and demolished in 1880 to make way for the new goods shed. The Northampton–Rugby section opened to passengers on 1 December 1881, followed by the line to Roade on 3 April 1882.

The Midland Railway reached Northampton from Wellingborough in 1866 by exercising running powers in retaliation for similar LNWR actions in the Burton area. The MR built its own station in Northampton over the road from Bridge Street, but the services did not cater for local traffic to Wellingborough, which remained an LNWR preserve until 1923. The MR's other line, acquired in 1885, but worked from its opening on 10 June 1872, was the Bedford branch, promoted as an independent line joining Bedford, Northampton and Weedon, but only authorised in 1865 to Northampton because of the difficulties of making a good junction at Weedon. The company built its own station in the garden of St John's Hospital, off Bridge Street, and built Guildhall Road as access. With its sharp curves and steep gradients, the branch was well suited for operation by the experimental BR diesel railbuses from 1958. At times they were crowded but a prolonged closure battle killed patronage, the line being closed for passengers on 5 March 1962, and for goods on 20 January 1964, except for the section from Hardingstone Junction to Piddington Ordnance Depot, which the army operated until 1981. St Johns Street station closed on 3 July 1939, after the crossover at Hardingstone Junction had been reversed to allow Bedford line trains to use Castle Station.

THE DAVENTRY BRANCH

A late development was the LNWR branch from Weedon to Daventry, which although proposed intermittently since 1845, was not authorised until 1885. It was opened with great rejoicing in Daventry on 1 March 1888, with six trains each way, taking ten minutes for the journey, compared with thirty by the horse bus, the return fare being 8d. There were 186 people on the 12.35 train which included a special coach for the corporation. At the inevitable banquet which followed, the mayor 'considered the railway was the greatest boon that ever reached the town of Daventry' (*sic*), and hoped for an increase in trade. This was no idle hope, for Daventry had been a flourishing old town before the opening of the L & B fifty years earlier, which robbed it of its through trade and prosperity; as the *Northampton Daily Reporter* commented, 'All its brilliancy and power has been lost by the seclusion which distance from the iron road entails.' The festivities continued with tea for 600 at 6.00pm that evening, followed by entertainment and dancing until 4.00am, the next day. Truly, continued the paper, Daventry was celebrating 'its place in the accessible civilization of the world'.

The railway, however, came too late to have any lasting effect on the town. The line was single, although earthworks allowed for doubling if traffic required, but even after the extension to Marton was opened on 1 August 1895, giving access to Leamington and Birmingham, the sharp curves and stiff gradients made through express working unlikely as an alternative to the well-established Rugby route, despite the hopes of the *Northampton Herald*. Daventry station was primitive, open to the fury of north-east winds so that '. . . on a cold day . . . with the snow a foot deep on all the countryside, there is probably not a colder station in the Midlands.' Thus commented the *Northampton Daily Reporter*, which also castigated the old Weedon station, with low, badly-paved platforms, as a 'positive disgrace'. On 25 January 1906, as an economy measure, the LNWR introduced a short-lived railmotor service accommodating fifty people, from Northampton to Daventry via Blisworth, promising new halts if traffic improved, but these never materialised. Weedon station and the branch were closed on 15 September 1958.

TWENTIETH-CENTURY DEVELOPMENTS

The most important development under the LMS was the choice of Northampton as a major freight sorting point. A new 24 siding marshalling yard was laid north of Castle Station in 1933, where freight from London to the Midlands and North West is sorted, this being easier than sending transfer freight trains from Willesden to Brent. BR has continued this policy, involving extensive use of the Market Harborough line as the connection to the East Midlands. This was why Northampton was chosen as the major interchange point between north–south lines and the 1944 projected new cross-country line from Yarmouth and Harwich to Worcester and Aberystwyth.

This concentration on freight meant indifferent passenger services on the main line. Complaints were being made in the early 1930s of slow services, resulting in an express timed to reach Euston in seventy minutes. In 1955 there were fourteen express and slow trains to Euston, the best time being seventy-four minutes, the worst, 2hr 20min. With the onset of electrification work, timings were increased, so that in 1963, trains were usually fifteen minutes slower. Services to Rugby and beyond were reduced from nineteen to sixteen.

The electrification of the Northampton loop proceeded with that of the main line, and new timetables were inaugurated on 18 April 1966. A smart new station was built, much appreciated by the town, and a basically hourly interval service of eighteen trains to London and Rugby or Coventry introduced. However, the service is now essentially 'outer suburban' and takes seventy-seven minutes to do the $65\frac{3}{4}$ miles to Euston. An 'Inter-City' service is impossible because of the concentration of freight through Northampton. Through freight trains including 70mph freightliner trains cannot be switched to the fast lines between Roade and Rugby because they would delay 100mph Inter-City expresses; they must follow the slow lines up from London into the Northampton loop. Similarly Inter-City trains would be excessively delayed by passing through Northampton, though the situation might alter following the proposed electrification of the Midland lines, which could involve the Market Harborough line.

The effects of Northampton missing the main line have been long-lasting. Its communications north and east depended on branch lines which were unable to survive increased road competition, in spite of the projected expansion of Northampton, Wellingborough and Peterborough, which made the East Midlands Study of 1966 call for better east–west communications; it suggested roads. (There is, however, talk of restoring Northampton–Leicester services.) Its passenger services to London and the West Midlands have taken second place to freight, but much of the freight does not originate in the town. Of the new industries that have come in recent years, like roller bearings, electronics, cosmetics and clothing, none are heavy industries vitally dependent on the railway. Since 1950, light engineering has displaced the shoe trade as Northampton's major employer, but its products are not railborne. Only the Esso storage depot has increased Northampton's own heavy freight traffic, though the cosmetics firm makes considerable use of the parcels facilities.

The first major railway influence on Northampton has been the electrified railway, which since 1966 has turned Northampton into a commuter town for London, Coventry and Birmingham. Its big planned expansion, to 230,000 inhabitants by 1981, was based equally on its position on the electrified railway, for passengers, and proximity to the M1 motorway, for freight. Although the increase has been slower than anticipated, reaching only 156,853 by 1981, commuter traffic is extensive, justifying seven trains to Euston in the period 07.11–08.13 and likewise in the $1\frac{1}{4}$ hours after 16.30, in the 1983 timetable. Each way one train takes under the hour, stopping once, and other fast trains have been put on, but the main off-peak timings are still depressing at over eighty minutes. A random example shows two trains leaving Euston at 15.00 : a Liverpool express and one for Northampton and Birmingham. The former calls at Milton Keynes Central (49 miles) at 15.36, twenty-five minutes before the Northampton train which has already stopped five times. As the Liverpool express has four more intermediate calls, would the extra twelve minutes via the Loop, to give Northampton both a fast journey and a northbound express, be commercially damaging? As it is, there are still no northbound trains other than to Birmingham, although at least the daytime trains there (but not the evening) are spared the all-stations trudge.

CHAPTER IV

Northamptonshire

In its 75th Anniversary Souvenir Edition in 1972 the *North-amptonshire Evening Telegraph* commented: '. . . if the boot and shoe industry was the county's backbone, the iron industry was its sinew.' The boot and shoe industry was long established and, as seen in Chapter III, was developing in Northampton before the advent of the railways. The iron industry, however, despite its local origins in Roman times, owed its reintroduction and subsequent development in the mid-nineteenth century almost entirely to the presence of the railways. From small beginnings in 1851 with scattered furnaces using local ore deposits, mining and smelting have been thoroughly exploited, culminating in the establishment of the giant Stewarts & Lloyds steelworks at Corby in 1934. This chapter will seek to relate the growth of the railway system and of the iron industry, dealing in particular with Central Northamptonshire, the most important area.

The Rockingham Forest area is the heart of the North-amptonshire field and had been an important iron-producing area since Roman times, ironworks at 'Corbei and Gretone' being mentioned in Domesday Book. However, in the six-teenth century, increasing demand for iron, still smelted by charcoal, conflicted with the demand for timber for the navy, expanding for war with Spain, so Elizabeth I forbade all iron smelting in Rockingham Forest. By the nineteenth century, iron smelting using coked coal was technically possible, but until mid-century there were sufficient deposits elsewhere of iron ore close to coal-producing areas to satisfy the increasing demands of the Industrial Revolution. In 1815, samples of Northamptonshire ore aroused no interest among ironmasters, and even at the Great Exhibition of

1851, samples from Woodford, on the edge of the Forest, were labelled as 'at present of no commercial value'. Local men thought differently, and the ore was once again being successfully smelted by 1853, its exploitation being led by Thomas Butlin at Wellingborough. Production of ore began on a small scale at various places in the county during the 1850s, producing in 1860 some 96,000 tons, but this was only 1·2 per cent of total UK production. However, with demand for iron and steel still increasing, by 1872 over one million tons of ore were being mined annually in the county, between six and seven per cent of the national total.

This great increase in production was considerably aided by the presence of railways. The Midland Railway main line was opened in 1857 to link Leicester with Hitchin, and so to London via the Great Northern Railway. It was not primarily conceived to exploit the mineral resources en route, for even in 1857 these were hardly known, but cuttings were dug through rich seams in the Desborough area; the railway company was not slow to develop their commercial possibilities. Conversely, two later lines were built to exploit the iron-ore deposits, first the Kettering, Thrapstone & Huntingdon Railway, then the MR's Kettering to Nottingham direct line, planned to exploit the ore field either side of the Welland Valley, as well as providing Nottingham with a faster line to London. The effect of this new industry on the towns and villages of central Northamptonshire has been considerable. Kettering was rescued from decline, Wellingborough rose from an ordinary village to an important town, while Corby New Town was created from a hamlet amid green fields.

THE MIDLAND MAIN LINE

Schemes for giving Leicester access to London and the south appeared early in railway history. George Stephenson was contemplating a branch to Derby from the London & Birmingham Railway near Northampton in 1830, and when in 1836 it became known that the Midland Counties Railway was preparing a link to Rugby to join the L & BR, then well under construction, an alternative line, the South Midland Railway, was proposed linking Leicester with Northampton, joining the L & BR at either Roade or Blisworth, and with a branch from Market Harborough to Stamford. The arguments in favour of this line as they affected Northampton and Market Harborough are discussed in Chapters III and VI.

In spite of some Parliamentary support, the SMR was passed over in favour of the MCR's Rugby extension, opened in 1840. Nevertheless, it was not long before a new connection southwards was being called for, as delays to passengers and coal alike were frustrating, while the inhabitants of Market Harborough and Bedford made very explicit their need for a railway. The result, during the Railway Mania, was the revival of the SMR, along with proposals for two other schemes. Of these, the Direct London & Manchester was really a non-starter, but the other, the Leicester & Bedford Railway, had powerful local backing. By this time, too, the MCR had amalgamated with other midland companies to form the Midland Railway, and was under the energetic chairmanship of George Hudson.

The SMR scheme of 1845 was wider than its 1836 plan, for two additional branches were planned, from Market Harborough to Bedford, and from Pytchley (near Kettering) to Huntingdon. Several connections would be made with the L & BR: at Northampton, with possibly an extension to the main line in the Roade area, near Irthlingborough, where the Huntingdon and Peterborough branches would cross, and at Bedford. Hudson invested £600,000 of Midland money in it, for it aimed at countering the proposed London & York Railway (authorised on 26 June 1846 as the Great Northern Railway) which seemed set to corner the traffic south of Nottingham by agreement with the Leicester & Bedford.

The Leicester & Bedford was nominally an independent concern, backed by influential local interests including William Astell, MP for Bedfordshire, and William Whitbread, the largest landowner along the route. They were anxious to see a line through Bedford to London, and were prepared to negotiate with either the Midland or the London & York, but receiving a more cordial welcome from the latter, tended to support York schemes. The London & York emerged during 1845 as the greatest threat to Hudson's empire, for it challenged his monopoly of the growing traffic between York and London. As such, it befriended the Leicester & Bedford by providing for a junction with it at Hitchin to allow through running to London.

In 1846 Parliament took a hand in this complicated game of railway politics, by favouring the anti-Hudson party. Not only did it push through the GNR's Act, but the House of Commons supported the Leicester & Bedford Bill while dismissing that of the SMR on the evidence of Robert Stephenson, who mistakenly said that London traffic from the SMR would travel over LNWR metals from Bedford. Furious activity by the SMR in explaining away Stephenson's error persuaded the House of Lords to reject the Leicester & Bedford Bill, only to encourage this party to try again the next year, backed this time by £750,000 of GNR money, half the total share capital. Before this could happen, Hudson called a meeting on 4 September 1846 at the Swan Hotel, Bedford, where he tried to reconcile the two local parties. No chairman had been appointed for the meeting and it broke up in disorder, with angry recriminations between Whitbread and the Midland's solicitor over the integrity of the SMR proposals. Another critic condemned the LNWR as 'only fit to carry charity children'.

Although the battle between the Hudson and the York parties concerned far wider issues than a local railway through Bedford and central Northamptonshire, Whitbread was determined that local interests would not be ignored. Accordingly he attended a conference at Derby in October with Hudson and Captain Laws of the GNR, where it was decided that the MR should purchase the Leicester & Bedford, while abandoning the SMR. Within two years the Midland would build the line through to Hitchin, making a junction there with the GNR which would offer no opposition to the Bill in Parliament. Still Hudson would not concede defeat, for he put into the Bill a clause seeking authority to cross the GNR in order to make a junction with his Eastern Counties Railway, then aiming for Hitchin from Hertford. Had this succeeded, Hudson's aim of controlling his own route to London would have triumphed, but Parliament realised his intention and deleted the clause. The Bill was passed on 9 July 1847.

After this flurry of activity during the Mania, the Midland failed to build the line to Hitchin within the stated five years. Nationally, money was in short supply, while the Midland's own finances were stretched under Hudson's unbridled ambition; in 1849 his fall nearly brought the Midland down with him. By the time John Ellis was secure as chairman, both the LNWR and the GNR had made inroads into MR interests, the powers under the 1847 Act had lapsed, and Whitbread was again making difficult noises.

The national economic climate was more favourable after the Great Exhibition of 1851, and consequently saw the revival of several local railway schemes, of which the Leicester & Bedford was one. Under Whitbread's able leadership, a deputation met Ellis at Derby, leaving the latter in no doubt that if they failed to obtain satisfaction from the Midland, then they would court other interested parties. This implied the GNR, which still aimed at access to Leicester and the Midland coalfield. The merits of this local scheme were still being subordinated to the wider issues of the Midland's independence and its desire for a route to London other than via Rugby. On this point the need was pressing, for in 1852 325,000 tons of coal alone passed through Rugby from the Midland, bound for the growing markets in London and the South, and the LNWR was hard put to accommodate it satisfactorily. Concurrently, Ellis was holding exploratory talks with both the LNWR and the GNR over amalgamation with the Midland, in order to obtain better facilities to London, for the Midland then could not afford to build its own line. In fact, a Bill was prepared for the 1853 Parliamentary session authorising the Midland's amalgamation with the LNWR, but Parliament was then suspicious of creating large railway monopolies and therefore rejected the Bill.

In view of the collapse of the amalgamation plan, the need for an improved connection with London, and the threat of GNR support for the Leicester & Bedford, coupled with a rising trend in Midland goods traffic and the possibility of tapping some iron ore traffic in Northamptonshire, Ellis had no difficulty in persuading first his board, and then the shareholders at Derby on 1 June 1853, to approve the extension of the Midland main line from Leicester to Bedford and Hitchin. In fact Ellis had long supported this extension, for on 14 July 1852 he had chaired the first meeting of the Leicester & Hitchin Extension Committee to survey a possible route and negotiate with favourable landowners. Whitbread responded by offering the necessary land to the company for its agricultural value of about £70 an acre—a valuable concession as over seven miles of the projected line would pass through his estates. The Duke of Bedford at Woburn followed suit.

The necessary Bill was passed on 4 August 1853 with little opposition, as the GNR had been bought off with useful concessions in Yorkshire, and had abandoned its plan for a branch from Sandy to Bedford. Thus was authorised a line which local interests had been calling for over the previous seventeen years, but which was built primarily to serve the wider competitive interests of the Midland. Nevertheless, in spite of the presence of the LNWR at three points en route, (Market Harborough 1850, Wellingborough 1845 and Bedford 1846) the line was of considerable importance in the economic devlopment of central Northamptonshire.

Even then difficulties were not over, for with the onset of the Crimean War, men and money were in short supply. The shareholders would only produce £1 million for the whole of the 63 mile line, inclusive of rolling stock, so, said John Ellis to the engineers, 'there are £900,000 to make your line with. If it can't be done for that, it can't be done at all . . . go and do it for £15,000 a mile.' And so it was, albeit with 'a great deal of "scraping"', to quote the engineers, a tribute to them and to Thomas Brassey, the main contractor. The result was only one tunnel, south of Bedford, but three major summits at Kibworth, Desborough and Sharnbrook, the latter reached by three miles of 1 in 120 going south. At Wellingborough the viaduct over the Nene caused problems, for the clay embankment pushed the completed abutments and wings forward, and although not a single brick was displaced, much rebuilding had to be done. Similar trouble at Sharnbrook Bridge over the Ouse caused foundations 25ft deep to be dug beside a 20ft deep river. In all, seven bridges had to be built over the Ouse in the seven miles between Sharnbrook and Bedford, as well as 60ft cuttings at Desborough and Sharnbrook. Labour problems occurred at harvest time when the need to use all available hands in the fields was as strong as in medieval England, labourers simply abandoning the railway workings for a time.

The Midland had adopted a distinctive architectural style for its stations but using different local materials: Glendon station was built in limestone, Desborough, $2\frac{1}{2}$ miles away, in ironstone; Oakley in red brick, Great Glen in white. At the main stations of Kettering, Wellingborough and Bedford, ridged glass and wrought-iron roofs were built over the platforms, resting on a decorated iron framework. Only Market

Harborough stood out, for the line used the LNWR station until 1884 when the new Joint station was opened further south in the fork of the lines.

The line was opened for coal traffic on 15 April 1857, for goods on 4 May, and for passengers on 8 May. On 7 May there were excursions to Leicester from Kettering, Bedford and Hitchin. The Kettering one took 300 people for 1s od (5p) return, in thirty-three coaches pulled by two locomotives decorated with evergreens. The Bedford train comprised thirty-two coaches and was graced with a band at either end, that nearest the locomotive being dressed in white uniforms! The day was observed as a holiday in Bedford, Kettering and Market Harborough, and another series of specials was run to Bedford and Hitchin, carrying 2,000 from Kettering and another 1,000 from Desborough, Isham and other small stations. The procession to Kettering station was led by eight girls from the parish Sunday School, followed by the boys from the National and Sunday Schools with their staff. The children were treated to the trip and, as the *Northampton-shire Advertiser*'s reporter observed: 'it was truely gratifying to observe their countenances lit up into joyous transports at their excursion.' Only 400 went on to sample the delights of Hitchin. Most detrained at Bedford, where the children were given bread and cheese, while selected adults enjoyed a good dinner with 'choice wines'. Wellingborough was more *blasé* about the whole affair, having been on a railway for twelve years.

The passenger service was originally of four trains daily each way, two stopping at all stations. In order not to offend the LNWR at Market Harborough, and elsewhere, the Midland put its passenger (except third class) and coal rates from Leicester to London the same on both the Rugby and Hitchin routes. Furthermore, through bookings were not allowed from north of Leicester to King's Cross, nor from intermediate stations between Leicester and Hitchin to intermediate stations between Hitchin and King's Cross. Trains for Hitchin were not to run north of Leicester, and it was not until 1 February 1858 that Midland passenger trains could run into King's Cross, goods trains following from 1 October. Meanwhile the Rugby route continued to enjoy through bookings and the bulk of the passenger traffic.

All three companies—LNWR, MR and GNR, saw their

freight traffic expand rapidly during the early 1860s, causing congestion into London. At Rugby in 1862 five miles of coal trains built up waiting to move south, despite the third track laid by the LNWR into London; there were frequent delays to the 2,382 Midland goods and 961 passenger trains running through to the GNR. Such problems, coupled with worsening relations with the GNR, all combined to make the MR present a Bill to Parliament in 1863 for an extension from Bedford to London. The opening of the new line in 1868 ensured that the Leicester–Bedford section became part of the Midland main line, and its services increased accordingly, with thirteen trains each way daily.

From the later 1870s, the main line was progressively quadrupled south of Kettering, with easier gradients going south. The new lines were to the east of the original tracks, but between Kettering and Wellingborough (both exclusive) the new lines were built to the west, which involved rebuilding Burton Latimer station—formerly Isham—in the same style as Corby on the Manton line. The original overbridges were built of red brick, but the new extensions were in blue.

The most important of these works was the Wymington Deviation, a 3½ mile line opened on 4 May 1884. It curves away east of the old line between Irchester and Sharnbrook stations, and tunnels for 1,860yd under the summit. The main aim was to give the heavy southbound coal trains, mostly hauled by small Johnson o–6–os, nothing steeper than 1 in 200 to climb as opposed to the existing three miles of 1 in 120, with the result that whereas they could only take thirty-one loaded mineral wagons over the original summit, they could take thirty-eight on the deviation.

KETTERING AND DESBOROUGH

Of the Northamptonshire towns and villages on the line, Kettering and Wellingborough developed most, although the development of iron ore mining brought increased prosperity to many other places. Kettering badly needed a new source of wealth, for it was in serious economic difficulties. In the early eighteenth century Kettering was 'a Place of Great Trade and very full of People; both of which are chiefly owing to the Woollen Manufacture.' In an age of bad roads, this worsted industry flourished, as the town was closer to London than its Yorkshire or East Anglian rivals, but as canals and turnpikes improved other areas' access to the capital, and with increasing competition from Lancashire cottons, Kettering's staple industry declined badly, and by 1821 half the 3,668 inhabitants were paupers. The shoe industry was developing, as elsewhere in the county, but not until after 1830. In 1851 Kettering's population was 5,125, third to Northampton and Peterborough but far behind both, and with no guarantee of maintaining it, for prices were high in the town as coal and other supplies had to be dragged over indifferent roads from railheads at Wellingborough or Market Harborough.

Even the discovery of iron ore on the railway did not immediately benefit Kettering. The ore was discovered at Desborough and Glendon to the north, in the railway cuttings, but Kettering lies mainly on embankments or level ground; it was not until about 1870 that it was realised Kettering also lay on a rich ore field. In 1871 quarrying began north west of the station and furnaces were built in 1878. The extensive narrow gauge railway here had many locomotives, one of which in the 1880s sported the name *Yum-Yum* from *The Mikado*, then highly popular in London. The furnaces finally closed on 24 May 1959, the quarries following on 24 October 1962.

Quarrying also began at Cransley, south-west of Kettering, in 1873, furnaces following in 1877. The MR opened a mineral branch to these on 19 February that year, taking away both iron and surplus ore. Within ten years the ore here was exhausted, and a new company opened quarries at Loddington, slightly further west, whither the MR extended its Cransley branch in April 1891, taking ore now both to Cransley furnaces and, in greater quantities, to Staveley. The metre-gauge lines at Loddington had unusual locomotives, one being from Cambrai in France, two being destined for Spain and one for Singapore, none having been sent. The Cransley furnaces were closed on 1 November 1957, the site soon being taken over by a large scrap merchant specialising in breaking-up redundant railway material including over a hundred steam locomotives, as well as coaches, wagons and London Underground stock. The majority of the scrap was taken away by rail all over the country, but especially to the

Plates 8 and 9 Change at Northampton: the second Castle Station *(above)* makes way for the third in 1966, whence a new semi-fast electric train departs for Coventry *(below)* past the goods shed, built on the site of the castle's keep. [Author.]

Plates 10 and 11 The railways and industry I: *(above)* a view from the road bridge of Corby ironworks about 1914; *(below)* one of Bass's engines working on to BR tracks past an old Midland signalbox in Burton. [Sir Frederick Scopes; S. A. Leleux.]

Birmingham and Sheffield areas until 1980. Beyond the furnaces the MR branch was lifted early in 1972, having been closed when the Loddington quarries closed on 6 July 1963.

This activity at Kettering after 1871 was reflected in a rising population. From 5,125 in 1851, it had doubled by 1881, and then rose by nearly a thousand a year to 28,653 in 1901. Over the last eighty years growth has been sustained but steady, the 1981 population being 45,356. Worries over the closure of the local furnaces have been offset by the rise of Corby and the introduction of light industries.

The opening of the Manton line for passengers in 1880 enhanced Kettering's importance as a railway centre, so that by 1903 it enjoyed twenty-six trains on the main line daily each way, some being Nottingham expresses. Other trains started at Kettering for the Nottingham and the Huntingdon lines, which respectively carried twelve down and ten up trains and five trains each way daily. Within less than a generation, Kettering had been put on the railway map and its prosperity assured. In 1973 it had twenty-one down and nineteen up trains daily, the semi-fasts taking about seventy-five minutes for the seventy-two miles from London, but with a best time of fifty-eight minutes non-stop. With the Manton and Huntingdon lines closed for passengers in 1966 and 1959 respectively, Kettering now serves as a railhead for a wide area, especially Corby; an Inter-City bus link to Peterborough via Corby and Oundle began in 1980.

Desborough was the first place on the MR to begin iron ore quarrying. Within months of the line opening, quarries were being worked. As the nearer supplies were exhausted, the miners went further afield, and the town expanded onto the abandoned workings. A population of 1,350 in 1851 had doubled by 1891. Other pits were opened in the area, including some in 1905 by the Desborough Industrial & Provident Co-operative Society Ltd, a unique venture for such an enterprise. In fact, some members feared 'the great capitalistic firms would undoubtedly boycott us as we were a Co-operative Society.' These fears proved groundless, as the ore sold well on the open market. Prior to 1914 output ran at 2,000 tons a week, and the Society employed 120 workmen whose annual wages bill was £7,000. During the 1912 coal strike, the furnaces and mines were badly hit. The Society tried to find work for all the men before being forced to lay them off, and even organised loans and charity. The slump of 1921 and General Strike of 1926 killed off all Desborough's pits except those supplying the Sheepbridge furnaces at Chesterfield with much of their ore, these closing at the end of 1966.

Lying in close proximity to the centre of Desborough, the station lasted well, being closed on 1 January 1968 along with the remaining three between Market Harborough and Leicester, (Kibworth, East Langton, Wigston). The other village stations between Leicester and Bedford had been closed by the end of 1960. Even so Desborough, the 'Co-op Town' and its partner Rothwell 1½ miles to the south, never developed as Kettering and Wellingborough did, their populations in 1961 being only 4,553 and 4,763 respectively, thrice and twice their 1851 figures.

WELLINGBOROUGH

With Wellingborough it is a different story. Originally its fortunes were built up on the wool trade, the annual Wool Fair being held into the present century, but with shoes taking over by 1800, when the population stood at about 3,000. This had risen to 5,000 by mid-century and the town had a secure place as the third largest shoe manufacturer in the county, a position it retained until Kettering took over a century later. The town was well served with coaches, having from 1810 a daily service to London for 16s od (80p) inside or 9s od (45p) outside, though these prices had risen by 1845 to about 4d–5d a mile inside or 2d–3d outside. The journey took up to ten hours. From 1839 one coach ran via Olney to Wolverton to connect with the 11.00am train from Euston, bringing passengers into Wellingborough by 4.30pm.

Wellingborough, then, was a thriving town when the L & BR opened its station, 1¼ miles out of town, on 2 June 1845. London Road Station, as it was known from LMS days, became the hub of a horse bus and carter service over a wide area of surrounding villages. There has always been a mill nearby on the River Nene; in 1880 it was taken over and rebuilt by Whitworths, who in 1969 brought in 25,000 tons of grain by rail from Tilbury, having previously shared this traffic between railway and canal via Northampton.

The real impetus came in the 1850s with Thomas Butlin's smelting of local iron ore, and the opening of the MR. In the thirty years after 1851 the population nearly trebled from 5,061 to 13,794, thereafter rising steadily to 30,583 by 1961. Although the Midland had to build Midland Road, opened in 1860, and to run horse buses to the Hind Hotel, to gain access to the town centre, the town has grown out towards this line in a way it has not towards the LNWR. The building of two separate furnaces, marshalling yards and engine sheds undoubtedly helped this by stimulating the need for workers' housing nearby, Midland Cottages for example, being built to house the station porters. With the coming of the London Extension in 1868, Wellingborough was roughly half way between the Erewash Valley and the capital. Accordingly, the MR built a large locomotive depot, always housing the biggest goods engines, which worked the heavy freight traffic passing through. A large hostel was built to accommodate engine crews unable to go home immediately. By 1980, with the end of the steam engine and loose-coupled goods train, the depot had no allocation of locomotives; one roundhouse (the wrong one!) was gone and the other was leased to a dried-fruit importer; the hostel was but a memory and the remaining marshalling yards were under delayed closure.

Butlin's first furnace was opened in 1852, but as his premises were cramped and had no rail access, in 1867 he opened two furnaces south of the MR station, producing nearly 400 tons of iron a week. By 1914 there were four furnaces producing up to 1,400 tons a week, but the post-war depression and General Strike killed them. Closed in 1926, they were dismantled in 1930, but foundry work continued, Morris Motors taking over and rebuilding the plant 1947–50. As British Leyland the plant employed some 800 men producing over a third of all BLMC cylinder blocks until its sudden closure in 1981. The output, though, was all road-borne, with only small amounts of coke and scrap arriving by rail.

Wellingborough's other furnaces were built in 1886 north of the station, the Midland building Neilson's Sidings to serve them. Ore came from quarries on Finedon Hill, brought down by narrow-gauge tramway. Segments for the tube tunnels of the Northern and Piccadilly Lines in London were cast here. Expansion before 1914 was followed by depression after 1920, although one furnace kept going until 1932. Then Stantons rebuilt the works which lasted until 1962 when Stewarts & Lloyds (owners since 1950) closed them as their integrated works at Corby was working below capacity. The tramway and quarries continued supplying Corby until 1966.

Closure of these furnaces threw 330 men and women out of work, but in the 1960s Wellingborough was designated as a developing town to take London overspill, and sufficient light industry such as printing, food processing and clothing manufacture was established to reduce unemployment to a minimum. The proposed population for 1981 was 85,000, although this was soon revised to 61,000 and then forgotten, for by 1981 it had only reached 43,899. Expansion brought greatly increased business in the passenger and parcels traffic, offsetting the decline in heavy freight following the closure of local ironstone mines. In 1968 some 72,000 passengers used the station, with traffic mainly to the London area. Twenty-five thousand parcels were despatched including clothing, cooked meats and books, while the station warehouses were full of tanned hides awaiting distribution. Altogether the station earned £68,000 from passengers and £326,000 from freight. HSTs further boosted business (see page 245).

A major loss on the freight side was the closure of the South Durham Steel & Iron Co's mines at Irchester and the Ebbw Vale (later Richard Thomas & Baldwin's) mines at Irthlingborough. The former were originally opened by Thomas Butlin in 1863, and closed finally on 6 June 1969. The extensive system, now partly converted into a country park, connected with the LNWR's Wellingborough station, and early on had sent much ore to Derbyshire; in the 1960s it was sending over 4,000 tons a week to Middlesbrough and Hartlepool. Unusually in the ironstone industry the Irthlingborough workings, opened in 1915, were actually mines, which honeycombed Finedon Hill for a total of forty-five miles, up to 100ft underground. About 4,500 tons of ore were sent out weekly until closure on 30 September 1965, three trains going to Scunthorpe weekly, and one daily to South Wales. A sintering plant was installed to crush and screen the ore, making it more economical to use, but by the later 1960s it was increasingly uneconomic to send low-iron-content home ores any distance, hence the closure of these and many other pits. The 300 men employed at Irthlingborough were mostly re-employed in other expanding local industries.

THE NORTHAMPTON BRANCH

The Midland opened a spur between the two Wellingborough stations in 1857, although it was not used for passenger services until 1 October 1866. It exercised running powers for all traffic over the LNWR to Hardingstone Junction, Northampton, where it built a short branch to a temporary single-platform terminus abutting onto Bridge Street. This was incorporated into the Midland's goods depot when the branch to St Johns Street Station was opened on 10 June 1872. A small engine shed, still standing, was built at the junction. The initial service was eight trains each way daily non-stop, three going on to either Leicester or London, and conversely. By 1901 there were twelve trains each way, all running to and from Kettering. In 1961 the service had contracted to nine push-and-pull trains from Wellingborough, (ten to Wellingborough) plus a through train to Nottingham, returning from Leicester. Sixty miles per hour was often reached with these units being pushed. Closure came on 4 May 1964 along with the Peterborough line. This latter had carried country children to and from Wellingborough's grammar schools— the 'Ringstead Prep' being a regular feature at the High School while the girls waited for the evening train home.

There were several ironstone workings in the Nene Valley, but none were long lasting, and gravel is now the main commodity dug. The Whiston and Earls Barton pits were stimulated by World War I and killed by the next depression. The Cogenhoe mines were open for over thirty years from 1858. Here ran a locomotive named *Alathea Choice*, after a local lady who was having an illicit love affair with its driver, her social inferior. All the pits had rail access.

THE HIGHAM FERRERS BRANCH

Higham Ferrers is an old market town which has failed to match the growth of neighbouring Wellingborough and Rushden. With only 965 inhabitants in 1831 it was already losing ground to Rushden with 1,245 inhabitants, for Higham (unlike Rushden) was effectively in the hands of the Duchy of Lancaster, which restricted building. From 1845 the towns were served by 'Higham Ferrers' station, later 'Irthlingborough' on the LNWR line, whence horse buses plied into the towns. Under one 'Bussy' Clarke, these continued into the present century. From 1857 the Midland's station at Irchester was nearer Rushden, but the towns remained without their own branch until 1893, although Rushden was expanding with the shoe trade.

Authorised in 1890, the new line was intended to link up with the Kettering to Huntingdon line at Raunds. A landowner near Raunds refused to sell land so the line was only built over the 3½ miles to Higham Ferrers, although the course of the planned extension could be made out in the former goods yard. Goods traffic began on 1 September 1893, passenger trains following on 1 May 1894. The initial service was six trains each way, increasing to ten by 1901, a third class return from Rushden to Wellingborough costing 5d. The Higham stationmaster had to send twenty pounds of walnuts annually to the St Pancras Hotel from a tree left growing by the station.

TRAFFIC AND STAFF AT RUSHDEN

	1904	*1913*	*1922*
Tickets issued	99,417	107,102	77,626
Including seasons	47	131	268
Income	£6,258	£8,415	£14,357
Parcels sent	59,583	83,058	121,251
Income	£1,537	£2,168	£9,477

	1901	*1913*
Merchandise, tons	41,540	61,022
Coal, tons	20,907	43,528

Staff:	*1902*	*1914*
clerks	7 at £384	9 at £910
carters	9 at £494	13 at £778
porters	6 at £314	10 at £567

Traffic and staff at Rushden. Labour was cheap and plentiful before World War I, so this single-platformed station could afford to employ thirty-two men for less than one senior stationman receives today

Higham developed in the ten years after 1891 as much as in the previous forty, but still with only a mere 2,540 inhabitants to Rushden's 12,453, the latter's being an increase of 5,000 since 1891. Traffic at the station reflected this growth, as the table shows, while staffing and salaries make interesting comparisons.

Passenger traffic on such a branch was an easy prey to regular bus services, succumbing on 15 June 1959 except for trains to Blackpool and Yarmouth on Saturdays in the town's holiday fortnight, which lasted until 1964. Freight continued until 1969; on 3 February the small amount of general goods traffic ceased, while on 3 November the iron concentrate traffic was transferred to Twywell on the Kettering–Thrapston line. This traffic was a by-product of the local sand and gravel industry, beginning about 1960. The steel industry liked it for its higher iron content (46 per cent to the 30 per cent of raw Wellingborough ores) and it was easier to handle. Until 1966 road tippers took it to Irthlingborough station, then from 6 July they used a tipping dock on the platform at Higham Ferrers, whence over 1,500 tons were despatched weekly. The traffic increased; in 1972 about 2,000 tons left Twywell weekly, roughly two-thirds to Irlam, the rest to Etruria.

THE KETTERING TO HUNTINGDON BRANCH

This was originally a South Midland scheme of 1846, as a branch to meet the Eastern Counties Railway at St Ives via a short connecting line at Huntingdon. This scheme failed with the demise of the SMR, to be revived in 1862–3 by the Kettering, Thrapstone & Huntingdon Railway, partly to exploit the ironstone fields in Northamptonshire. The Midland were to work the line from the beginning, with running powers over the Great Eastern Railway to Cambridge via St Ives. It was opened to goods on 21 February 1866 and to passengers on 1 March, but was not vested in the MR until 6 August 1897. The line, with sharp curves and gradients of 1 in 70 ran through sparsely-populated country, many stations being badly sited. Thrapston was the largest town with an 1851 population of 1,183, but the slow growth to 1,747 by 1901, and subsequent stagnation indicate that the railway was only of marginal importance. Raunds demonstrates this clearly. Always an important small town, its population increased from 1,870 to 3,811 in the fifty years after 1851, yet it was two miles from its small station, and its shoe industry was not vitally dependent on good adjacent rail transport.

Passenger services consequently were light, ending on 15 June 1959, with never more than four daily trains throughout each way, plus one or two to Thrapston only. Two each way sufficed during World War II, though afterwards it did boast a summer Saturdays-only train from Birmingham and Leicester to Clacton, calling at Thrapston. It used to be said that if one missed the train one could take a taxi and catch up with it at the next station.

Intermediate freight traffic did not justify leaving the line open beyond Kimbolton from 15 June 1959, or between Twywell and Kimbolton from 28 October 1963. However, ironstone greatly contributed to the line's traffic, just as the line allowed many quarries to be opened up. The Woodford mines were opened first, by General Arbuthnot, who had sent the ironstone samples to the Great Exhibition. There was a plan to open two blast furnaces in the grounds of Woodford House, but this came to nothing. Furnaces were, however, erected further east at Islip in 1871 beside the MR. Here the largest narrow-gauge tramway system in the ironstone field developed, with over ten miles of track. The pits were intensely worked until 1947, but by then all equipment and furnaces need major overhaul so Stewarts & Lloyds decided to concentrate on Corby, not far away. The furnaces had closed in 1943, the mines in 1952. Other quarries existed prior to 1914, but only those at Cranford survived all slumps. This extensive system straddled the MR, and in places 60ft of overburden needed removing. Using modern machinery, the Staveley Coal & Iron Co was sending two train-loads of ore away daily to Hartlepool. This traffic ended on 4 July 1969, leaving only the iron concentrate traffic from Twywell, at 2,000 tons a week, using the line until 1978.

THE CORBY LINE

Corby is the local steel town *par excellence*, owing its existence to its position on the richest part of the ore field, which in turn owed its exploitation to the building of the Kettering–Manton–Nottingham line in the 1870s.

The potential wealth of Rockingham Forest was realised in the 1860s, and foundations of four furnaces were laid below Neville Holt Hill, beside the LNWR Market Harborough–Stamford line. These came to nothing through financial difficulties, but the deposits had aroused the interest of four railway companies, the Midland, the LNWR, the GNR, and an outsider, the Manchester, Sheffield & Lincolnshire, as part of their wider schemes in the East Midlands. The full story of the rivalry is narrated in Chapter VI. Here it will suffice that a joint MR and MS & LR line from Doncaster to Rushton (north of Kettering) was proposed in 1874 to counter a joint GNR and LNWR line from the Nottingham area to near Market Harborough. This line was ultimately opened in stages between 1878 and 1883, and had spurred the MR to devise a new line from Nottingham to Rushton via Manton, authorised in 1875, the Doncaster line having been abandoned. With slight deviations from the original route, the line was opened for goods between Glendon, 1½ miles nearer Kettering, and Nottingham on 1 November 1879; local passengers followed on 2 February 1880, through trains from St Pancras to Nottingham and beyond on 1 June that year. Between Manton and Melton Mowbray the route ran over the Leicester–Peterborough line, opened in 1848.

Earthworks on the line were heavy, as it crossed several valleys, but nine tunnels and a long viaduct ensured that the steepest gradient was 1 in 142, and most less than 1 in 200. The crossing of the Welland Valley involved a major tunnel either side (Corby, 1,920yd; Glaston, 1,842yd) and Harringworth Viaduct, 1,275yd long, with 82 arches of 40ft span and a maximum height above the valley of 60ft.

As a through passenger route it was designed to give Nottingham a more direct link with London, and in 1903 it was carrying over a dozen express and stopping trains each way daily, the latter connecting at Kettering with Leicester main line expresses; it succumbed to rationalisation in 1966, when Corby and Gretton stations were closed on 18 April and most expresses were diverted away. There was some public outcry, but the station at Corby had never been rebuilt when Corby New Town was developed during the 1930s away from the railway. A frequent bus service to Kettering satisfied Corby's needs, and the former is now designated 'Kettering for Corby'. Intermediate traffic was inevitably a prey to bus competition, Harringworth and Geddington stations, the latter miles from anywhere, closing on 1 November 1948.

It has always been an important freight route, many southbound mineral trains being routed this way after 1880 to avoid congestion at Leicester and to benefit from the easier gradients than those of the old main line. In itself the line south of Manton generated considerable traffic in iron ore and other minerals, mines extending from Harringworth down to Glendon, and mostly still exploited until the rundown of Corby furnaces 1980–1.

The Glendon workings date from 1863, and progressively moved east as the Manton line was built. In 1903 a local mining entrepreneur, James Pain, expanded and modernised the workings, receiving an offer to build furnaces between the Leicester and Manton lines. Pain refused, and the offer was taken up by Lloyds Ironstone at Corby. With increasing overburden to remove, Pain introduced mechanical diggers, but at first they could not distinguish between good ore and dross, so more than one truckload of worthless material was consigned to the furnaces. Up to 10,000 tons of ore were being sent weekly along the main line to Corby in the 1970s.

The adjacent Storefield pits opened in 1898 supplying the Bennerley ironworks in Derbyshire. For many years there was a ramshackle narrow-gauge tramway, whose elderly locomotive had to rest for ten minutes en route up to the MR exchange sidings with the four wagons. Greasing was rudimentary: an old man sat in a trench beneath the rails 'fatting the wagons' by slapping grease onto the axles as they ran over the top. After being closed for eleven years, the South Durham company took over the workings in 1940, but by 1971 it was no longer profitable to send ore to Middlesbrough, and they were closed on 15 September.

A thick seam of ore revealed during the digging of Corby tunnel and cutting was quickly exploited during the 1880s. At this time Corby's population was 845. There was no reason why Corby should not have remained just another mining village, but from 1885 the pits were operated by the progressive and experienced Lloyds Ironstone Co, which introduced the first steam digger into the industry in 1895, and then in 1910 opened two blast furnaces. The population had climbed to 1,356.

In 1923 Stewarts & Lloyds Ltd, tube manufacturers, bought Lloyds Ironstone (no relation) as part of an expansion plan involving the control of raw materials supplies. Then to remove their Glasgow works' dependence on imported steel, S & L decided to move it onto the iron ore field, where the company would construct an ironworks, steelworks and tube-works, choosing Corby because of the estimated 500 million tons of ore locally available. The depression delayed building of the £3·3 million works from 1930 to 1932, but by 1934 they were in production, fully so by the end of 1937. Over 1·7 million tons of ironstone were mined and 182,500 tons of tubes produced in 1938. The labour force rose from under 800 in 1932 to over 4,000 in 1939, of whom a third had come from other company works, and a half were locally recruited. The population in 1931 was still only 1,596, but by 1939 it was the biggest 'village' (in local government terms) in Britain with a population of over 12,000. The 1950s and 1960s saw further rapid advances, so the 1971 population stood at 47,994. Production in 1973 was about 450,000 tons of tubes annually, which BR handled. To produce these required over one million tons of coal from South Yorkshire and the East Midlands, 250,000 tons of limestone from Derbyshire and 30,000 tons of steel scrap from British Steel Corporation works in Leicestershire and Staffordshire, all brought in by BR, as were 200,000 tons of ironstone from Glendon. Most iron ore, though, was transported over the extensive internal system from a wide area, earlier pits at Gretton and Harringworth having been integrated into the Corby network. A walking dragline weighing 1,650 tons and capable of lifting twenty-seven tons in one go was installed in 1952 to remove the hundred feet of overburden. Since 1934 Fisons had been using slag in making fertilisers, at a plant behind the steelworks. The firm exported quantities to Eire and Germany by rail, amounting to some 10,000–15,000 tons annually.

Periodic recessions in steel produced worries of depression in Corby, so from the 1960s light industries such as potato-crisp manufacture were attracted, although most of their products were almost entirely road-borne. These fears were finally realised in 1980 when the international troubles in the steel industry forced BSC to rationalise its plants still further. After the summer, ironstone quarrying was run down and the last of Corby's furnaces was blown down in March 1981.

While demolition men cleared the site, supplies of steel coil for the tube making, which was reprieved, began to flow in from Teesside (page 248). With government backing, a new industrial estate has been opened, but as the official emphasis was on 'new roads to serve Corby' it was obvious that the railway connection was considered irrelevant. Not so with another ambitious plan, to create a huge futuristic leisure complex on American lines on the steelworks site. As this anticipated three million visitors a year, a revived passenger link would be needed. It is always possible that a northward extension of the 'Bedpan' electrification to Wellingborough and Kettering could embrace Corby (page 245).

Northamptonshire was producing over five million tons of iron ore in 1957, mostly rail-borne. Even in 1962 richer foreign ore only equalled home ore in tonnage used, and expansion was anticipated in the Midlands fields. However, with the advent of bulk ore carriers and higher rail freight charges, the steel industry found it cheaper to use foreign ores. Midlands ironstone mining was dead; Northamptonshire's dozen blast furnaces were destroyed and a staple industry was at an end.

CHAPTER V

Leicester

'A very fine town, spacious streets, fine inns, fine shops and containing, they say, thirty or forty thousand people. It is well stocked with jails...' was how William Cobbett described Leicester in 1830 in *Rural Rides*. It had long been an important and prosperous city, based on the hosiery and footwear industries from the seventeenth century. This prosperity was not continuous, as poor transport facilities hindered expansion, and while these industries were still domestic, they were badly hit by the industrial depressions of the 1830s and 1840s, with a fifth of the population on poor relief. Hence Chartism was rife in Leicester, and its jails well used.

Leicester has always dominated its county. Over half of the county's population lives within seven miles of the city centre and Leicester with its 1981 population of 279,791 is over five times larger than Hinckley (55,273) or Loughborough (47,647); in Cobbett's day Leicester was four times their size. While the railways did not create this situation, they have certainly aided Leicester's sevenfold growth since 1830. Earlier, turnpiking, improvements to the River Soar (Loughborough Navigation 1778; Leicester Navigation 1794) and the long-delayed completion (1814) of the Grand Union Canal towards Rugby had aided Leicester's development.

At its peak in the 1820s, the Leicester Navigation was carrying 56,000 tons of coal annually for Leicester, 59,000 tons for other markets and 11,500 tons of other goods, but the coal was chiefly from beyond the Trent. It was cheaper to bring it the thirty miles by canal from South Derbyshire than the dozen miles overland from West Leicestershire. The Leicestershire coal owners tried to retaliate with two tramways and the Charnwood Forest Canal down to Loughborough, opened in

1794, but the canal reservoir burst its banks in 1799 and was never repaired. Thereafter some collieries closed, while others sent their output into Warwickshire via the Ashby Canal, opened in 1804, but this did not satisfy the more enterprising owners, among them William Stenson at Whitwick.

<h2>LEICESTER & SWANNINGTON RAILWAY</h2>

Stenson was interested in deep mining, but this was obviously uneconomic unless he could sell his coal cheaply. Resenting the Derbyshire dominance over the Leicester coal market, in 1828 he visited the Stockton & Darlington Railway at work and found the answer. Thus the Leicester & Swannington Railway was born, backed by his Whitwick partners and John Ellis, a local landowner and friend of George Stephenson. George and Robert walked over the route and thought that the line would be profitable because it would carry granite, building sand and bricks for the expanding city as well as coal and lime. George backed this judgement by buying £2,500 of shares, although he preferred Robert, then aged 25, to be engineer. This and Ellis's chairmanship was settled at the first meeting of the promoters at the Bell Hotel, Leicester, on 12 February 1829. The railway was authorised in May 1830, with £90,000 capital which later had to be raised to £140,000. About two-thirds of this was raised locally, while George obtained the rest from his friends in Liverpool. The line was to be built in five years which was generous, for in spite of difficulties with contractors, the first section was opened within two years.

The 16 mile line ran from the west bank of the Soar near West Bridge to Swannington, then a village of 549 inhabitants in the middle of the coal-mining area. Its route included inclines at Bagworth and Swannington and the tunnel at Glenfield, 1 mile 36yd long, which the locals found so fascinating that gates had to be installed to keep them out. Intermediate stations were at Glenfield, Ratby, Desford, Merry Lees and Bagworth; only that at Bagworth, built like a toll house, is still standing. The branches to collieries, authorised in the Act, were in fact built by the coal owners.

The 11 mile lower section, from Leicester to Bagworth, was ready first and ceremonially opened on 17 July 1832. The directors sat on boardroom chairs placed in a wagon, while

others sat on planks, or stood. A small brass cannon was fired
when entering and leaving stations, while the band played
and flags waved bearing slogans 'cheap coal and granite',
'warm hearths and good roads', and 'may the triumph of
science prove the blessing of the people'. Unfortunately,
according to the local legend, the locomotive stuck in Glenfield tunnel with its chimney fouling the low roof. The band
stopped playing, the light bonnets, veils and dresses of the
ladies, and shirt fronts and faces of the men were covered in
smuts; an unscheduled stop was made by Glenfield Brook
while the company washed, using handkerchiefs as towels.
Nothing further untoward happened, and refreshments were
taken at Bagworth, cold meats for the men, cakes and wine
for the ladies. An observer noted that only water was unavail-
able for the guests and that otherwise ale, porter, cider, sherry
and champagne were abundant. There was also dinner for
fifty gentlemen on their return to Leicester.

The regular passenger service began next day, with three
trains each way. A coach connection was soon operating from
Bagworth to Ashby-de-la-Zouch. Passengers were provided with
octagonal brass tokens which were given up and used again.
The next year services extended to Ashby Road (Bardon
Hill) on 1 February, and to Long Lane (Coalville) on 22 April
for coal, and 27 April for passengers. Railway inns were used
on the latter section instead of station buildings, while
passengers were expected to walk the forty-three chains length
of Bagworth incline, at a gradient of 1 in 29. Passengers were
not wooed by the company, which only added coaches, as they
put it, 'to some of the coal trains for the convenience of
communication with the villages adjacent to the railway.' It
may have carried 443 passengers a week in 1838, but between
January and June 1843 passengers only contributed 5·1 per
cent in receipts while in January 1836 2,913 wagons of coal
ran to Leicester. Wages were good, a fireman receiving 3s od
(15p) a day plus 6d (2½p) for every trip he made as a driver.

There were still three return trains daily in 1910 between
West Bridge and Desford, but they were withdrawn on 24
September 1928. Goods trains, finally serving only a few coal
merchants and an oil depot at West Bridge and the Groby
granite quarry siding, lasted until 29 April 1966. Mixed
trains ran until 1888.

The Midland bought the line in 1846 as part of a through

route from Leicester to Burton, but the Bagworth incline and Glenfield tunnel were obstacles. The incline was bypassed by the 2 mile Thornton deviation built as part of the doubling of the track between Coalville and Desford, completed in March 1848. Then on 1 August 1849 the Desford to Leicester (Knighton Junction) line was opened. It was preferable to build a new line to join the existing Leicester–Rugby line south of Leicester than to double Glenfield tunnel and extend the old line across Leicester from West Bridge station, which was rebuilt in 1893.

The effect of the line on the Swannington area will be examined in the wider context of West Leicestershire in the next chapter. The immediate result in Leicester was that Derbyshire coal, selling at 18s 0d (90p) a ton, was undercut by 7s 0d (35p) by Swannington coal of the same quality. The angry Derbyshire coal owners, faced with losing 160,000 tons of coal traffic a year, sought revenge.

THE MIDLAND COUNTIES RAILWAY

Every week the coal owners of the Erewash Valley, which separates Nottinghamshire from Derbyshire, met at the Sun Inn, Eastwood, to discuss business and then take refreshment. At their meeting on 16 August 1832, a month after the opening of the L & SR to Bagworth, they considered ways of countering this threat to their virtual monopoly of selling coal in Leicester. Meetings with the canal companies who carried Erewash coal to Leicester had been very unproductive, as the canal companies were most unwilling to shoulder alone the burden of rates reduction, while the coal owners were unwilling to lower their prices. So the Eastwood meeting resolved: 'There remains no other plan for our adoption than to attempt to lay a railway from these collieries to the town of Leicester.'

Their original plan was for an extension from Pinxton to Leicester, then to Rugby, of the existing tramway from Mansfield. Sufficient subscriptions however were unforthcoming locally so the promoters turned to the North West, as the Swannington people had. The Liverpool men, however, were less interested in local schemes than in formulating a national system. Their own Liverpool & Manchester Railway was operating; their London & Birmingham was before

Plates 12 and 13 The railway as employer: *(left)* the lampfiller at work at Leicester Central; *(right)* moving up the ranks, two Midland ticket collectors pose at Luton. These pictures were taken soon after 1900 when the railways still provided sound, if not well-paid, employment for many thousands of men from all classes. [S. W. A. Newton collection, Leicester Museum; Luton Museum.]

Plates 14 and 15 The Railways and industry II: (above) Snibston Colliery, Coalville; (below) the tall towers of the ABM maltings at Louth dwarf the wagons of malted Lincolnshire grain bound for Scottish whisky distillers. [Author.]

Parliament; there were plans for a Grand Junction Railway linking Birmingham with Liverpool and Manchester, and others for a railway from Leeds to Derby. The major gap was from Derby to the South which could well be filled by a railway from Derby to the L & BR at Rugby, via Leicester, with a branch to Nottingham, and another to Pinxton from the Derby–Leeds line. This broader scheme was called the Midland Counties Railway, and its prospectus was issued in November 1833, requiring capital of £125,000. The original Pinxton–Leicester scheme had required a mere £32,000.

The Liverpool financiers considered this sum insufficient to appeal to Parliament, and so increased it during 1834 to £600,000. As they now were virtually financing the MCR, they had Charles Vignoles appointed engineer in 1835 in place of William Jessop, ordering him to make a fresh survey. Vignoles' report in 1836 revealed the need for improvements in the plans, so capital was raised to £800,000, then to £1 million, of which nearly half came from Lancashire. Among the local shareholders were the then Prime Minister, Viscount Melbourne, and John Ellis of the L & SR.

While these financial arrangements were progressing, a call arose from Northampton and Market Harborough that the MCR should come their way. Strong arguments were advanced, ranging from the extra traffic to be gained from agricultural produce and Northampton's merchandise to the desirability of avoiding Kilsby Tunnel. The route to London was only four miles shorter than via Rugby, so this was insufficient to sway the MCR away from the Rugby route, as their main aim was access to Birmingham as much as to London. In the event, this was a short-sighted decision, as in 1839 the Birmingham & Derby Junction Railway was opened, before the MCR, while the two companies amalgamated in 1844. The direct Leicester–Birmingham line came in 1864, so the Leicester–Rugby line was of less use as a Midlands outlet to Birmingham than was planned. The opening of the Leicester–Hitchin line in 1857 did not immediately harm through traffic southwards, but the London Extension of 1868 effectively turned it into a rural branch.

The MCR's Bill entered Parliament during 1836, and although passed that same year, it was not unscathed. Opposition was inevitable from the canal and some landowning interests, but what nearly wrecked the Bill was the hostility of the North Midland Railway, whose Bill for a line from Derby via Chesterfield to Leeds was also before Parliament. The MCR's Erewash Valley branch to Pinxton pointed north, and the Eastwood men hoped to extend it towards Chesterfield. This would roughly parallel the projected NMR, which feared that it might have to join the MCR near Chesterfield and thus lose not only twenty miles' worth of rates, but also a junction at Derby with their Birmingham line friends. The possibility of the NMR joining the canals to defeat the MCR worried the 'Liverpool Party', so that they dropped the Pinxton Branch to save their Bill. To them the Eastwood men were dispensable; their line could be locally promoted. Thus had the MCR developed, and thus its Bill was passed in 1836. The Leicester–Rugby section was to be delayed a year to allow further thoughts on the Northampton routes. None materialised.

Strangely, the Corporation of Leicester opposed the scheme, as it feared damage to its water conduit and depreciation of the value of the South Fields as building land. However, the ratepayers held a meeting on 11 February 1836, maintaining 'that a railway passing through Leicester communicating with the London and Birmingham Railway would be highly advantageous to the town.' The Bill passed Parliament without the Corporation's support and the ratepayers were proved correct.

There were few engineering problems, other than the need to keep the lines above the flood plains of the Trent and Soar. As the section between Derby and Nottingham was the easiest, and likely to bring in useful revenue, work was concentrated there, so that opening was effected on 4 June 1839. The section from Trent Junction to Leicester was opened with much ceremony on 5 May 1840, followed with no ceremony eight weeks later, on 30 June, by the Leicester–Rugby portion, on the same day that lines to Leeds and Hull were opened. Through traffic began at once, and quickly picked up, one train on 9 July consisting of twenty-two coaches.

The effect of this railway on Leicester was great. Almost immediately, Derbyshire coals were arriving at 12s 0d (60p) a ton which, although slightly higher than Swannington coal, was still competitive. Leicester's own manufactured goods could find far wider markets than hitherto, which was of great

advantage after the slumps of the 1840s, making mechanisation of the footwear and hosiery industries worthwhile in
the 1850s and 1860s. The growth of the town's population
reflects this rising prosperity, for over the thirty years to
1861 it increased by 70 per cent to 68,000. By 1857 the town
had expanded beyond the railway to the south, and steadily
followed it east, along the Humberstone and Belgrave Roads.

The MCR was also useful to Thomas Cook of Leicester,
an ardent supporter of the Temperance Movement. While
walking from Market Harborough to a great temperance
meeting in Leicester: '. . . a thought flashed through my
brain, what a glorious thing it would be if the newly developed
powers of railways and locomotion could be made subservient
to the promotion of temperance!' At the meeting he broached
the idea of hiring a special train to take supporters to another
meeting at Loughborough three weeks hence. 'The meeting
roared with excitement.' So on 5 July 1841 some 500 people
crammed into over twenty open coaches for the 11 mile
journey, for a shilling return. Cook concluded: '. . . All went
off in the best style, and in perfect safety we returned to
Leicester; and thus was struck the keynote of my excursion,
and the social idea grew upon me.' Cook's was far from being
Britain's first excursion train, but from it was born the travel
agency known the world over, whose head office remained in
Leicester until 1879.

The MCR station in Campbell Street, large and handsome
in the classical style, although with only one long platform
inside, was replaced further west by the present, larger
London Road Station in 1892. The old site, absurdly large
in 1840 according to critics, was too cramped by the 1870s,
while even the new one has been a bottleneck for freight. The
initial service was six trains each way, five going on to
London from Rugby, three having come from Hull, one from
York and two from Nottingham and Derby. The best time to
London was 4½ hours, which compared well with the ten
hours by the fastest coach. As was expected, the coaches soon
faded out, going first to the secondary routes, and then serving
as horse buses.

THE MIDLAND RAILWAY

The Midland Railway was created in 1844 out of the amalgamation of the MCR, the Birmingham & Derby Junction Rail-

way and the North Midland Railway, under the aggressive chairmanship of George Hudson. His aim was to monopolise rail travel in the East Midlands and to the North East, building his empire on York and Derby. But such a monopoly was an invitation for competitors, with whom Hudson spent the next five years battling, either with branches to tap new eastern areas before others got there, like the Syston & Peterborough, or with projected lines to put competitors off, like the South Midland Railway, which Hudson used to fight off the Great Northern's challenge to Leicester via the Leicester & Bedford Railway. Both the SMR and the Leicester & Bedford were viable local projects, but as explained in Chapter IV, they were overtaken by the widereaching aims of Hudson and the GNR and quietly dropped when they had served their purpose.

From 1852, John Ellis, new chairman of the Midland, had chaired a Leicester & Hitchin Extension Committee while local interests were again vocal and the GNR again showed a desire to reach Leicester. As a result, the Midland line was extended southwards from the Rugby line at Wigston, to the GNR at Hitchin. It was opened with the usual celebrations on 7 May 1857, although coal traffic had been running since 15 April and goods traffic from 4 May. In fact it was the coal traffic which found the new line most useful, for the LNWR's own traffic between Euston and Rugby was growing quickly, causing increasing delays to Midland traffic. In the long term the Midland only transferred delays to its traffic away from the LNWR onto the GNR, and only the building of the London Extension solved the problem. This was opened for goods traffic in September 1867, while express passenger trains began working to St Pancras on 1 October 1868.

This affected Leicester far more than the Hitchin Extension, which was long treated as a branch, for all through bookings from north of Leicester had hitherto to go to Euston. Now there were twelve expresses daily from St Pancras, with eleven up; two of these ran non stop between Kentish Town and Leicester (and conversely) in 2 hours 14 minutes. By this time Leicester was an important Midland junction, lines to Peterborough being opened throughout in 1848, to Burton in 1849, and to Nuneaton and Birmingham over the South Leicestershire Railway (an LNWR creature) to Hinckley in 1864. They are fully discussed in the next chapter.

For nearly a thousand years Leicester has vied with Nottingham and Northampton in size and importance. With the development of water transport in the late eighteenth century Nottingham took the lead, but the railways put Leicester firmly ahead for most of the nineteenth century. Whereas both Northampton and Nottingham were on branch lines, for Derby was the important junction of the MCR, Leicester became well served from all directions. Not until Nottingham was on its own loop line from Kettering, from 1880, was it able to overtake Leicester. For forty years up to 1901 Leicester increased its population by 30 per cent every decade. Equally important, industry grew, encouraged by both easy rail access to national markets, and the supply of male labour, for the hosiery industry employed more women. Engineering particularly developed, first as the handmaid of the newly mechanised hosiery and footwear industries and then independently.

THE GREAT NORTHERN RAILWAY

The GNR had cast covetous eyes on Leicester and the neighbouring coal field since the 1840s, but only got there when it joined the LNWR, which wanted access to Nottingham. The result was the GNR & LNWR Joint line from Market Harborough to the Nottingham–Grantham line, with a purely GN branch from Marefield Junctions to Leicester Belgrave Road, opened on 1 January 1883. Passenger services were never lavish as traffic failed to come up to expectations. There were four daily return trains to Peterborough, reduced to three by 1910, when the Midland was running six. The GNR trains were cut out as a war economy measure from 1 April 1916 and never restored. The Leicester–Grantham service enjoyed five down and six up trains, rising to seven down by 1910. There were also a return workmen's service from Lowesby and sundry market day extras.

Two World Wars thinned these services down by 1950 to two return trains to Grantham connecting with main line expresses, and the workmen's train from John O'Gaunt. The Midland route was more attractive to passengers, and closure of the GNR line came on 7 December 1953, although the workmen's service ran until 29 April 1957 when Midland Red at last provided a suitable bus service. Even so, holiday trains were run to Mablethorpe and Skegness until 9 September 1962.

These holiday trains ran during the three summer months, with a return working on Saturdays to Skegness and to Mablethorpe, and a return to Skegness on Sundays. Extras were often run. Most trains called also at Humberstone, Thurnby, and Melton Mowbray, but with a 25mph speed limit on the branch because of the poor track progress was sedate, needing three hours to reach Mablethorpe. In 1959 there were forty-four trains to Skegness carrying 12,074 passengers and twenty-eight to Mablethorpe with 7,963 passengers.

A large goods warehouse, still standing, was erected at Belgrave Road, but goods traffic was never heavy, being mainly in leather, footwear, hosiery, grain and potatoes, the latter coming in bulk from Lincolnshire. This agricultural traffic declined from 1929, while the footwear and hosiery had declined by 1914, following the opening of the Great Central. There was also a coal train from Colwick for the Leicester Gas Works, half-a-mile from Belgrave Road. Transhipment was necessary, and ultimately the gas company found that doing this manually was too expensive, so it asked the GN to install tipping facilities. The GN refused on grounds of cost so the gas company approached the Midland, who willingly provided bottom-opening wagons and hoppers. From 1 June 1964 access to Belgrave Road was via a spur from the Midland at Humberstone, allowing the line on to Melton Mowbray to be closed. This spur was on the site of the original one put in when the line was built, but rarely used. Final closure came on 2 April 1969.

THE GREAT CENTRAL AND THE TWENTIETH CENTURY

The route of the Great Central's London Extension paralleled the Midland throughout Leicestershire from Loughborough to Rugby. In Leicester the GCR built a large station to the west of the city centre, consisting of an island platform with two bays at each end. Most striking was the pair of large water tanks at each end of the station. The city was well built-up, so the GCR had to run its line on a viaduct over a mile long through the central area. Even so, it had to rebuild 300 working-class houses and avoid a good Roman mosaic pavement. It was an expensive business. A locomotive depot and sixty-six acres of yards were established to the south.

The GCR route, opened on 9 March 1899, came too late to be of any significant influence on Leicester. Its greatest use was to open up direct access to the South West via Banbury. Trains from Leicester to Oxford were running from 1900 and soon extended. Otherwise in its heyday it offered a competitive service to London and the North Midlands with the Midland.

At 103 miles the Marylebone route to Leicester was four miles longer than that of the Midland. In 1905 it carried fourteen down trains, two stopping, five semi-fasts and the rest expresses, giving Leicester a best time of 108 minutes, only three minutes longer than by the Midland route, although the latter, serving more traffic centres, carried more trains. Northwards the GCR had the edge over the Midland, with a 4 mile shorter route to Nottingham. Of its thirty-two down trains, six were non-stop covering the $23\frac{1}{2}$ miles in 23–28 minutes, while only one Midland express could manage 30 minutes.

So while the Midland provided variety of destinations, the GCR provided speed. Thus it continued after Grouping, for while the Midland line, as the poor relation of the old LNWR, was left with its legacy of Derby's small engine policy, the LNER ran big engines on the best trains. On the whole, the LMS was the more important, for it brought in 380,000 tons of coal a year, its principal goods depot at Queen Street handled over 400 wagons daily, while fourteen non-stop trains were provided on the London service. After World War II arrears of maintenance on the ex-GCR were less quickly rectified than on the busier East Coast main line, and it tended to receive locomotives long overdue for overhaul. Relegation to the status of a secondary main line was therefore inevitable under BR, and when modernisation came in the later 1950s, the greater versatility of the Midland main line made it the obvious choice. Diesel haulage of expresses began in 1962, with a regular-interval service to Leicester from 1966. These consisted of an hourly express, non-stop to Leicester, and thence to Derby or Nottingham and beyond, plus an hourly semi-fast to Leicester, connecting there with the express, and continuing to Nottingham or Derby. The best 1973 time from London to Leicester was 84 minutes by twelve trains, and from Leicester on to Nottingham 29 minutes by nine trains.

Meanwhile, the GCR was fading out. On 4 March 1963 local stations were closed and services were reduced to three semi-fasts between Nottingham and Marlyebone, plus Nottingham–Rugby locals, and expresses via Banbury. Then in 1966 everything closed south of Rugby leaving only six locals, which finally succumbed on 5 May 1969. During June 1965 a spur was laid to the Burton branch by the locomotive depot, and goods traffic ceased between Leicester and Quainton Road.

While Leicester's prosperity has been considerably aided by its good railway position, its physical growth has been aided by the tram, then the bus and private car. The Corporation bought-up the small horse tramway system in 1901 and electrified it in 1904–5. The trams were very popular, being more convenient for suburban areas than the few suburban stations. The railways had done little to promote suburban stations and services, and so lost heavily, traffic at Humberstone Road falling by a half between 1902 and 1910.

Leicester has become an important railhead for its county, as many small stations were closed in January 1968, the Burton line on 7 September 1964, and the Rugby line (the old MCR) on 1 January 1962. However, it remains an important junction for North–South and West–East services. The 1983 timetable showed thirty expresses each way for London, with a new best time of seventy-two minutes. Northwards, fourteen expresses served Derby and eighteen Nottingham, of which thirteen terminated at Sheffield and three at Leeds. Eastwards, eleven trains went to Peterborough, five going on to Norwich and two to Cambridge. Sixteen trains took about an hour to trundle to Birmingham and there were sundry locals to Bedford, Melton Mowbray, Nottingham and Derby.

CHAPTER VI

Leicestershire

The Soar Valley divides Leicestershire in half, as well as providing the early route for canals and railway. To the west, the country is more industrialised, with the Leicestershire coalfields, Charnwood Forest stone quarries, Hinckley's hosiery factories and Loughborough's engineering works. Although the canals were important in stimulating industry, their penetration was hindered by the hills, and it was left to the railways to develop the industrial potential of this part of the county. The eastern part is also hilly in character and most railway building was delayed until the 1870s; it remains agricultural although ironstone mining has been important.

THE COALVILLE AREA

Although one of Britain's smaller coalfields, contributing only $2\frac{1}{2}$ per cent of the total UK output in 1967, the Leicestershire field, centered on Coalville, has been important locally for two centuries, first for domestic fires, and now for generating electricity. Granite quarrying too has long been important, mainly on the eastern side of Charnwood Forest, while limestone quarries are scattered throughout the area, and fireclay is important in the far west, around Moira and Swadlincote.

The earliest coal pits were in the Coleorton area, where the seams came close to the surface, but their continued existence was threatened by the influx of Derbyshire coal brought to Leicester by the Loughborough Navigation, opened in 1778. Although the Leicestershire coal owners were able to delay the completion of the Leicestershire Navigation until 1794, its opening forced them in to building their own canals, but with the disadvantage of being on the wrong side of the hills of Charnwood Forest. The immediate results of this were the promotion of the unsuccessful Charnwood Forest Canal to take Leicestershire coal via Loughborough into Leicester, and the development of markets in Warwickshire served through the Ashby Canal. Both canals needed a network of feeder tramways to penetrate their hilly hinterlands.

The Charnwood Forest Canal was opened in 1794. A tramway with an average gradient of 1 in 78 brought traffic down from the canal terminal at Nanpantan into Loughborough, a distance of 2¾ miles. It was engineered by William Jessop, using smooth rails and flanged wheels. At the western ends, other tramways connected the canal at Thringstone with limestone quarries at Cloud Hill and collieries at Swannington and Coleorton. Although coal brought to Leicester by this roundabout route was cheaper than by direct overland cartage, it nevertheless needed three transhipments en route and could not compete effectively with Derbyshire coal. A burst reservoir in 1799 brought the closure of the Charnwood Forest Canal along with Leicestershire's first railway, and caused a minor recession at Swannington. The Leicester Navigation proprietors planned a railway over this 'Forest Line' in 1834, but nothing came of the proposal until 1883 when the LNWR-controlled branch to Loughborough was opened, using part of the old canal course.

The Ashby Canal was opened in 1804 from near Moira to the Coventry Canal south of Nuneaton. This gave Leicestershire coal and lime access to the central Midlands and to London where coal from Moira colliery, sunk in 1804, was popular. An extensive system of tramroads was necessary, authorised in the canal's Act, and opened by 1802. From the canal basin at Willesley one tramway passed Ashby on its 8½ mile main line to Ticknall limestone quarries. A 3¾ mile branch led to collieries at Lount and the Cloud Hill limeworks beyond Worthington. The Ticknall Tramway was engineered by Benjamin Outram, a partner of Jessop. He built several tramways and urged a common gauge of 4ft 2in for, as he told the Ashby Canal Committee in 1799: 'it is exceedingly probable the Railways will soon become general for the transport of Merchandise thro' the commercial parts of this kingdom.' Outram laid plate rails on stone blocks whose course can still be followed in places, beside the Ashby road out of Ticknall.

South of Ashby the tramway was closed in 1850, but the Ticknall line lingered on until the last biennial trip ran on 20 May 1913. The Cloud Hill branch was rebuilt in 1839 with a combined plate-and-edge rail, from the limeworks to the junction with the Coleorton Railway at Worthington. Ultimately in 1874 the Midland, owners of both canal and tramways since 1846, rebuilt the section from Ashby to Worthington as part of its Ashby–Derby branch, the Cloud Hill section being lifted in 1891.

Improved mining methods in the 1820s allowed deeper pits to be dug, at Ibstock, Whitwick, Bagworth and Snibston, but better transport was needed to Leicester if these developments were to be fully exploited. So, as related in the previous chapter, William Stenson, a partner at Whitwick Colliery, promoted a railway to Leicester backed by his partners, John Ellis and George Stephenson. George's son, Robert, was appointed engineer to the line, and took an active part in developing the coalfield, being responsible for digging a successful deep mine at Snibston.

The opening of the Leicester & Swannington Railway throughout came in November 1833, although trains had been operating from Leicester to Bagworth from 17 July 1832, and on to Coalville from 22 April 1833 (27 April for passengers). The immediate effect was to stimulate more mining along the course of the railway which in turn encouraged new settlements to develop, as many existing villages were too far away to house the miners. The best example is Coalville, where there was no settlement until the late 1820s, while old villages like Shackerstone or Market Bosworth stagnated or declined.

Coleorton Colliery reopened after thirty years, which encouraged the building of the Coleorton Railway. Since 1832 the L & SR directors had considered extending the line through Coleorton to Cloud Hill limeworks, thus meeting the Ticknall Tramway. Although George Stephenson was asked to take a view of the neighbouring country and report on the possibilities of an extension, the board dropped the idea. Sir George Beaumont thereupon wrote to the L & SR directors that he would promote a railway linking his Coleorton Colliery to the L & SR if the company would pay for the Act. The result was the Coleorton Railway, opened in 1834 with horse traction, from a junction with the Ticknall Tramway at Worthington to the foot of the Swannington incline although it never made a physical connection with the L & S. It carried coal and lime.

The opening in 1840 of the Midland Counties Railway from Derby and Nottingham to Leicester and Rugby ended the brief monopoly of Leicestershire coal on the Leicester

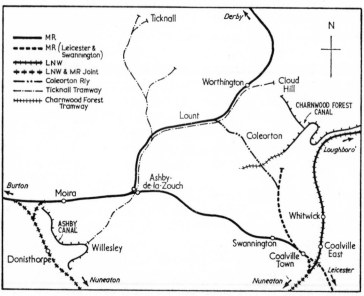

The Swannington Area. The early exploitation of this coalfield was aided by several canals and railways

market. Although it could compete effectively with Derbyshire coal, by 1844 output was declining and new markets were being sought, while a railway was surveyed from Desford south to Broughton Astley on the MCR with running powers thence to Rugby. However the L & SR was in a good strategic position with the Railway Mania developing, forcing Hudson's new Midland Railway to buy the line in 1846, in order to prevent hostile incursions into his 'territory'. Within three years the section from Coalville to Desford had been improved and incorporated into the Leicester–Burton line, opened throughout on 1 August 1849. As a physical part of the growing Midland Railway, access to nationwide markets was now possible. Output from the Leicestershire coalfield reached 439,000 tons in 1854, and passed the million ton mark by 1867.

The Swannington incline, at 1 in 17, was always cable worked, drawing loaded wagons up with a large stationary engine. Traffic was never heavy, especially as the neighbouring collieries were worked-out and closed. The Coleorton Railway ceased working during 1860, becoming a siding from the Ashby–Derby line, opened in 1874. Calcutta Colliery was the last to be closed, in 1892, but a powerful pumping engine had to be installed to keep its workings free of water, as they joined others. Coal wagons then had to be lowered down the incline for the pumping engine, until the plant became electrically operated in 1947, when the incline was closed on 14 November. In 1952 the original engine went to York Railway Museum.

The future lay with the newer, deeper pits from Coalville southwards, Ellistown pit being sunk in 1875, the settlement following in 1877. Coalville, however, had become the focal point of the area, forming an urban district in 1892, which incorporated Whitwick and parts of Swannington. In the 1901 census it was the third town in Leicestershire with 15,281 inhabitants, while the 1911 census noted that the large population increase, to 21,880, was due to the extension of the railway wagon works and colliery development. After World War II the rise of Hinckley pushed it into fourth place, reflecting the great reductions in labour force in recent years in both mining and the railways, the 1961 population being 28,250. Most of the coalfield's annual output of over four million tons is used in the Midlands, two-thirds being rail-borne, making the line very profitable. In 1964 an hourly train of up to 1,000 tons left Coalville for Drakelow Power Station, Burton-on-Trent, while a daily train of over 1,000 tons left for Leamington. Other trains served London, Hams Hall Power Station at Coleshill, and Peterborough. There were eight through passenger trains in 1910, nine in 1955, but these were withdrawn on 7 September 1964, although Ashby-de-la-Zouch Station, a classical masterpiece from 1849, has been recommended for preservation. The line also carried beer traffic from Burton to London. The gradients have become steeper due to mining subsidence, that up to Swannington from Coalville being particularly notorious.

The wealth of the Leicestershire coalfield had early encouraged rival schemes to the Midland Railway's routes, the major one being a line from Atherstone to Burton via Ashby, with branches to Moira, Ticknall and Breedon. Hudson fore-stalled this in 1846 by obtaining an Act for a similar line, which then lapsed, and for buying the Ashby Canal and its tramways for £110,000. This profitable canal continued in importance until the railway paralleled it in 1873, when traffic declined.

The next challenge came from the LNWR in 1866, when it sponsored the London & North Western & Midland Counties Coalfields Railway from Nuneaton to Ashby via Market Bosworth. The Midland replied by successfully asking Parliament to revive its 1846 powers, but in the event it joined with the LNWR to build a line from Hinckley to Ashby via Moira, with a branch from Shackerstone to Coalville and a connecting spur from Stoke Golding to Nuneaton. All the lines were built, but the section from Stoke Golding to Hinckley was never used. The rest was opened on 1 September 1873. The line served collieries at Donisthorpe and Measham as well as giving the LNWR access to those in the Moira and Swadlincote areas.

Finally the proposed railway over Charnwood Forest, dropped in 1834, was revived in 1874 as the Charnwood Forest Railway, with substantial LNWR backing. Originally it was to connect with the MR at Coalville and Lough-borough, but this was altered to a junction in Coalville with the LNWR/MR Joint line and a terminus at Loughborough Derby Road. The LNWR saw it as a feeder line, while the promoters hoped it would aid landowners to develop the area, encouraging tourism and industry. For the tourist there was 'charming scenery and a bracing climate', plus the ruined priory at Grace Dieu, where a halt was provided. Otherwise the line offered an outlet to the Birmingham area for the hosiery of Loughborough, Shepshed and surrounding villages, coal from Coalville, granite from Bardon Hill and Shepshed and lime from Thringstone, together with farming produce and timber. It was opened on 16 April 1883. In 1906 the LNWR wanted to join it to the GCR at Loughborough, but refused to pay for the flying junctions on which the GCR insisted.

These railways completed the industrial development of the Coalville area. Their passenger potential was unable to match road competition, services ending on 22 September 1930 between Ashby and Derby, and on 13 April 1931 between Ashby, Burton, Loughborough, Shackerstone and Nuneaton. As mineral lines they served into the 1960s, although everything is now lifted between Shackerstone and Loughborough, Ashby and Worthington and south from Measham, apart from the short section preserved by the Shackerstone Railway Society as the Market Bosworth Lt Rly.

Swadlincote sprawls over the hills at the western end of the coalfield. Now having a population of 23,388, it has grown from 1,076 in 1861 on the basis of the several local mines and the extensive fireclay deposits which have developed the important tile, pottery and pipeware industries. Served first by tramways from the Ashby Canal at Moira, it then lay on a branch from the Burton–Leicester line, opened on 1 June 1864. This was extended to Woodville on 1 May 1883, and back to the Leicester line near Moira on 1 September 1884. In 1910 the loop enjoyed six trains daily from Burton, most going on to Ashby. Although it lost its passenger services on 6 October 1947, a through train from Desford to Blackpool still called on summer Saturdays until 1962.

In spite of its status as a railway junction, and the industry flourishing in its neighbourhood, Ashby-de-la-Zouch has remained a quiet historic town, mainly because there is no local coal. Its population of 4,400 in 1831 has only doubled, with two thirds of the increase since 1931. In addition to the main line it was connected to Burton by the Burton & Ashby Light Railway, a 3ft 6in gauge electric tramway owned by the Midland, opened from Burton to Swadlincote on 13 June 1906, and to Ashby on 2 July 1906. After a short life, road competition killed it on 19 February 1927.

The railways aided the development of granite quarrying as well as of coal mining and limestone quarrying, enabling the area to sell over one million tons in SE England in 1900. Charnwood Forest granite is too hard for dressing as building stone, but is ideal for railway ballast and roadstone. Although much is now taken away by road, large quarries at Mountsorrel, Cliffe Hill and Bardon Hill are still served by rail.

Loughborough's early prosperity depended on hosiery and on coaches, handling over thirty daily. The opening of the Soar Navigation in 1778 lowered coal prices by forty per cent, stimulating further industrial growth. Loughborough then flourished as Leicestershire's second town, with over 10,000 people in 1831. Unfortunately, the opening of the L & SR

removed the through coal traffic on the Navigation, the opening of the MCR killed the coaching traffic, while the domestic
hosiery industry was in the doldrums. The town stagnated for
thirty years, despite the Midland and the establishment of
the famous bell foundry in 1840. Once the hosiery industry
was mechanised from the 1860s, Loughborough's railways
helped it to become a major centre, unlike neighbouring
Shepshed. Renewed prosperity was further aided by the establishment of the Brush Works in 1880. This firm specialised
in electrical equipment, especially tramcars, then a rising
market, and also built a few steam locomotives and railcars—
the railways' answer to tram competition in cities. Since World
War II it has built many diesel locomotives for use at home
and abroad. In forty years Loughborough doubled its population to 21,000 in 1901, becoming a borough in 1888, and
doubled it again in the next seventy years.

SOUTH LEICESTERSHIRE

Like West Leicestershire, the area south of Leicester was
adequately opened up by railways from an early date, but
unlike the west there is little indigenous industry. The railways therefore have served this agricultural area *en passant*
rather than specifically tapping its resources. It is also becoming a commuting area for Midland cities, but by road, for on
the two surviving lines all the small stations have been closed;
even the Greater Leicester suburb of Wigston (population
31,900) lost its last station in January 1968.

The first line in the area was the Midland Counties Railway, opened on 30 June 1840 to a temporary station at Rugby
Wharf, the junction with the London & Birmingham not
being completed for another three weeks. As a trunk railway,
it was not to cross turnpike roads on the level, but when
building the necessary bridges the approach roads were not
to be steeper than 1 in 30, and overbridges were to clear the
highway by 16ft. As one of the pioneer railways various other
provisions were written into the Act. The railway was to be
screened from turnpikes to avoid frightening the horses and
thus endangering the coach passengers, with a £25 daily fine
for non-observance. The public were liable to a £5 fine for
trespass or for driving cattle along the line. Landowners
beside the railway could cross it freely only until occupation

bridges had been made. The table of rates on page 106 shows the wide variety of goods these railways expected to carry.

At Broughton Astley, the stationmaster's house was rebuilt from an existing one, and was reputedly haunted. The halt at Leire was opened on 4 April 1925 after wrangling with the LMS over the need for a stopping point. The villagers subscribed over £100 in 1924 towards the cost.

Once the Midland had its own independent route to London, from 1868, through traffic ceased to use the line except as a diversion. It generated little goods traffic which was not susceptible to lorry competition. In 1910 there were five return trains from Leicester to Rugby and seven by 1955 with Saturdays seeing them well used. Extensive track renewals were due in 1961 yet were not justified by the traffic. The TUCC suggested abandoning freight traffic and using a diesel for local passenger services. BR rejected this idea as the Great Central line was only three miles away, although loss of local services was likely there also. Passenger and freight services were withdrawn on 1 January 1962.

The next line south of Leicester was the Midland's extension to Hitchin, designed to relieve congestion at Rugby, and opened on 8 May 1857, although coal and freight traffic had begun earlier. In Leicestershire it followed substantially the route of the South Midland Railway of 1836, when Market Harborough and Northampton were unsuccessfully calling for the MCR to be diverted their way.

Commercial interests in Market Harborough maintained that if the town lost trade through the opposition of the landed interest, it would decline to a dirty country village like Lamport. If the landowners' parks were affected, then they could plant trees to hide the view. A contemporary broadsheet then answered the landowners' objections by pointing out that their rents could be reduced by a third if commerce went via Rugby, that the Swannington Railway had cut coal prices by a third, that animals would arrive at market in a better condition, therefore fetching a higher price, that wider markets would be available for their wool and grain, that far from farmers losing manure through the decline of horses, the railways would need horses for local cartage, and could also bring to farmers cheap fertilisers from towns, as well as manufactured goods they needed. The railway was indeed seen as all things to all men! In hoping for a reduction in coal

For all dung, compost, and all sorts of manure, lime, and lime-stone, and salt, and all undressed materials for the repair of public roads or highways ; and for all coals, per ton per mile, one penny farthing :

For all grain, corn, coke, culm, charcoal, and cinders, all stones for building, pitching, and paving, all bricks, tiles, slates, clay, sand, ironstone, and iron ore, pig iron, bar iron, rod iron, hoop iron, sheet iron, and all other similar descriptions of wrought iron, and iron castings not manufactured into utensils, or other articles of merchandize, per ton per mile, one penny three farthings :

For all sugar, flour, hides, dye woods, earthenware, timber, staves, and deals, metals, (except iron,) nails, anvils, vices, and chains, per ton per mile, two-pence halfpenny :

For all cotton and other wools, drugs, manufactured goods, and all other wares, merchandize, articles, matters, or things, per ton per mile, four-pence :

And for every carriage of whatever description, having more than two wheels, and not being a carriage adapted and used

for travelling on a railway, and not weighing more than one ton and a half, per mile, five pence ; and if having only two wheels, per mile, four pence :

For every horse, mule, or ass, per mile, five pence :

For every ox, cow, bull, or neat cattle, per mile, two pence :

For every calf or pig, per mile, three farthings :

For every sheep, lamb, or other small animal, per mile, one halfpenny :

This comprehensive table of rates from the Syston & Peterborough Railway's Act of 1845 shows the wide range of traffic which the railways were expected to carry, to the general benefit of the community prices, the broadsheet included an interesting exhortation on the advantages of cheap coal for the labouring classes, for in giving them warmth, it brings cheer, thus avoiding both drunkenness out of cold misery, and the temptation to steal fuel, which could bring a man ultimately to the gallows!

The ancient market town of Market Harborough was until 1840 an important coaching centre with twenty-three per cent of its working population as servants and another thirty-two per cent in hosiery. The coaching traffic, however, was threatened by the MCR, so Market Harborough needed a railway in compensation, but the MCR went to Rugby instead. With the failure of the SMR in 1836 and 1845–6, Market Harborough stagnated, its population remaining around 2,300 for thirty years. The coming of the LNWR's Rugby & Stamford Railway in 1850 was of no immediate influence. Seven years later this was joined by the Leicester–Hitchin line, and had a branch to Northampton opened on 16 February 1859. Then light industry developed, such as corsetry, and a cattle market was established. By 1881 the population had reached 5,300 and has increased steadily to 13,000.

The present Market Harborough Station was opened on 14 September 1884, its dignified domestic Georgian style contrasting with the Victorian Gothic of the Hitchin Extension stations. The original station was LNWR property, for the Hitchin line ran over LNWR metals for $\frac{3}{4}$ mile. This caused congestion, especially after the opening of the London Extension and GN Joint line, so on 26 June 1885 the Midland opened its new line crossing over the LNWR. At the new Joint station each company had its own stationmaster, the LNWR man also looking after GNR business.

The Rugby & Stamford Railway was one of several branches planned by the London & Birmingham Railway. As it followed the Avon and Welland Valleys, engineering works were light but level crossings numerous, which was to be a serious drawback in the manpower-conscious days of the 1960s. It was opened as single track to Market Harborough on 1 May 1850, on to Rockingham on 1 June as double track, finally to join the Midland at Luffenham on 2 June 1851. Rockingham station is on the edge of Caldecott, a far more substantial village, but lacking the influential Castle. Traffic was thin until excursion tickets for the Great Exhibition made the line better known.

In the competitive 1870s, the LNWR's route from Birmingham to Peterborough required reversal at Blisworth and was four miles longer than the Midland's route via Leicester. The GNR also wanted to run through trains between Peterborough and Leicester. Accordingly the LNWR doubled the Rugby–Market Harborough section and built the Seaton–Wansford line over the watershed into the Nene Valley, cutting fifteen miles off its route. It was opened on 1 November 1879. Immediately the Seaton–Luffenham section was relegated to a single-track branch line while the direct Rugby–Peterborough route became a secondary main line, carrying a through Birmingham–Harwich service until 1939, and latterly Birmingham–Yarmouth trains, as well as a night mail. Post-Beeching rationalisation has kept only the Midland line into Peterborough from the west. This now carries the through services, while the LNWR line and the Luffenham branch were closed on 6 June 1966.

Seaton was also the junction for the LNWR's $3\frac{3}{4}$ mile Uppingham branch. Headmaster Thring of Uppingham School noted in his diary in 1860 that a railway was being discussed, but as Manton station served Uppingham adequately, nothing was done until the 1890s. Traffic began in September 1894 with some goods trains and school specials; public services began on 1 October. Patronage was never consistently heavy; although the school was under contract to the LNWR to use the line, local people increasingly used the better Midland services at Manton, and it was not unknown for a train to be cancelled for total lack of passengers. Freight traffic was also meagre, especially as the school blocked the expansion of the local ironstone quarry after 1918. The push-and-pull service was withdrawn on 13 June 1960, school specials and goods trains lasting until 30 May 1964.

Leicester's Birmingham line originated in 1846, when the Coventry, Nuneaton, Birmingham & Leicester Railway was authorised to build a line from Nuneaton to the Midland at Wigston. The powers lapsed, to be revived in 1859 for a branch from Nuneaton to Hinckley, a hosiery town of 7,000 inhabitants. In 1860 the South Leicestershire Railway, an LNWR creature, was authorised to extend this branch to Wigston, with running powers into Leicester over the Midland, in return for allowing the Midland running powers over the SLR and on to Coventry, and authority to build a line from Nuneaton to Whitacre. This could give the Midland a direct route from Leicester to Birmingham, rather than via Rugby, Coalville or Derby, and the LNWR would get access to Leicester. From Nuneaton to Hinckley was opened 1 January 1862, and on to Wigston on 1 January 1864. The Midland opened its line to Whitacre on 1 November 1864, and then the Wigston South Curve (authorised in 1869) in 1872 to allow through running from London to the SLR. Over the next ten years there were through trains from St Pancras to Birmingham, but they could not compete with the LNWR route, shorter by twenty miles. The branch to Enderby granite quarries opened in 1890. Blaby station was burned down in 1913, some say by the Suffragettes, being replaced by a simple wooden structure.

The railway rescued Hinckley from stagnation. The hosiery trade had always dominated the town, but this had a long lean period from the 1830s and Chartism had been powerful. The opening of the SLR coincided with mechanisation of the hosiery industry; factories concentrated in towns, particularly where there was a railway and the footwear industry followed. By 1901 the population had reached 11,000, since when it has quadrupled, making it the second largest town in Leicestershire, although with only twelve trains each way in 1972, compared with Loughborough's twenty-two.

The Great Central Railway had no influence in South Leicestershire at all. The only sizeable community served was Lutterworth, which previously had relied on the MCR's station at Ullesthorpe. Its population of 2,500 in 1841 was swollen by the builders of the MCR, after which it declined steadily throughout the century. The coming of the GCR had no effect, the population in 1961 being only 3,700. It lost its station on 5 May 1969.

EAST LEICESTERSHIRE

This hilly area was not opened up by the railways until the late 1870s as seemingly it had little to offer. Even then it was railway politics that caused the lines to be built, though they were to profit immediately by extensive ironstone workings on the Wolds. The exception was Hudson's Syston & Peterborough Railway through the Upper Wreake Valley and the Vale of Catmose.

Melton Mowbray is the only important town, the distribution centre of Stilton Cheese from the Vale of Belvoir
(over the Wolds), the home of pork pies, and the centre for
foxhunting, the 1831 and 1841 censuses attributing the rise
of population to the popularity of hunting, bringing in grooms
and their families.

The Great Central, although not serving the area directly,
recognised the popularity of hunting by offering first class
Hunting Season Tickets from London, available to convenient
stations for three, four or six months, the rates to Quorn
& Woodhouse, for the Quorn Hunt, being £10 10s 0d (£10.50),
£14 3s 6d (£14.17½), and £21 respectively. Publicity brochures
were issued listing the hunts, their meeting places and the
nearest stations. Special trains for passengers and horseboxes
would be run as required.

With the Syston & Peterborough Railway, Hudson aimed
to tap the traffic from Peterborough and the Fens via his
Eastern Counties Railway before his arch-rival, the London
& York Railway could reach there. The route was roundabout
partly to keep to the valleys, partly to serve population centres
en route, for, as Hudson said, 'a line should bend to the
population, and not leave the towns.' He was frustrated by
Lord Harborough, who utterly refused to have a line through
Stapleford Park. The towns however supported the project,
especially as during the last winter a sharp frost had created a
fuel famine, with coal rising to £2·00 a ton.

In November 1844 Lord Harborough's retainers prevented
the surveyors from making good measurements in his park
by a series of running battles, with the immediate result that
several men were fined. The Midland however got its Act in
1845, which provided for a tunnel under his Cuckoo Plant-
ation. Because of inadequate surveying, the tunnel fell in,
destroying sixty trees, and Harborough prevented the digging
of a cutting. The buying of the canal in 1845 as trackbed
had not placated him and he obstructed the surveying of the
authorised deviation, so the Midland unsuccessfully sued a
hundred of his men for assault.

The section from Syston to Melton Mowbray was opened
on 1 September 1846, and from Stamford to Peterborough
on 2 October 1846, but Harborough's obstruction delayed
opening from Melton to Stamford until 1 May 1848. The
deviation at Saxby (Lord Harborough's Curve) was too sharp

for the Midland expresses when the Melton–Manton section became part of the Kettering–Nottingham main line in 1880, so in 1892 it was eliminated by agreement with Harborough's successor.

Since rationalisation the line has become the main west–east artery, although the Beeching Report had threatened it. Since 1880 though, the western portion to Manton, had been an important by-pass round Leicester for through mineral trains, rejoining the old line near Kettering. The Nottingham passenger trains were taken off in 1966, leaving the line with eight return trains, mostly through workings.

In the early 1870s four railway companies had designs on East Leicestershire. The GNR wanted access to Leicester, the LNWR to Nottingham and its coalfield. The Midland regarded these areas as its preserve, but in countering these threats, saw the utility of a direct London–Nottingham line. The Manchester, Sheffield & Lincolnshire Railway was after any access southwards. All were hoping to tap the ironstone reserves.

In 1872 the Midland obtained its Act for a line from Nottingham to Saxby, on the same day that the GNR got one for a line from Newark to Marefield, the Lords having deleted the section on to Leicester, (the GNR had taken over the locally-promoted Newark & Leicester Railway scheme). The LNWR then joined the GNR to extend the Marefield line southwards to Market Harborough, and revive the Marefield–Leicester branch. This alarmed the Midland, which joined the MS & LR in promoting a line from Doncaster to Rushton, near Kettering. This line was authorised in 1874, but was of no real use to either, and so abandoned. The GNR/ LNWR line was also sanctioned in 1874, so the Midland put forward a new Bill for a line from Kettering to Manton, authorised in 1875. This was of greater potential than the GNR/LNWR route, which ultimately they were loath to build.

The Midland route involved two lines, from the main line at Glendon Junction, Kettering, to Manton on the S & PR, then leaving that line at Melton Mowbray for Nottingham. Both were opened for goods traffic on 1 November 1879, for local passenger trains on 2 February 1880, and for through expresses on 1 June 1880. The Leeds and Bradford trains tended to run this way, leaving the Manchester ones to run via Leicester. As the line crossed the watersheds, earthworks were heavy, especially in Rutland. Out of nine tunnels in fifty-one miles, four were longer than ¾ mile. Passenger services succumbed in 1966 with the coming of regular interval expresses via Leicester. The southern section is still an important freight line.

The GN & LNWR Joint line ran from Welham Junction, on the LNWR line north of Market Harborough, via Melton Mowbray, to Stathern Junction, where it split, one line running north-west to Saxondale Junction, the other north-east to Bottesford, both on the GNR Nottingham–Grantham line. GNR branches led from Bottesford to Newark, and from Marefield to Leicester. The Newark line was opened first through Stathern to Melton, on 30 June 1879. Then came the section on to Welham Junction on 15 December 1879, finally the Leicester branch on 1 January 1883.

The *Leicester Chronicle* approved the line as a great convenience for travellers, and described the imposing station at Melton Mowbray as 'a perfect model of convenience and comfort.' A price war began with the Midland, while through services were tried between Newark and Northampton, including one from Leamington to Scarborough in July 1883. By 1910 the basic services were six daily return LNWR trains from Northampton to Nottingham, including a through coach from Melton to Euston, and seven GNR trains from Leicester to Grantham (six back). Additionally, there were three return GNR trains from Leicester to Peterborough via the Medbourne and Fletton curves, opened in 1883. The Peterborough trains disappeared in 1916, while other services were reduced by wartime economies. By 1950 competition from the Midland line services for through traffic, and buses for local traffic, had so pruned passenger traffic and services, that closure was inevitable on 7 December 1953. Patronage was not helped by the use (until 1944) of the dingy and inconvenient London Road low-level station in Nottingham which was primarily a parcels depot after 1900. Before World War I hunting specials were common; John O'Gaunt Station was renamed in 1883 after a local fox covert; certain fences were not to be above 3½ feet high, to placate the hunting interest.

The line was an important goods route, while also contributing much local traffic. The LNWR was able to tap the East Midlands coalfield, and ran seven daily coal trains to Willesden, with seven other freight trains to the South Midlands. There were regular mixed freights from Camden to Doncaster, including a wool train going on to Bradford. Stone trains ran from Northamptonshire to Scunthorpe. Until 1939, a hundred trains a day used the line, but these were reduced after nationalisation, until by 1960 they were being rationalised on to other routes, closure coming piecemeal 1962–8.

Local traffic was mainly agricultural. Milk traffic was centred on John O'Gaunt, which sent up to four tanks daily to London; it now goes by road. Cattle traffic was such that a passenger train might pick up sixteen cattle trucks en route. Stilton cheese was sent regularly from Scalford to the House of Commons.

Ironstone, though, was most important. The outcrop at Tilton was exploited from 1885, stone going to Holwell ironworks from 1918. Most supplies came from the Wolds north of Melton Mowbray, being tapped both by the Joint Line and the Midland. The supplies were known before 1855 when the Clay Cross company considered mining here, but abandoned the idea as the nearest railway was six miles away. Then a civil engineer preparing the Midland's Survey for the Nottingham line in 1873 noted the redness of the soil and sent samples of rock to the Staveley company, which found them acceptable. In 1876 the Midand opened a branch from Asfordby to Holwell, allowing Staveley and Stanton ironmasters to exploit mining there. Furnaces were opened at Holwell in 1881 using local ore. This Holwell Iron Company encouraged the GNR to open a mineral branch from Scalford to Waltham-on-the-Wolds on 5 April 1883. This was extended to rich reserves at Eaton in 1884. Then in 1887 the Midland extended its Holwell branch to Wycomb Junction on the Waltham branch to bring ore over to the furnaces from Eaton, this becoming the main exit for the stone going to Stanton and Staveley works in Derbyshire. Extensive industrial railway systems developed, one from near Harby & Stathern taking over part of the GNR's Eastwell branch, opened in 1885 off the Eaton branch, but never used. One quarry at Eaton used a pair of vertical-cylindered locomotives, and then two French ones, of which *Cambrai* is to be kept at Irchester. In the early 1950s 650,000 tons of ore were leaving these Leicestershire quarries annually; in the late 1980s coal should be leaving the mines here instead.

CHAPTER VII

Nottingham

The 'Robin Hood' express linked St Pancras and Nottingham between 1959 and 1962, emphasising the connection between the outlaw and the town. In fact until the seventeenth century, Nottingham was important in enforcing law and order in the unruly North. Thereafter the town's favourable position at the southern edge of a major coalfield and beside the navigable River Trent encouraged the growth of industry. England's first recorded 'railway' was laid in 1604 linking coal pits at Wollaton (within the town boundary from 1877) with the Trent. The lace industry developed during the same century and the hosiery industry, especially using cotton, from the later eighteenth century. For several centuries Nottingham had developed in competition with Leicester and Northampton. All three towns grew steadily during the eighteenth century but Nottingham, enjoying its position on the Trent at a time when water transport was of great importance, was in the lead. It lost this pre-eminence to Leicester in the first half of the nineteenth century, as it was unable to expand physically. Also from the beginning of trunk railway development, Nottingham effectively was on a branch while Leicester was on a main line. Although subsequent lines radiated out from Nottingham—to Lincoln, Grantham or Mansfield—they too were branches. The first main line reached Nottingham in 1880 as the Midland's loop from Kettering, followed by the Great Central's London Extension in 1899.

Nottingham undoubtedly benefited from both these lines, as will be seen, but two earlier factors were responsible for reviving the town's prosperity. The belated enclosure of the town fields from 1845 allowed the town to expand, although appalling slums remained, even after the Great Central Railway pulled many down, plus the workhouse, in its drive through Nottingham. Physical expansion was vital because of the mechanisation of the lace industry in the 1840s and hosiery industry in the 1860s. In 1871 Nottingham's population, by now 88,000, overtook that of Leicester. The 100,000 increase recorded in the 1881 census was due to the enlarging of the town boundaries in 1877, when suburbs like Basford and Bulwell were taken in.

The coming of the railway in 1839 was useful to Nottingham. Without it, the town would have lost ground even further to its rivals, and probably have remained heavily dependent on two trades which themselves were subject to the vagaries of fashion and international trade. Nottingham was already notorious for its violent radicalism, which increased in the depressed 1840s. But the railways did not create the 'New Nottingham' of which contemporaries spoke at mid-century; instead they made possible the ultimate diversification of the town's industries, enabling local firms such as Jesse Boot's pharmaceuticals, John Player's tobacco products and Raleigh bicycles to reach national markets. Light engineering also followed the mechanisation of the lace and hosiery trades.

Nottingham then was far from being either the product of the Industrial Revolution, like many Lancashire towns, or of the railway age, like Grimsby, although both forces were influential in the long term. Rather, local factors had most influence on Nottingham's belated development in the nineteenth century, as was the case at Luton. The story was different for the coal and iron industries, stretching from Nottingham's own doorstep away to Chesterfield, but that will be dealt with in the next chapter. The railways of modern Nottingham, and away to the east and south, will be discussed here.

THE MIDLAND COUNTIES RAILWAY

As discussed in Chapter V, the Midland Counties Railway was originally a coalowners' scheme to enable their Erewash Valley coal to compete effectively on the Leicester market. It would bring Nottingham little at first that was not transportable by canal, for as a local trade directory commented in 1834:

few commercial towns possess greater facilities for transporting merchandise, or have more direct communication with the inland navigation of England than Nottingham.

However, as local industrialists realised, it would bring goods more quickly, and in better condition. This especially concerned the booming lace industry which looked to Somerset and Devon for raw materials; these often came by sea because of the lack of adequate inland transportation from the West Country—a protracted journey with the added risk of damage by salt water spray. Consequently, when the MCR's Bill was before Parliament, favourable petitions were presented from the Town Council and the 'bankers, merchants, manufacturers, traders and inhabitants of Nottingham', countering opposition from the various canal interests.

The MCR's Bill, as authorised in 1836, involved lines from Derby to Nottingham and from Trent—then as now a non-existent place near Long Eaton—to Leicester and Rugby. When it was realised that Nottingham would in effect be on a branch line, and that Derby was going to become a major railway junction, for lines from Derby to Birmingham and Leeds were both authorised within a month of the MCR, local feeling ran high. As a member of the Corporation put it:

> Nottingham, from its geographical position, might and ought to have been made a point through which the direct line of railway from South to North should pass . . . That benefit has been lost to the town in consequence of the neglect and indifference with which the subject has been treated. The neighbouring town of Derby has completely outstripped us in the race for railway advantages.

He was well received. However, it was the Lancashire financers who could dictate the early railway geography of the Midlands, as local finance had been insufficient. They preferred Derby as it was closer to Birmingham than Nottingham. They saw Nottingham, and its adjacent coalfield, as a feeder area.

As the MCR needed income as soon as possible, it concentrated on building the easiest section first, from Derby to Nottingham, which was opened with much ceremony on 30 May 1839. To the accompaniment of church bells and military music at the station four trains prepared to leave Nottingham for Derby. As each did so, the band played the National Anthem. Thousands watched the spectacle along the $15\frac{1}{2}$ mile route. After an hour in Derby the trains returned, and the 500 guests enjoyed the lavish buffet, speeches and toasts, with the band still busy. On the second return trip to Derby, one train reached 40mph. Next morning's *Nottingham Journal* welcomed the railway with the hope that '. . . new days are coming to Nottingham—that a new impetus is now being given to the long declining affairs of our ancient town . . .' It also called for the enclosure of the town fields so that the full benefit of railway communication could be gained.

Public services for passengers, parcels and van goods began the following Tuesday, 4 June. The station was built in The Meadows just outside the town, so horse buses provided a connection to the centre. Trains left for Derby at 7.00am, 11.00am, 3.00pm and 7.00pm, the fares being 4s od (20p) first class, 2s 6d ($12\frac{1}{2}$p) second class. The intermediate stations were at Beeston, Long Eaton, Breaston and Burrowash (*sic*). The advertisement announcing this ended with the stern comment, 'No gratuity is allowed to be taken by any servant of the company.'

Nottingham gained access to Leicester when the section from Trent was opened on 4 May 1840; London, via Rugby, could be reached from 30 June 1840. The journey however was tedious, for all passengers over the Leicester line from Nottingham had to travel first to Derby. The opening of Trent station on 1 May 1862 ended this unnecessary travel; either passengers changed trains or coaches were detached. This did not affect excursion trains which were very popular. The Nottingham Mechanics Institute organised one to Leicester at 3s od (15p) return three months after the railway opened. It was so successful that the MCR ran one there on 24 August. 2,400 people were carried in sixty-five vehicles, the train taking three hours to do the twenty-seven miles. The lesson of these ventures was not lost on Thomas Cook.

THE LINCOLN LINE

In 1844 the MCR amalgamated with the other two Derby companies into the Midland Railway under the energetic leadership of George Hudson, who controlled the railway route from Rugby to York. His monopoly was threatened by rivals, particularly the London & York Railway which would open up Lincolnshire and Eastern Nottinghamshire. In order to make the London & York appear unnecessary to Parliament, Hudson planned branches to Lincoln and Peterborough, which were both authorised in 1845, although they failed in their aim of preserving Hudson's monopoly, for the London & York was authorised in 1846 and many Mania schemes were put forward for that area.

George Stephenson engineered the Nottingham–Lincoln branch, which offered no major difficulties as it followed the Trent Valley to Newark. In fact the railway was made in eight months, although it was not opened until 3 August 1846. Two special trains of guests reached Nottingham, one with Hudson, the Midland Chairman, from Derby, the other with Ellis, Vice-Chairman, from Leicester. At 09.26 Hudson's train, of thirty-five first class carriages, left for Lincoln, followed by Ellis's, sixteen similar carriages, at 10.15. Hudson stopped at Newark, but Ellis ran straight through, taking an hour to do the thirty-three miles. After champagne and light refreshments the parties returned to a large champagne lunch in the Nottingham engine shed. Another journey to Lincoln followed, this time in a violent storm, where a good dinner was eaten. Regular traffic began next day with four trains each way plus the night Lincoln mail. The heavy rain of the third had weakened the track, which subsided at Gonalston crossing, beyond Lowdham, throwing an engine into the ditch, killing the fireman.

Stephenson had recommended that the line begin twenty-six chains west of Nottingham station, so that trains would back out of the terminus, then run past it to Lincoln. This was soon found to be awkward, so a large new station was planned on the Lincoln line east of Carrington Street which was to cross the station throat on a bridge. This new station was opened on 22 May 1848, with an impressive frontage in Station Street. The original Carrington Street station became goods offices, which are still on the site, although of the original buildings only the gateway survives.

Newark-on-Trent was the principal town en route. This market town of ten thousand people in 1841, was an important centre for malting, milling and brewing, there being twenty maltings and twenty corn mills. It also had a large coal trade. The Midland built a handsome small station by the castle,

NOTTINGHAM RAILWAY STATION.

INTERIOR OF NOTTINGHAM RAILWAY STATION.

NOTTINGHAM PASSENGER STATION.

PRINTED & PUBLISHED BY T. STEVENSON &C ENGRAVERS &c MIDDLE PAVEMENT.

Early Nottingham Stations. (*top* and *centre*) The original MCR
station (1839–48). This was replaced by a new building (*bottom*)
over the road (1848–1903), on the same site as the present station

although with the opening of the 'Towns line' in 1852 the
GNR station near North Gate, larger but less impressive,
became more important. The Midland crossed the GNR on
the level; the south-to-east spur was not constructed until
1965.

The growth of Newark was slow—the population had
barely increased by half by World War I. The railway found
Newark flourishing, and merely replaced water and road
transport for carrying its grain from the Vale of Belvoir. An
important recent development is the building of Staythorpe
power station beside the railway and Trent west of Newark,
burning coal from the Leen Valley and Cotgrove Collieries.

THE SOUTHWELL BRANCH

As the railway bypassed Southwell, a single-track branch was
opened in 1847 from Rolleston Junction over the 2½ miles to
this small ancient cathedral city. At first a shuttle service
connected with most Lincoln line trains, but by 1853 the
service was down to one horse-drawn train a week. Steam
services were restored in 1860 and the branch was extended to
Mansfield in April 1871. Southwell station was then rebuilt
in stone, the original wooden building being transferred to
Beeston—even the Midland sometimes made economies in
stations. The extension line was important in opening-up the
coalfield east of Mansfield; increasing coal traffic in the 1920s
led the LMS to double the original branch and put in the
west curve at Rolleston Junction to allow through workings
to Beeston sidings. Most of the twenty trains on the Southwell
line in 1910 ran to Newark.

The branch had character. The push-and-pull train was
affectionately known as 'The Southwell Paddy'. The 08.55
departure (after the last war) was popular with businessmen
as it connected into a Nottingham express. The Clerk to
the Nottinghamshire County Council was a regular patron of
this service, but once it went without him. He insisted that
the train be brought back to Southwell for him, while the
express was kept waiting at the junction, and so it was! The
previous Southwell train carried grammar school children to
Newark, and then it shunted vans. Once this took so long that
instead of preceding the Nottingham express back to Rolleston
Junction, the 'Paddy' followed it, and the express had to

Plates 16 and 17 Prosperity to decline: the railway still played an important part in the community when this picture was taken at Habrough (above) in the early 1930s; the train had to draw up twice at the short platform. But Uppingham (below) never used its branch line fully. [T. E. Routhwaite; Ian L. Wright.]

Plates 18 and 19 Nottingham scenes: *(above)* a late 1890s view of the Midland's station showing the GCR's bridge under construction; *(below)* a Manchester-Marylebone express runs into Victoria past the sandstone cliffs in the 1930s. [Nottingham City Library; T. G. Hepburn.]

wait at the junction while the branch train dashed up to Southwell and back. Locomotive crews often caught rabbits along the line for their dinners, either shooting them or pelting them with lumps of coal. It was not unknown for the crew of the first train on the branch to reach the signal box controlling the west curve before the signalman. On those days the crews would operate their own signals. The line closed to passengers on 15 June 1959.

The main line was not bereft of excitement, for the Nottingham express was due into Midland station at the same time as one from Grantham at Victoria station. From Netherfield to Trent Junction the trains ran side-by-side and racing was common, with commuters cheering on their own train. In LMS days Lincoln services regularly ran on to Derby, and have been extended to Crewe by BR. There was also a through Lincoln–Bristol train and Lincoln–Bournemouth coach before World War II.

THE GRANTHAM LINE

During the Railway Mania, the Nottingham Corporation resolved to try to end the town's branch line position. The Council Railway Committee was formed, and examined thirty-five railway projects affecting the town. Two projects especially took its notice. The Nottingham, Erewash Valley, Ambergate & Manchester Railway would run from Nottingham via Bulwell, Alfreton and Ripley to Ambergate, where it would join the projected Manchester, Buxton & Matlock Railway. Eastwards an associated company projected the Nottingham, Vale of Belvoir & Grantham Railway, while a rival promoted the Nottingham & Boston Railway. In September 1845 these three schemes were amalgamated into the Ambergate, Nottingham & Boston & Eastern Junction Railway. The Erewash, Cromford and Nottingham Canal proprietors, as well as local merchants and manufacturers backed the scheme. The second scheme that the Council considered was the grouping of the Grand Union Railway, Grand Union Extension Railway and Nottingham, Boston & Grand Union Railway, which would produce a line similar to the Ambergate's west of Nottingham, and running through Grantham to King's Lynn in the east, with a branch to Boston. However by the end of 1845 the line west of Nottingham had been abandoned, and a public meeting in Grantham had declared for the Ambergate company. This was duly authorised in 1846, whereupon the Grand Union merged with it. Another Ambergate company merger in 1846 was with the Nottingham Canal, where traffic had declined over the previous five years from 12,183 tons to 8,965 tons.

Although subsequently most of the AN & B & EJR's route was built, the undertaking was over-ambitious in the circumstances prevailing after the Railway Mania, when finance was restricted. It began by building the Nottingham–Grantham section, but even here economised by starting the line at Colwick from a junction with the Midland's Lincoln line. Running powers were obtained into the Midland's Nottingham station. In 1849 an extension of time was needed, and a Bill authorising the abandoning of the lines west of Nottingham and east of Grantham was passed. Opening came, with large crowds, on 15 July 1850. The initial service of four trains each way daily proved too optimistic, being reduced to one daily after a fortnight. All the intermediate stations except Netherfield & Colwick were opened then.

From its authorisation, the Ambergate railway was poised between the rival Midland and Great Northern Railways. The GNR tried to acquire it in 1846 and 1847, to gain access to Nottingham. The Midland likewise tried in 1851, to preserve its monopoly there by preventing such access. The key figure was Graham Hutchinson, a large GNR shareholder, who realised the strategic importance of the Ambergate company to the future of the GNR. He cornered Ambergate shares and was responsible for defeating the Midland attempt of 1851; likewise when the GNR approached the Ambergate board with another amalgamation offer, Hutchinson ensured its acceptance and an immediate working agreement was made. The Midland was not prepared to accept this, and used a legal loophole in Chancery to obtain an injunction preventing the GNR from working the Ambergate traffic.

Matters came to a head when the GNR, anticipating the opening to passengers of its 'Towns line' on 1 August 1852, advertised through services from King's Cross to Nottingham. These would be quicker than the Midland's, which was not surprising in view of the latter's trek via Derby. The first GNR train accordingly ran into the Midland station where Midland locomotives, which had both preceded and followed it in from Colwick, closed-in on the 'intruding' locomotive after it had run round its train. According to spectators it was like an elephant hunt. The GNR driver made a sporting charge at his captors in a hopeless attempt to get away, but he was evicted from his steed which was borne away in triumph and locked in a shed. As a final indignity, the rails were removed and there the locomotive stayed for seven months.

The Midland claimed the GNR was infringing the Lord Chancellor's injunction, while the GNR maintained that the Ambergate people had hired the engine. The Ambergate company soon complained that the Midland was obstructing its locomotives and 'their booking clerk threatened with expulsion'. The Midland tried unsuccessfully to obtain a further injunction to prevent the Ambergate company from using the Midland's station, then harassed the Ambergate company so that it had to convey goods traffic out to Colwick by cart. Finally in 1854, at the second attempt, the Ambergate company was authorised to be leased to the GNR for 999 years as from 2 April 1855. A new station was to be built beside London Road, and served by an independent line roughly parallel to the Midland's from Colwick. These were opened on 3 October 1857, and a connection at Colwick was removed.

The ornate London Road station served as the headquarters of the AN & B & EJR until 1923 when, as the Nottingham & Grantham Railway & Canal Company, (since 1860) it was absorbed into the LNER. From 1900 it lost most of its services to the new Victoria Station, increasingly becoming a goods depot. The last passenger services were transferred on 22 May 1944, but the station still stands substantially as built, serving as a major parcels depot, while Ambergate Street nearby is a reminder of the old company.

The strategic importance of this line was implemented during the 1860s when the GNR tried to break the Midland's monopoly of the coal traffic between the Derbyshire–Nottinghamshire coalfield and London. The GNR was forced to build its own line for this which was authorised in 1872 from Colwick to Derby and beyond, with a branch to Pinxton. A year later the line from Newark to Bottesford, and the joint line with the LNWR through Leicestershire were authorised. Between them the lines generated considerable mineral traffic which was dealt with at new sorting yards laid out at Colwick.

The Pinxton line was fully operational in 1876, while in 1878 were opened the Derby line, Colwick yards and locomotive shed and Netherfield station to serve the growing railway township. The yards were extended in 1889–91, giving twenty miles of sidings on 150 acres of land. The Bottesford West Junction to Newark line was opened on 1 July 1878, followed before the end of 1879 by the joint line from Saxondale and Bottesford North Junction through to Welham Junction near Market Harborough. The LNWR established its presence with a goods depot in Nottingham, now the site of a housing estate, and a locomotive shed at Colwick, closed in 1928.

The Newark line trains numbered six down and seven up in 1910. These were gradually reduced to an evening return train after World War II, which was diverted to Grantham in 1955. The LNWR was responsible for the Joint Line passenger services from Nottingham, running six trains through to Northampton in 1910. Rather surprisingly, the LNWR did not seek running powers into the new Victoria station in 1900, which did not help patronage of their trains. When these were finally diverted there from London Road in 1944, it was too late, and the two daily return trains to Market Harborough (one going on to Northampton) ceased running on 7 December 1953.

The Grantham services were frequent until the economies of recent years pruned them to fourteen each way, including the through Harwich–Manchester boat train. The GNR had run three return through services to King's Cross, two coming from Sheffield, and the LNER ran a Pullman express from King's Cross to Nottingham and Sheffield for a short time in 1924, but the existence of the GCR route from 1899 curbed these services. One up King's Cross train remained well into BR days.

Excursion traffic was important as the working week was reduced. The connection between Allington and Barkston East Junctions was opened in 1875 to allow through running to the East Coast, avoiding Grantham. Although originally seen as a freight link, it was invaluable for seaside excursions following the rise of Skegness and Mablethorpe from the 1880s. Between the wars evening excursions from Nottingham to Skegness at 2s 6d (12½p) return were so popular that often six trains were needed. After nationalisation, excursions and Summer Saturday extras came from LMR stations like Coalville or Alfreton. These had to reverse into London Road Goods Yard to gain the Grantham line, which took half an hour. The old Ambergate company's connection was only restored in 1965; the Grantham services were transferred into Midland station when Victoria station closed in 1967. The Racecourse station nearby was closed on 8 December 1959 after 102 years.

Rationalisation of the plethora of lines around Nottingham in the 1960s reduced the importance of Colwick yard, which was closed in 1970. The growth of merry-go-round and block coal trains and decline in the number of collieries has meant less sorting of wagons, which can be done at Toton for Leen Valley traffic. This has reduced goods traffic on to the GNR main line going south to London or north to Immingham, but traffic still moves into East Anglia, and the opening of the Cotgrove colliery branch in 1960 has generated more traffic. This branch leaves the main line just south of Colwick on a triangular junction, of which the westward arm is carried on an impressive concrete viaduct. Further east the GNR opened ironstone branches from Belvoir Junction to Denton in 1883 and from High Dyke Junction to Sproxton and Stainby in 1916–22, but the recession in English iron ore mining brought their closure 1972–4 (but see page 248).

THE MANSFIELD LINE

Whereas the Ambergate company might have brought Nottingham main line status, its contemporary, the Mansfield line, was envisaged solely as a feeder line. The Midland promoted it in 1845 to tap the Leen Valley collieries and planned a triangular junction at Nottingham to allow southbound coal trains to avoid Nottingham station. It was authorised in 1846, and in 1847 further authorised to purchase Jessop's Mansfield & Pinxton Railway which would parallel the line over four miles north of Kirkby-in-Ashfield. The branch was opened to this point on 2 October 1848 and on to Mansfield on 9 October 1849. Traffic was boosted over the 1848 opening as it coincided with Nottingham Goose Fair week, but fares were not competitive, as the Midland charged 4d third class for the $2\frac{1}{2}$ miles out to Radford.

Within the 1877 boundaries of Nottingham there were

stations at Lenton, closed in 1910, Radford, Basford and Bulwell. These last three areas were separate villages which expanded with the development of Nottingham's industries. Bulwell was also a centre for making bricks and flowerpots, using the very red clay dug close to the railway. At Basford Junction the Kimberley branch diverged west to join the Erewash Valley line at Bennerley Junction. The passenger service, comprising in 1910 six return trains running through to Ilkeston Town, lasted from 1882 to 1917.

Mansfield lies fourteen miles by road from Nottingham, but is seventeen by rail. Moreover with eight intermediate stops the ten all-station trains in 1955 took up to fifty-five minutes for the journey. Even the 'express' took thirty-seven minutes, ten minutes longer than in 1932. Eight of the trains ran on to Worksop, but all were withdrawn on 12 October 1964.

THE GNR EXPANDS

Nottingham gained four useful railways in the thirteen years 1839–52, but it was the developments in the last quarter of that century that really put Nottingham on to the railway map. The GNR took the initiative with its 'Derbyshire lines', then the Midland responded to foreign incursions into its territory with a new main line to Nottingham, and finally the Great Central swept through on its London Extension. It is perhaps ironical that little remains of these lines which at last brought Nottingham real express services, except perhaps the spirit, which has promoted the great accelerations over the original MCR lines in the later 1960s.

The GNR's Derbyshire lines were primarily after coal, to break the Midland's monopoly of the Derbyshire–Nottinghamshire coalfield. Added attractions were the towns of Ilkeston, Derby and Burton (and even distant Stafford). The full development of these lines is discussed in the succeeding chapters, but here it can be noted that passenger services between Nottingham and Pinxton began on 1 August 1876, to Derby and Burton on 1 April 1878, up the Leen Valley from Bulwell to Newstead beside the Midland's Mansfield branch, on 2 October 1882, and on the Leen Valley Extension to Shirebrook (South) on 1 November 1901.

It was remarkable that until 1900 trains for the Derbyshire lines left Nottingham going east, before going north at

Colwick. By the time they faced west at Daybrook, some $3\frac{1}{4}$ miles direct distance from Nottingham, they had travelled $7\frac{1}{2}$ miles, and from Colwick on a line increasingly choked with coal traffic from Annesley. It was to remedy this situation, and to open up new residential development in NE Nottingham, that local businessmen formed the Nottingham Suburban Railway in 1886.

Their line, authorised that year, ran from Trent Lane East Junction, where the GNR crossed the Midland, northwards to Daybrook, saving $3\frac{1}{2}$ miles. The GNR was to operate the line from the beginning, and could buy it after ten years, although it never did. Nor did it route all its local passenger services over it, as was originally intended. The GNR and the Midland were unhelpful; the Midland wanted the NSR's overbridges to be 50ft wide, while the GNR insisted on a flyover at Trent Lane, to avoid fouling the Grantham line, and an extra span to cover three extra tracks which might be (but never were) needed later. Finally, a farmer at Sherwood had to be appeased by adding ten yards to the tunnel to avoid disturbing his stackyard. These extra expenses and the heavy earthworks, much through sandstone, increased the cost by a third.

Construction took two years, opening early on 2 December 1889. No GNR directors graced the scene but various officials did, as well as the contractor who claimed he was still in possession, despite a legal injunction to prevent him from interfering with the opening. His agent stopped the train at Trent Lane Junction, claiming that the GNR was trespassing. The GNR ignored him and he had to jump out of the way, but not before laying his red flag on the rail in protest. On the return journey it was found that the contractor was travelling without a ticket.

The initial service was of ten down and nine up trains to Daybrook, four going on to Newstead, but the residential development failed to come as expected. The opening of the GCR's direct line up the Leen Valley rendered the NSR unnecessary, as GNR trains joined the GCR at Bulwell Common or Bagthorpe Junction, via connections built so that the GNR could use the Joint station, opened on 24 May 1900. A revised train service gave five trains to Basford & Bulwell and three to Shirebrook. Then the development of electric trams by Nottingham Corporation hit traffic at the NSR stations, so that by 1914 many trains ceased to call there. They were closed as a wartime economy measure on 1 July 1916. In pre-war days the line was part of a circular route for Shirebrook trains, running mostly via Bestwood Junction, Bulwell Common, Nottingham Victoria and Thorneywood. The LNER initially only ran four daily trains over the NSR; the heavy gradients of 1 in 49 and 1 in 70 made it difficult to work with small locomotives.

The partial collapse of Mapperley Tunnel on the Gedling line in 1925 brought all Leen Valley trains over the NSR, while a royal visit to Sherwood in 1928 brought thirteen special trains carrying 6,834 children and teachers, but that was the end. The single passenger service over the line ceased in 1931 while goods traffic was down to a thrice-weekly goods serving the brickworks at Thorneywood. A bomb severed the line just north of the Midland bridge in 1941; the hole was never repaired and the whole line was abandoned in 1954.

Although the Gedling line had been used by MS & L trains for Nottingham from 1892 when it opened its extension between Staveley and Annesley, (GNR trains ran from Nottingham to Staveley from 1893) this line, like the NSR, declined as a passenger route when the Joint station was opened in 1900. In 1910, of the ten down Shirebrook line trains, half went via Gedling, three via the NSR, and two direct. Otherwise down traffic was confined to an early morning Pinxton local and thirteen Basford & Bulwell locals, half of which ran after 17.00 from Victoria. The Derby line enjoyed sixteen down trains and the Pinxton branch eight, direct from Victoria. The GNR gave Nottingham through trains to Heanor, Ilkeston, Derby, Burton and Stafford. The LNER withdrew the Burton, Stafford and Heanor services in 1939 and diverted the Leen Valley services over the GC line in 1931. In 1955 there were still four down Saturday trains to Shirebrook North (withdrawn in 1956), four down locals to Basford North (formerly Basford & Bulwell) via Gedling (withdrawn in 1962) twelve to Derby (withdrawn in 1964) and seven to Pinxton (withdrawn in 1963).

THE MIDLAND MAIN LINE

The first stage in improving Midland access to Nottingham was the building of the Radford–Trowell loop, opened on 1

May 1875, giving direct access to the Chesterfield line. There were severe slacks at either junction and the line is steeply-graded, so that progress then and now was sedate.

Meanwhile the Midland was interested in exploiting the Leicestershire, Rutland and Northamptonshire iron ore field, and in 1872 was authorised to build a line from London Road Nottingham to Saxby on its Syston–Peterborough line. At the same time the LNWR, GNR and MS & LR were all after lines in this area, which alarmed the Midland. The outcome was a further Midland line from Manton (on the S & PR) to Glendon, north of Kettering, authorised in 1875 along with deviations to the Nottinghamshire line which would now join the S & P at Melton Mowbray. The GNR/LNWR Joint line was authorised and built at the same time.

These two new sections opened to goods traffic on 1 November 1879 and to local passenger trains on 2 February 1880. Express trains from St Pancras, usually the Leeds, Bradford and some Scottish ones, began running on 1 June 1880. The distance from St Pancras to Nottingham was one mile shorter and the gradients easier than by the old route to give an easier journey for heavy mineral trains, coal running south or iron ore moving north. This was done at the expense of heavy earthworks as the line crossed the valleys rather than running along them.

Local traffic along the line was never heavy and was not encouraged, so that the line could be kept clear for express and freight trains. Many of the intermediate stations in Nottinghamshire were closed by the LMS. The buildings at Widmerpool have been converted into a public house. Local Nottingham to Melton Mowbray trains numbered eight in 1932, with two more going on to the M & GN via Saxby, one bound for Yarmouth. This was a popular route for Summer Saturday holiday expresses from Lancashire to the Norfolk Coast, and in reverse, pre-war strawberry specials from the Fens to Nottingham. The M & GN trains were withdrawn on 2 March 1959 and the last express service on 1 May 1967.

As an express route this line could bring Nottingham within $2\frac{1}{4}$ hours of London by 1905. There were six up expresses in 1910 and nine in 1932 and 1955, when the best time was $2\frac{1}{4}$ hours (worse than 1905!) and the worst, for an express, of almost three hours. Other expresses could still be joined at Trent and Derby.

THE GREAT CENTRAL

As its name suggests, the Manchester, Sheffield & Lincolnshire Railway was a northern concern, but under the aggressive chairmanship of Edward Watkin its eyes turned first to
Nottingham, and ultimately to London and even to Paris.
As the railways were still monopolising inland transport in
the 1890s there was just room for a third main line from the
East Midlands to London, but no one saw either how international conflict would distort the British economy in the
twentieth century nor how quickly the railway's monopoly
would be effectively challenged by road transport. Within
a generation of its opening, the GCR was an expensive
luxury, certainly into London.

Nottingham benefitted considerably from the GCR, more
than anywhere else on the extension, although Sheffield and
Leicester found it very useful. Watkin was determined to gain
a central site for the Nottingham and Leicester stations,
although this involved the destruction of much property. Also
at Nottingham this involved heavy earthworks including
some 2,250 yards of tunnelling and nearly a mile of viaduct.
Victoria station was in a vast cutting from which 600,000
cubic yards of sandstone were excavated with a tunnel at
either end. Carrington station was also between two tunnels
while Arkwright Street was on the viaduct. While driving
Victoria Street tunnel (the most southerly) the men pierced
the strongroom of a bank and the rock cellars of two public
houses; at the first they drank freely of the contents, but at
the second they found only bottled ginger and herb beer.
They also discovered the old dungeons below the old Guildhall plus the remains of long-executed criminals, which the
Corporation reburied.

The Great Central was opened on 15 March 1899 for
passenger traffic, but as the main station was not ready,
Arkwright Street served as the main town station, and Carrington for northern local services. The GNR had ultimately
consented to join in the construction of the joint station and
built a connecting line entirely on a viaduct, from Trent
Lane West Junction to Weekday Cross Junction at the south
end of Victoria Street tunnel. A new station was built beside
its London Road terminus, becoming London Road High
Level. Neither company could decide on a name for their

new station, Central being anathema to the GNR. The town clerk found a solution, as the station was opened on the Queen's birthday, 24 May 1900. This decision would probably have come naturally earlier in her long reign.

The station occupied thirteen acres of land and 1,300 houses including twenty public houses had to be demolished to make way for it. The land alone cost £473,000, while the final sum exceeded £1 million. The building was impressive, especially from within and contained twelve platforms, in the form of two large islands with double bays at either end. But as *The Railway Magazine* contributor commented in 1932, 'The station is a good deal more pretentious than its traffic warrants.' There were then about sixty departures from either end daily, while the proximity of the double track tunnels created an operating bottleneck. Furthermore, all southbound freight traffic, which was heavy, passed through the station, while shunting had to extend into the northern tunnel. This was on a rising gradient of 1 in 130, with no ventilation shafts because of the property above, so it was frequently foul. All incoming trains treated it with great caution.

The GCR offered Nottingham nine good trains to London in 1905, the best taking 2¼ hours, similar to the Midland's. The situation did not change much into the 1930s. In addition there were several cross-country services—five each way in 1932 —leaving the GC at Woodford Halse, and serving variously Aberdeen, Edinburgh and Glasgow, Newcastle, Leeds, Bradford, York and Hull, Bournemouth and Southampton, Cardiff and Swansea, and Bristol, Plymouth and Penzance. As all these trains ran through Sheffield, Nottingham and Leicester, the net result was an unbeatable train service between these towns. Although the Midland line had more trains to Leicester in 1932, they took a good forty minutes for the 27 mile journey, whereas the standard GC line time was twenty-seven minutes non-stop for the 23½ mile journey. Similarly, at thirty-eight miles the GC route to Sheffield was only 2½ miles shorter than the Midland route, but at fifty minutes was quicker than the Midland's.

In addition to the thirteen expresses in 1932, there were fourteen stopping trains to Leicester from Nottingham, eight for Sheffield via Chesterfield and fourteen to Mansfield, on the line opened in 1917. This branch was again preferable to the Midland, with a best time of twenty-eight minutes and a normal time of forty minutes, ten minutes quicker than the Midland route. It still carried eight down trains in 1955, but lost them in 1956.

In spite of being well patronised and amid much criticism, the GC line lost its London expresses in 1960, although it had suffered as the poor relation of the prestigious GN line since 1945. Many saw this as the beginning of the end, and from 4 March 1963 the line lost all its local services between Nottingham and Sheffield, again the best patronised; all the intermediate stations except New Basford were closed. Through freight was withdrawn in 1965 and the next stage was complete closure south of Rugby and between Bulwell Common North Junction and Annesley Junction, with diversion of the through cross-country expresses via Derby and Birmingham on 5 September 1966. This left a shuttle service between Nottingham and Rugby, which was diverted to the re-opened Arkwright Street station from 4 September 1967 when Victoria was closed. These services ended on 5 May 1969, leaving the two daily freight trains from Ruddington ordnance depot and Gotham gypsum mines (branch opened 1900) running into Victoria Street tunnel and reversing down the GN spur to London Road. These were withdrawn when the Loughborough spur to the Midland line opened in April 1974. Nottingham Council developed the Victoria Centre on the station site.

With the decline in coal, steel and fish traffic plus the greater line capacity provided by diesel locomotives and sophisticated signalling, it was inevitable that duplicating routes would be phased out. By the mid-1960s GC line traffic could be diverted on to Midland routes via Toton or Birmingham. But the reduction in passenger services left a void for Nottingham which BR was very slow to fill.

MIDLAND AND MODERN SERVICES

By the 1880s Midland station employed 170 men, including twenty clerks, thirty porters and a dozen men in the parcels office. This busy place handled thirty thousand parcels a month, especially from the lace trade, and about five thousand parcels daily before Christmas. 'Parcels' included animals such as the fierce gorilla bound for Loughborough. This got loose in its van, so it was sent on to Nottingham. Here it bit the parcels clerk across the thigh and ran out into the street, hotly pursued by staff and dogs. It was cornered in a timber yard but kept bowling the dogs over with its fists. Finally two men got a chain over it and sent it back to Loughborough.

The opening of Victoria Station put the Midland to shame. Their station, adequate in 1848, was ridiculously cramped by 1900, with only three platforms, and unattractive to passengers. But it took a locomotive derailment to make the Midland respond to the GC's challenge. It knocked down a cast iron pillar, bringing down part of the train shed. An entirely new station was built with a handsome terra-cotta frontage facing Carrington Street. Its five through platforms and a bay coped adequately with the 162 daily departures.

After 1966, improvements were gradually made to Midland line services. By 1973 there were twenty expresses to London, some fast from Leicester, taking just under two hours, others stopping en route but also connecting into the fast ones at Leicester. Going north, Nottingham was still not adequately served as more of the Sheffield trains ran direct down the Erewash Valley line. Eight trains went north, five to Sheffield in fifty-six minutes, and one each to Alfreton & Mansfield Parkway, Manchester and Glasgow. Additionally, three night trains ran to Sheffield and Glasgow via Derby. The re-routing of the Harwich–Manchester boat train via Nottingham in 1973 doubled Nottingham's continental revenue, while local services revived as roads became more congested, especially around Trent Bridge, although the Midland's disused Kettering line bridge had a road laid across it to ease this.

The 1983 timetable showed services to sixteen destinations as scattered as the West and East Coasts, Scotland and Birmingham. The HSTs provided sixteen up and seventeen down services for London with an improved best time of ninety-nine minutes. Northwards twelve trains served Sheffield, of which one went on to Leeds, one to Barrow-in-Furness and two to Glasgow/Edinburgh, the last three running via Manchester and Preston; the Harwich boat train remained. Of the local services, fifteen went to Lincoln (one going on to Cleethorpes), thirteen to Grantham (four continuing to Skegness, one to Boston and two more terminating at Bingham), twenty-two to Derby (twelve proceeding to Crewe and six to Birmingham) and one to Birmingham via Leicester.

CHAPTER VIII

The North Midland Coalfield

Coal has been mined along the Erewash Valley at least since the thirteenth century and probably earlier. Its exploitation always depended on adequate transport to market, for only cheap coal would be burnt in quantity as a domestic fuel. As initially only water transport could offer cheap bulk cartage, the first mines developed were those with access to navigable rivers.

Huntingdon Beaumont, squire of Wollaton (west of Nottingham), was the first known English coal owner to tackle the problems of carrying coal over bad roads: by 1604 he had laid down two parallel lines of wooden rails between his pits and the Trent, on which to run horse-drawn waggons. It was not until later in the eighteenth century that these early waggonways or tramways became widely used as canal feeders, and several were built to serve the Nottingham Canal. Out of them developed the independent railway.

The development of railways stimulated both coal mining and the development of heavy industry on the coalfield. They had several advantages over canals: they were less restricted by physical obstacles; they could reach easily even wider national markets; and as locomotives grew more powerful, they could carry more at once.

This can clearly be seen in the North Midland coalfield. First access to the Trent, then the building of the Erewash, the Cromford and the Nottingham Canals by 1800, encouraged mining and the establishment of small iron furnaces. Railways were essential by the 1830s to maintain the coalfield's profitability, as the important Leicester market had been cornered by the Leicestershire coal owners using their new railway from Swannington. When the railways came in the

1840s the coal mines multiplied, new iron furnaces were established, and existing furnaces grew larger. Another wave of railway building in the forty years after 1870, initiated by the Great Northern Railway's desire to tap this profitable area, hitherto a Midland preserve, resulted in the extending of the coalfield eastwards, up the Leen Valley, around Mansfield, and finally into Sherwood Forest. This process is still continuing, with Bevercoats Colliery opening in 1965.

As the Erewash forms the county boundary between Nottinghamshire and Derbyshire, this chapter will deal with the coalmining areas of both counties, from Trent, up the Erewash Valley and beyond to Chesterfield and Staveley, and then up the Leen Valley to Mansfield and into Sherwood Forest.

TRENT JUNCTIONS

There is no village called Trent, but in the meadows by Long Eaton the Erewash Canal meets the River Trent, and the Erewash Valley, Derby, Nottingham and Leicester lines converge, as conceived by the original promoters of the Midland Counties Railway.

These coal owners from the Erewash Valley wanted a railway from their collieries to Leicester in order to regain their dominant position in that coal market. Branches would link Nottingham and Derby, and an extension deeper into the coalfield at Pinxton was mooted. Unfortunately they could not raise sufficient capital locally, and the proposed Pinxton extension was seen as a threat to another scheme, the North Midland Railway, from Derby to Leeds via Chesterfield. The northern financiers who rescued the MCR project abandoned the whole Erewash Valley line in order to avoid NMR opposition. Although these tactics were successful, and the MCR Bill was authorised in 1836, the Erewash Valley men were still without their railway and Leicester market. The MCR was duly opened between Derby and Nottingham on 30 May 1839, and to Leicester on 4 May 1840 via junctions at Sawley in the west, and at Long Eaton station in the east. The two lines met at Trentlock Junction (now Trent Junction), in the south.

The Midland Railway, the creation of the 1844 amalgamation which included the MCR and NMR, was able to revive the Erewash Valley line, opening it to Codnor Park on 6 September 1847. It left the MCR lines at Long Eaton Junction, giving direct access to Nottingham, and at South Erewash Junction for Leicester traffic. Two difficulties soon arose: there was no direct access to Derby, and a level crossing was created at Platts Crossing over the direct Derby–Nottingham line.

As the mineral traffic increased, Platts Crossing became a dangerous nuisance, and the next year the Midland was authorised to build a new north-to-west curve near Trent Junction, but as the company was short of money this was delayed until 1862 when the Trent Junctions were re-modelled. This Sheet Stores Curve allowed Platts Crossing to be taken out, for Derby–Nottingham trains could also use this curve. A new station was built and also another curve from the original Derby–Nottingham line, to allow Derby–Leicester trains to use the new station. The final addition in 1901 was the high-level goods avoiding line from Toton, with its spur to the Nottingham line at Attenborough Junction, separate tunnel under Red Hill, and spans over the Trent.

In the 1880s Williams thought that the opening of the Manton loop to Nottingham would spell the end of Trent as an interchange station. In fact it lived on as such until 1 January 1968, and was still handling nearly a hundred passenger trains daily in 1961. The end of local services and consequent recasting of the timetables in the mid-1960s ended its usefulness. Its system of curves and the Manton loop meant both London and Manchester trains could leave the station in either direction. Uninitiated passengers found this most confusing.

Freight workings, over 300 trains daily, could also be confusing as all coal trains to Castle Donnington and Willington power stations, and to Birmingham and Derby, had to use the station. Before the days of the power signal box at Trent, wrong train information to one signalman could—and did—result in a long Toton–Castle Donnington coal train being held at Trent South Junction to await a train from Leicester, yet still fouling South Erewash Junction. If the Leicester line train, bound for Nottingham, turned out to be unexpectedly long, it would be held at South Erewash Junction, yet still fouling Trent South Junction.

The Midland built its sheet stores and sack stores at Trent. At the former, 10,000 wagon tarpaulins were made annually

Plates 20, 21 and 22 Nottinghamshire locals: *(top)* 'The Southwell Paddy' at Rolleston Junction; the round-ended stations were a feature of the Lincoln line; *(centre)* a Mansfield train arrives at Bulwell Market, while *(below)* a Shirebrook (North) train pulls out of Sutton-in-Ashfield (Town). [T. G. Hepburn *(all)*.]

Plates 23 and 24 Derbyshire scenes: *(above)* a down express hurries through Cromford station in the summer of 1911; *(below)* a quiet moment at the busy terminus at Wirksworth, where substantial milk traffic supplements the heavy stone traffic. [BR, LMR; Locomotive Publishing Co.]

and 90,000 repaired. On the permanent staff of the sack stores were a dozen women to darn holes in the company's 450,000 grain sacks and six cats to keep down the attendant rats.

Today the built-up area extends from Nottingham westwards through Beeston to Long Eaton and Sawley, and northwards up the valley through Stapleford to Ilkeston. When the railway came, the main communities were Beeston with some 2,800 inhabitants and Long Eaton with 1,900. For several years Trent station was without road access, and even now the only inhabitants live in the railway cottages. Both towns were slow to grow, Long Eaton's population increasing by one between 1841 and 1851. Both towns developed from the 1870s but as much under the influence of Nottingham as of the railway, although the sleeper depot and Toton marshalling yards each offered employment.

Long Eaton can boast three separate stations carrying that name. First was the original MCR station, which added 'Junction' when the second Long Eaton station on the Erewash Valley line was opened in 1847. For ten years this station was called Toton for Long Eaton, reverting to its original name on the closure of the first station in 1862, when Trent was opened. The second station was closed in 1967 and the name transferred to Sawley Junction station, which had been opened in 1888. Further east, Attenborough station was opened as a roadside halt in 1864, and benefitted greatly from the large wartime ordnance depot established at nearby Chilwell. However it could still be described as a roadside station in the 1930s despite enjoying twenty-six trains daily. Beeston had fifty-five daily, which encouraged commuter traffic.

TOTON SIDINGS

Toton sidings have developed at the lowest point of the Erewash Valley line. The two yards act as the focal point of the Nottinghamshire, Derbyshire and South Yorkshire coalfields, and have a wide distribution area—to Peterborough and the east, to London and the south, and to Birmingham and the west. Williams in 1884 described Toton's growth:

> . . . twenty years ago it was nearly all fields. There was just the up and down passenger line, one siding and a weighing machine, over which a mineral train could be passed. . . . As the mineral business increased, fresh sidings were added, and a night as well as a day staff of men was provided.

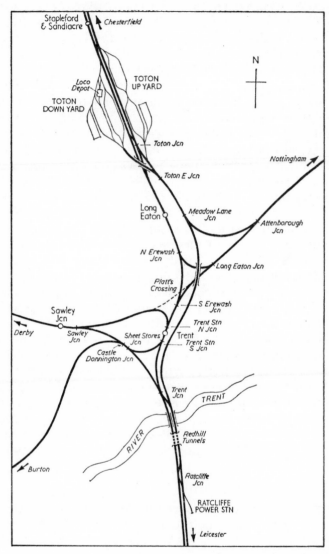

The junctions at Trent

On the down side, dealing with returning empties, there were five reception roads and seventeen sorting sidings in 1884. Full wagons are dealt with on the up side, where in 1884 there were nine reception roads and sixteen sorting sidings. Much shunting was done by horses; about forty were sufficient in summer to handle the 18,000 wagons a month. In deep winter, when grease might freeze in the axleboxes, it could take two or three horses to move a single wagon. During the winter some 26,000 wagons were handled a month.

Hump working began in 1901, which considerably speeded wagon sorting. In the 1930s a thorough modernisation of both yards was planned, and completed in May 1939 for the down yard. Work on the up yard was interrupted by the war and not completed until 1952. Diesel shunters were then extensively used, and the thirty-five sidings in the down yard could handle nearly 5,000 wagons a day. Actual reconstruction in the down yard was kept to a minimum, but in the up yard sixteen miles of track were completely taken up and replaced with twenty-seven miles, within two years. Four fans of sorting sidings were laid, comprising thirty-seven roads, plus eleven arrival lines and twenty storage roads. These up sidings received up to seventy trains daily in 1952 and despatched sixty; between them, the two yards handled two million wagons a year.

During the 1960s coal traffic declined sharply as oil imports increased and as natural gas replaced town gas. In addition, the eight local power stations are supplied directly from collieries, consuming half of the sixteen million tons of coal produced locally. Ratcliffe-on-Soar power station at the south end of Red Hill Tunnel, for example, burns up to 100,000 tons of coal a week and is fed continuously by 1,300 ton coal trains on the merry-go-round principle. (It also produces 20,000 tons of fly-ash weekly, which is taken by train to Peterborough.) This has left surplus capacity at Toton, enabling it to take over traffic formerly handled by rival company yards at Annesley (GCR) and Colwick (GNR).

THE EREWASH VALLEY RAILWAYS

Fifteen years after its inception, the Erewash Valley line was opened by the Midland Railway on 6 September 1847 from Trent to Codnor Park. The Pinxton extension was realised when the line was extended there through Pye Bridge on 9 October 1849. Through working to Mansfield was possible as the Midland rebuilt the original tramway, also re-opened that day.

The impact of this line on the industry of the valley area was enormous. It virtually created two major ironworks, and began the systematic exploitation of the concealed coalfield. Reference to the graph below will show how coal shipments out of the valley doubled in the five years after 1849, and again in the following decade, and how much this was due to the railways; canal traffic dropped by two thirds over the next twenty-five years.

Although there was a small furnace at Stanton during the Napoleonic Wars, it was unimportant. The history of the works really began with the erection of three furnaces in 1846 while the railway was being built. Within two years the

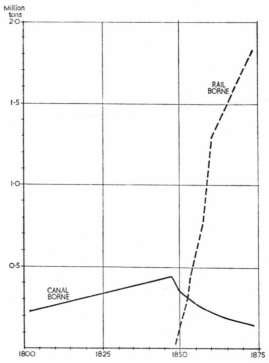

Coal tonnages leaving the Erewash Valley (1800–75). The Midland Railway was able to aid coal production here on a scale impossible for the canals

works was producing annually over 10,000 tons of iron. During the 1860s it began importing ore from Northamptonshire, mining its own ore there from the 1870s. The works enjoyed connections to both the Midland and the Great Northern Railways.

The other ironworks stimulated by the railway was at Codnor Park. The Butterley Company had been established by Jessop and Outram above the tunnel on the Cromford Canal in 1790. Tramways linked it to the canal, which it had helped to promote, and to its coal and iron mines. Soon it was the largest in Derbyshire. It followed its coal seams two miles eastwards, and established three new furnaces alongside the new railway, which again it had helped to promote. Annual output by 1848 was nearly 10,000 tons. The company produced materials for railway construction, especially bridges. Probably its most famous work was the ironwork for the trainshed at St Pancras station.

The profitability of the Erewash Valley coalmines led the Great Northern to cast covetous eyes on this Midland preserve. When the GNR proposed a branch from Colwick to Codnor Park in 1862 the Midland bought it off by offering it some traffic via existing lines in Nottingham. After its London Extension was opened in 1868 the Midland was no longer dependant on GNR goodwill in London. It therefore ended the 1863 agreement, virtually excluding the GNR from the Nottinghamshire coalfield. Faced with the loss of £50,000 revenue annually, and desiring to break this Midland monopoly, the GNR proposed in 1872 a more far-reaching scheme of railways than their 1862 one.

From Colwick the line went north to tap the Duke of St Alban's undeveloped Bestwood coalfield, then lacking rail access, before veering west to Kimberley and the Erewash Valley. At Awsworth Junction, one line ran north through Eastwood to Codnor Park and Pinxton; the other continued west through Ilkeston to Derby, Burton-on-Trent and Stafford using running powers over the North Staffordshire Railway. This line would give the GNR coal outlets both east and west,

Kimberley, then a small town of 4,000 people, had actually petitioned the GNR for a railway. Ilkeston also welcomed it. The Midland's Erewash Valley line, seeking coal before passengers, had skirted this town, which was served by a branch line opened on the same day as the main line. But the facilities were poor and people said that they would rather walk to the Junction than use the branch; indeed from 1870 they had to, for the Midland closed it to passengers. In spite of Stanton ironworks, Ilkeston had only grown slowly during the 1850s and 1860s, and was still known for its lace and hosiery. However, the recent building of the Bennerley furnaces was an added attraction to the GNR, whose line served the town well from 1878 to 1964. In 1910 Derby could be reached in fifteen minutes or Nottingham in fourteen minutes by GNR, whereas the Midland services took at least twenty-two to Nottingham, and over an hour to Derby. Ilkeston's population rose by 5,000 each decade between 1871 and 1901. (The corresponding GNR line times in 1955 were sixteen and twenty-five minutes, for the 9 mile journeys; no wonder the line went out of business!)

The GNR scheme was authorised in 1872, and the Pinxton line was begun first to bring in coal traffic. It was not ready for opening until August 1875 because of the heavy earthworks involved between the Leen and Erewash Valleys. Indeed, even after opening to mineral traffic, the deep cutting at Kimberley was unfinished, and a temporary line with gradients of 1 in 35 had to be laid alongside. Even so, in the first six months of 1876 115,000 tons of coal were carried, justifying the project. Passenger services began running to Pinxton on 1 August 1876.

The Derby line from Awsworth Junction was begun in 1875 and opened fully on 1 April 1878. It crossed the Erewash Valley on a long lattice viaduct. Ironically, Eastwood, the home of the Midland Counties Railway, was better served by the GNR, who also laid sorting sidings there. At Pinxton the GNR and Midland stations were adjacent. Unfortunately, the very success of the line was disastrous here, for mining caused the departure platform to subside, and all departures in later years used the isolated and windswept bay platform. Closure came on 7 January 1963, followed by the Derby line on 7 September 1964. Goods traffic was progressively cut back, ending finally in 1968.

The Midland responded to the GNR threat by building several branches and connecting lines. The mines at Shipley, west of Ilkeston, were linked to the Midland at Stanton Gate by a line opened in 1870. On 1 May 1875 the Trowell to

Radford cut-off was opened to allow quicker access to Nottingham, and on the same day the line from Pye Bridge to Ambergate (Crich Junction). This was primarily a goods line, to divert the increasingly heavy traffic in meat, grain, fruit and timber from the Americas, imported via Liverpool and other Lancashire ports, away from the congested Ambergate–Derby–Trent line. Already freight from the West Riding was diverted down the Erewash Valley line at Clay Cross, and could regain the Birmingham line at Repton using the Castle Donnington line, opened throughout in 1873.

The next step was to re-open the Ilkeston Town branch on 1 July, 1879, followed on 12 August by the branch from Bennerley Junction to Kimberley and Watnall, where it joined the branch from Basford Junction to Watnall Colliery, opened in 1877. Passenger services over this Kimberley branch began on 1 September 1882, but never seriously rivalled those of the GNR.

On the hills west of the Erewash Valley lie the twin mining towns of Heanor and Ripley. These grew steadily throughout the nineteenth century and into the twentieth, reaching 24,000 and 18,000 population respectively by 1951. Heanor attracted both companies, with the Midland first by thirteen months. The GNR branch, opened to passengers on 1 July 1891 was an extension of its Shipley (Nutbrook Colliery) branch, opened to coal traffic from Ilkeston Junction in June 1886.

The Midland branch approached Heanor from Ripley, and was part of a plan to put Ripley on a through line, as the Midland did not favour terminal branches in the coalfield. Although authorised separately in 1884 and 1886, the Ripley–Butterley and Ripley–Heanor lines were opened together on 2 June 1890. The section on to the main Erewash Valley line, and spur into separate platforms at Langley Mill, were opened on 1 October 1895.

Ripley's first railway was the branch from Little Eaton, opened on 1 September 1856 and serving collieries nearby at Denby and Marehay. Hitherto these had been served by an even older line, the Little Eaton Gangway, engineered by Outram as a 4ft 6in gauge plateway, and linking these collieries to the Derby Canal. Opened in May 1795, it finally closed in July 1908. The branch was connected to the new line in Ripley, giving access to the new station sited in the centre of the town. The original station, further east, became a goods yard.

In 1910 Ripley was served by nine trains to Heanor and Langley Mill, eight to Butterley and seven to Derby. In 1917 the Langley Mill to Butterley trains were withdrawn as an economy measure but were reinstated in 1920. Trains were again halted by the General Strike on 4 May 1926, and were not reinstated. Derby–Ripley services were withdrawn on 1 June 1930, except for excursions. Goods traffic was withdrawn gradually : Heanor–Ripley and Ripley–Butterley in 1926, from Heanor in 1951 (coal 1970) and Ripley in 1963, although Denby still sends out coal. The GNR Heanor branch enjoyed ten down and nine up trains in 1910. These were withdrawn on 30 April 1928 except for a workmen's service, which lasted until 4 December 1939. Goods traffic continued until 1963.

Before World War I local train services were heavy along the Erewash Valley, with up to fifty each way using various routes, terminating usually at Ilkeston or Chesterfield. The Kimberley branch carried six trains to Ilkeston, one going on to Chesterfield, and six to Nottingham. The Butterley line carried fourteen eastward and eleven westward trains, some branching off to the Ripley line, and including one down and two up expresses between Nottingham and Manchester. The Pinxton line carried eleven Mansfield trains, many connecting badly at Pye Bridge, and twelve up trains, two going through to Nottingham. In spite of this profusion of services, passengers from Nottingham to Ilkeston and the northern Erewash Valley stations preferred to use the more direct GNR trains.

World War I killed the Midland's Kimberley branch on 1 January 1917, and the track west of Kimberley was lifted for use in France. Depression in the mining industry between the wars, coupled with the growth of bus services across the valley seriously affected rail patronage. The fate of the Ripley lines has already been noted. 16 June 1947 saw the end of passenger services on the Butterley and Pinxton lines, except for a daily return workmen's service between Mansfield (Kirkby-in-Ashfield 1964–5) and Nottingham, and the final closure of the Ilkeston Town branch. Although there were still eight down and seven up local trains along the main Erewash Valley line in 1955, intermediate stations were quietly cut out, so that these services ceased to run from 2 January 1967. Alfreton station was re-opened as Alfreton & Mansfield Parkway on 7 May 1973, to serve Inter-City trains. Four thousand passengers a week used the station, where nine London expresses call, while in addition the area's new light industry supplied 450 parcels weekly including whole car engines. Ten years later traffic was still steady. The Butterley branch is being revived as a working museum of the Midland Railway (see page 235).

THE CLAY CROSS AREA

The Erewash Valley line became a through route to the north when the extension line was opened for passengers on 1 May 1862 between Pye Bridge and the ex-NMR at Clay Cross. Goods traffic had been running for six months.

The Bill for this line envisaged mineral branches to Tibshelf and Blackwell. The Blackwell branch was ultimately built privately, opening about 1871, although the Midland bought it in 1876 and extended it two miles to Huthwaite, obscuring in the process remains of tramways which had once linked these pits to the canal at Pinxton. A new community grew up at Blackwell, where the population rose from 542 in 1871 to 2,195 in 1881, and increased by 1,000 in each of the next two decades. A station was opened in 1881 and a locomotive depot, Westhouses, soon after. Talk of extending this line to the Mansfield line at Sutton-in-Ashfield came to nothing.

The Tibshelf branch, extended to Teversall, was built by the Midland, opening on 1 May 1866. An extension to Pleasley was opened on 2 April 1877, and on to Mansfield Woodhouse on the Worksop line on 1 May 1886. This has remained an important colliery branch, although long cut east of Pleasley. Both the GNR and the MS & L were interested in the collieries along this line, the former opening its Teversall branch (no regular passenger service, only miners' trains) in 1897 and the Leen Valley Extension line to Pleasley in 1898. The MS & L concentrated on Tibshelf, where two branches were opened off its Annesley extension in 1892 and 1894. Passenger services over the Midland line were meagre, comprising four return trains between Mansfield and Pye Bridge, withdrawn from 28 July 1930.

The iron works and coal mines at Clay Cross again owe

their development to the railway, with George Stephenson as the driving force. When he was building the North Midland Railway, Stephenson decided to use Dronfield coke for the locomotives; it was used locally in the iron furnaces and was available at Clay Cross. He and others, including Hudson, sank pits at Clay Cross, and built coke ovens, but by 1847 the Midland Railway was obtaining better coke from Durham, and Clay Cross coal was not favoured on the East Midlands market. To save his enterprise, Stephenson erected iron furnaces to use the local coal, although initial difficulties were experienced in smelting the local iron ore. These supply problems were finally overcome when Northamptonshire ore was brought in during the next ten years.

The Clay Cross company was later responsible for building the Ashover Light Railway. This 2ft 0in gauge line was authorised in 1919, and formally opened on 6 April 1925, using rails and equipment reclaimed from wartime use in France, hence the six American Baldwin locomotives. The 7½ mile line from Clay Cross was built primarily to serve stone quarries between Stretton and Ashover, but as from Stretton the route passed up the scenic Amber Valley, it was popular with hikers, the new feature of the 1920s. Five thousand passengers were carried in the opening week, which was also Easter week, but the increase in cars brought regular passenger services to an end in 1930. A summer-only passenger service continued until 1936, with Stretton being the usual interchange station with the LMS, which the ALR followed to Clay Cross. By this time mineral traffic was far more important, having been stimulated by the railway. The line closed on 31 March 1950.

The small mining town of Clay Cross is actually on top of the 1 mile 26 yards long tunnel which the NMR had to drive under the watershed of the Amber and Rother rivers. The station was 1½ miles away, north of the junction. More collieries were served by the Wingfield–Pilsley loop which was opened in 1871, which area was also tapped by the MS & L in 1892.

CHESTERFIELD

Unlike most of the towns in the coalfield, Chesterfield has a long history, being until the nineteenth century the chief market for iron and lead, and the second largest town in

Derbyshire. Its canal was opened throughout in 1777. The town was fortunate in its geographical location in the Rother Valley, as when George Stephenson surveyed the route for the NMR, he was interested in finding the easiest route between Derby and Leeds, irrespective of what towns might lie roughly en route. To secure easy gradients he preferred to use the river valleys such as the Amber and Rother and for this reason ignored Sheffield, as in his opinion the ground between Sheffield and Chesterfield was unsuitable for railways. The Midland found this out when building the direct line from Chesterfield to Sheffield, opened 1 February 1870. This involved stiff gradients and the 1 mile 266 yard Bradway tunnel.

The opening of the NMR between Derby and Masborough on 11 May 1840 was without any ceremony, celebration being reserved for the full opening to Leeds on 30 June that year. As the NMR was an important link on both the north-south and north-east to south-west trunk routes, Chesterfield has always enjoyed a good main line train service. In 1973 one could travel through to Edinburgh and Plymouth, and even Penzance in summer, not to mention nineteen trains to London. In 1910 one could go no further west than Bristol without changing, but instead one could go through to Aberdeen, but with only five through trains to London. The original NMR station was rebuilt in 1870 and 1964–5.

Chesterfield was not as well served by the Manchester, Sheffield & Lincolnshire Railway. In 1884 the Staveley Iron Company suggested that the MS & L should build a branch from its main line to Chesterfield, partly over the Chesterfield Canal. The Bill for this was withdrawn when the Midland suggested negotiations for running agreements for iron ore trains from Frodingham to Staveley. However as these protracted negotiations finally produced only running powers for passenger trains, the MS & L decided on a new line from Beighton, where it joined the Midland near Sheffield, to Chesterfield, via Staveley. This Bill was thrown out by the House of Commons, but local support ensured the authorisation of a second Bill in 1889, which revealed the MS & L's intention of reaching Nottingham. Chesterfield was to be on a branch from this line linking Beighton with the GNR at Annesley. Between 1892 and 1894 seventeen colliery branches were opened between Beighton and Annesley.

MS & L trains first ran into Chesterfield on 4 June 1892, three days after public traffic had begun between Beighton and Staveley Town. The line down to Annesley was opened to goods traffic on 24 October 1892, while passenger trains began running from Staveley Town to Nottingham London Road (GNR) on 2 January 1893. Even before it was opened, proposals were in hand to make the Chesterfield branch into a loop, and the necessary connection to Heath was opened on 3 July 1893. However, apart from an evening Leicester–Cleethorpes express, Chesterfield in 1910 was served only by local trains, thirteen going north to various destinations on the GC, ten going south, mostly to Nottingham, but one to Loughborough. The main difference by 1955 was the drop in train services, with only seven each way, and none going north between 09.24 and 16.30. They ended on 4 March 1963.

At the same time that the MS & L was beginning to tap the coalfields around Chesterfield, another very ambitious company was formed with the same object, although on a grander scale. This was the Lancashire, Derbyshire & East Coast Railway, which although not reaching either end of its name, and with less than ten miles of route in Derbyshire, was nonetheless of considerable importance in opening up the Nottinghamshire coalfield. Whereas the GCR route through the coalfield has now been obliterated in many areas, the LD & ECR route east of Langwith is still important.

The driving force was William Arkwright, who wanted to develop the coal reserves on his estates east of Chesterfield. Other coalowners were enthusiastic and the Dukes of eastern Nottinghamshire lent their support. As various local schemes for opening-up the coalfield had come to nothing, and as east-west communications were poor, this line would allow coal to be shipped out either way; westwards to Warrington via the High Peak, Buxton and Macclesfield, or eastwards to new docks at Sutton-on-Sea via Lincoln. Branches would reach Sheffield and Manchester, to give a total route of 170 miles at a cost of £5 million. Watkin of the MS & L furiously described it as a mad scheme, but then Parliament in 1891 had just thrown out his Bill for the London Extension while authorising the LD & ECR.

As only £320,000 was actually subscribed—with three-quarters of that coming from the Great Eastern Railway, which was always anxious to tap a coalfield to increase its revenue—the middle section from Chesterfield to Lincoln, plus the Sheffield branch, was begun first, as here were the collieries. Engineering works were heavy as the line crossed the valleys, and included the 1 mile 864 yard Bolsover Tunnel, which was always troublesome and ultimately brought about the line's closure between Chesterfield and Langwith Junction on 3 December 1951. Earthworks would have been even heavier on the Peak District section, including a viaduct over Monsal Dale nearly 300ft high. The impecunious company regretfully abandoned this section in 1895. Nor did it build the Lincolnshire section, but it still kept the full title for reasons of prestige.

Full opening of the truncated main line was delayed until 8 March 1897 by Bolsover Tunnel. Colonel Yorke of the Board of Trade said that it was one of the best constructed lines he had ever inspected. As coal was the main traffic, passenger services were infrequent, with six trains out to Langwith Junction but only three thence to Lincoln. Chesterfield Market Place was the line's headquarters, and the General Manager lived nearby. He would discipline any driver he caught racing down the bank into the station. With four platforms, passenger facilities were more than generous. An impressive viaduct crossed both the Midland and GC lines together on the edge of the town.

When the GCR bought the LD & ECR in 1907, it put in connections to its own main line at Duckmanton (near Arkwright Town station) and goods traffic continued to use these to reach Market Place until 1957.

Chesterfield has taken full advantage of its rail facilities. The local Sheepbridge Coal & Iron Company was founded in 1863, with its large works beside the Sheffield line. Heavy engineering works have also been established. From 11,231 inhabitants in 1841, the population has grown steadily, trebling in fifty years, and now standing at 70,546. Stephenson, who had put the town on the railway map, sank several coalpits in the area and also leased nearby Tapton House, overlooking his railway. Here he spent his active retirement growing grapes, peaches, apricots and pineapples in vast hothouses. He carried on a friendly rivalry with Joseph Paxton at Chatsworth, who later conceived the idea of the Crystal Palace during a Midland Railway board meeting. Stephenson would send boxes of fruit down to his officials at Ambergate, always demanding that the boxes be returned. They were, in first class compartments. He died in 1848 and was buried in Holy Trinity Church, Chesterfield. All the shops were closed on the day of his funeral.

STAVELEY

Staveley, five miles from Chesterfield, is another town that benefitted greatly from the railway. The NMR came this way in 1840 when the town boasted over three thousand inhabitants. Iron production there had been carried on at least since the seventeenth century, and a furnace erected on the Chesterfield Canal in 1778 was sending pig iron into Staffordshire. Then in 1840 Richard Barrow bought the furnaces, enlarged them and connected them to the railway. The opening-up of the Northamptonshire iron ore fields by the Leicester–Hitchin line stimulated production, and Barrow benefitted further when his ore could come directly up the Erewash Valley extension. This caused Barrow to reorganise his works again, forming the Staveley Coal & Iron Company. During the 1870s the company began to work its own ore in Northamptonshire, while over half a million tons of ore left there for Derbyshire in 1871. The Staveley company was also mining 700,000 tons of coal a year from its five pits by 1863.

As a result of this industrial activity Staveley had grown steadily, reaching 10,000 inhabitants by 1891, and double that now. By then, as was described earlier, the MS & L was interested in the area, with the encouragement of the Staveley Company. The first goods trains, using contractors' locomotives, ran to Staveley works from Beighton on 1 December 1891; public traffic between Beighton and Staveley Town began on 1 June 1892. A large locomotive depot and ninety-nine staff cottages were built here, and five colliery branches opened.

Only the Midland struck eastwards from Staveley, by purchasing coal lines privately constructed and extending them towards Mansfield. One line opened in 1888 ran through Clowne to Elmton and Cresswell on the Worksop line, the other, completed finally in 1890 through Bolsover to Pleasley on the Westhouses line. Through passenger services between Chesterfield and Mansfield were begun on 1 September 1890, but only with three daily each way on each line. Those on the Bolsover line succumbed on 28 July 1930, those on the Clowne line, down to one return, on 5 July 1954, when services between Chestefield and Sheffield through Staveley were also withdrawn. Staveley lost its GC line services on 4 March 1963. Coal traffic continues on parts of all three lines.

RAILWAYS UP THE LEEN VALLEY

The waters of the River Leen once supported many bleaching factories, but more recently these have been overshadowed by the opposite commodity, coal. At its peak, the lines of three railway companies ran up this valley, to tap the lucrative coalfield.

The first was a coalowner's line from Awsworth to Cinderhill, whence coal was carried into Nottingham by cart. This was extended in 1844 to a wharf on the Nottingham Canal at Radford and was opened with due ceremony, as the *Nottingham Review*, in describing the special trains reported: '... the first, [of two carriages] tastefully decorated with flowers and evergreens, contained a lovely display of female beauty; the gentlemen occupied the second carriage.' Serving several local mines, the line was eventually connected to the Midland's Mansfield branch near Basford.

The Mansfield line was planned by the Midland in 1845 to tap local coal reserves and was authorised in 1846. The next year it purchased Jessop's Mansfield & Pinxton Railway, and it opened as far as Kirkby-in-Ashfield on 2 October 1848. As this coincided with Nottingham Goose Fair, the line did well that week, and the connecting two-compartment horse tram on the M & P was unable to cope with the flood of passengers; many walked. After that, patronage was slight, as at first the fares were uncompetitive.

From Kirkby the Mansfield line was to follow the course of the M & P, which was rebuilt with a few deviations to make it suitable for locomotive working. The M & P was authorised in 1817 as a feeder line to the Pinxton arm of the Cromford Canal, for it would have been too expensive to extend the canal to Mansfield. Mansfield was then as much noted for stone and lime, and these, as well as the coal, would be able to enjoy a wider market. The first load of coal was carried over the line and ceremonially burned in Mansfield on 13 April 1819. The day was treated as a public holiday, with several thousand people from neighbouring villages thronging the town, where the church bells rang continually.

The line used 3ft long fish-bellied edge rails and at first bullocks provided the motive power. Although coal provided the main traffic, amounting to some 50,000 tons in 1833, for many years the stone traffic from Mansfield was important. This was boosted after 1834 when Mansfield stone was used in the rebuilding of the Houses of Parliament. Many other commodities were carried, including 565 tons of manure in 1833 when the line paid a nine per cent dividend. Passenger traffic, on market days, began in 1832.

Although the Midland was authorised to buy the M & P, two London & York-backed railway companies actually did so, hoping to enable the latter company to enter the Erewash Valley. However they readily sold out to the Midland, and work on converting the whole line to locomotive traction, including some deviations of route was completed for opening throughout from Codnor Park, through Pinxton and Kirkby to Mansfield on 9 October 1849. Local enthusiasm was slight, as the *Nottingham Journal* commented:

> Our Mansfield friends have not shown great spirit in the preparations to commemorate the opening, there being not so much as a single banner of any description, and the only sign of approval or disapproval on the first train leaving the station was the braying of an ass.

But Mansfield had seen it all before. The arrival of the first steam engine on 24 August caused more excitement, when many spectators had taken a ride on the empty stock working.

Direct access from the M & P to Kirkby-in-Ashfield station only came in 1891 with a major deviation, while Sutton-in-Ashfield did not receive its station, on a short branch, until 1 May 1893, in response to competition from the proposed GNR Leen Valley extensions. Although this ¾ mile branch enjoyed twenty return trains in 1910, some running through to Mansfield, it lost them three times: from 1917 to 1923, for four months after the General Strike in 1926, and from 26 September 1949, although an unadvertised workmen's service only finally ceased running on 1 October 1951.

The Leen Valley coalfield is concealed beneath limestone and sandstone beds, requiring expensive deep shafts before it can be worked. For this reason the Erewash Valley area was tapped first, and it was not until rising demand and improving techniques were present in the 1870s that coal here was worth exploiting. Allport, the Midland's General Manager, admitted in 1873 that until very recently its Leen Valley line carried little traffic, but that he now hoped to send out one million tons of coal annually. This increased traffic inevitably stimulated the competitive instincts of the GNR, whose coal trains began running south from Bestwood Colliery in July 1881 and from Annesley Colliery that October on its own line. Passenger services began on 2 October 1882.

Ten years later, as has been noted above, the MS & L reached the GNR at Annesley from the north. The GNR was not happy with the MS & L's line seeing it as a future London extension. However, the GNR could not prevent its authorisation, especially when the MS & L gave an assurance that such an extension was not contemplated. The hollowness of this assurance was demonstrated when the MS & L deposited a Bill in 1890 for an extension from Annesley to Quainton Road. Although it took three years to have the Bill authorised, opposition from the GNR was discouraged by confirmation of an offer of long-coveted powers over MS & L metals to Sheffield. So the third line, a main line, was built down the Leen Valley, and its first coal trains ran on 26 July 1898.

At Annesley, the MS & L laid sorting sidings to accommodate 1,665 trucks, with extra land for extensions if necessary. A locomotive depot was also erected, but as Ahrons commented acidly:

> The gentleman who 'found' Annesley as a site for an engine shed, and who ought to be awarded an FRGS for his pains, omitted to 'find' a site on which to build houses.

As most of the railway workers lived in Basford and Bulwell, they were transported to work by the 'Annesley Dido', formed of ancient carriages usually hauled by obsolete locomotives. Similarly, local miners had their 'Paddy Mails', unadvertised trains of elderly stock with wooden seats.

In 1960, when Annesley yard comprised eighteen down and nineteen up sidings, traffic was heavy, both in local coal, and through bananas, fish, steel and iron ore. The south end saw forty-seven arrivals and fifty-eight departures; the north end eighty arrivals and sixty-four departures. Much of the traffic handled did not originate from the Annesley area, and therefore could be diverted on to other routes; local collieries could be connected to the Midland line. All through freight ended in June 1965, with complete closure in September 1966.

Three separate sets of passenger services were unnecessary up the Leen Valley. Those on the GN line were withdrawn on 14 September 1931, on the GC line on 4 March 1963, and on the Midland, on 12 October 1964. Incredibly slow, they lost out easily to road competition. Coal traffic ceased on the GNR in 1968, leaving the Midland alone once more, truncated at Annesley (to save maintenance on Robin Hood's Hills Tunnel) and serving seven collieries. These included

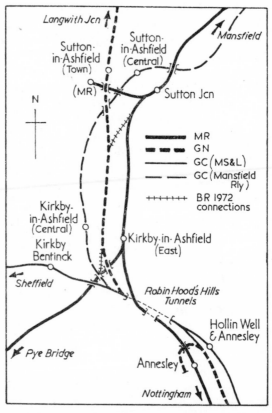

The twin Ashfield towns were served by competing railways as that part of the coalfield was opened up in the later nineteenth century; only the Pye Bridge–Mansfield line remains, for freight only

Calverton, connected by a BR branch opened in 1952, after the sinking of the colliery had been delayed by the war.

Of the twin Ashfield towns, Kirkby had lagged behind Sutton, yet as a junction of some complexity was better served by railways. Both towns grew with the opening of the coalfield, but only slowly until the 1890s, when the population of each rose by 5,000. Similarly both have stagnated with the decline of mining.

MANSFIELD

Mansfield, with its population of 58,949, is amongst the largest towns in the country without a railway station. Now the second town in Nottinghamshire, it had risen to fourth place, after Newark and Radford, after the arrival of the M & P. Radford was absorbed into Nottingham in 1877, while Newark, in spite of its position on two important lines only grew slowly as a market town. Mansfield stagnated after 1831 at about 10,000 inhabitants: being at the end of an indifferent branch it did not share in population movements to the bigger towns. Stone and hosiery remained more important than coal until the major opening up of the local coalfield after 1870. Then the town expanded, overtaking Newark by 1891, and virtually doubling in size between 1871 and 1901.

The first new railway out of Mansfield was to Southwell, primarily for goods traffic and to forestall any GNR ambitions. It opened on 3 April 1871 with a meagre two return passenger trains daily plus two others on market days. Although the timetable will not bear this out, by local repute farmers on Mansfield trains could alight at Rainworth station, walk a mile to the nearest public house and back to drink two pints of ale, and still catch the same train. Another oddity of the line soon after opening was a through train from Southwell to Buxton, then the farthest-flung town in the Southwell diocese. Unfortunately not enough of the faithful made the pilgrimage to their cathedral to make the service pay, and it was soon withdrawn. Normal passenger services to Southwell ended on 12 August 1929 although race and other excursions continued to the end. Coal traffic east of Rainworth had ended by 1965.

The Midland's next move was to end Mansfield's terminal status by extending the Leen Valley line on to Worksop, giving a northern outlet on to the MS & L for Mansfield coal, linking yet more collieries en route. This line opened on 1 June 1875 (goods three months later), and involved a third new station in Mansfield and a fifteen-span stone viaduct over the town. Mansfield Woodhouse Station was described as a 'pleasant contrast to the dreary and disheartening dens which used to be put up for the punishment of travellers in the early days of railway enterprise'. The line is still a major coal artery, although devoid of passenger services since 1964.

By 1890, when the Staveley line was open, Mansfield was a railway centre but under a not over-efficient Midland monopoly. Local interests wanted this broken, although neither the MS & L nor GNR was interested. The LD & ECR did propose a branch but was bought off by running powers over the Midland via Warsop curve (1899). Ultimately local enterprise built the Mansfield Railway, linking the GCR at Kirkby-in-Ashfield and the LD & ECR at Clipstone. Authorised in 1910, coal trains began running south from Mansfield Colliery in 1913, but full opening was delayed until 2 April 1917. Passenger services initially were three each way between Nottingham and Ollerton worked by the GCR, but by 1939 had increased to fourteen down and twelve up, with a through Leeds–Bournemouth express. These declined considerably after 1948 to eight down and seven up, including three on to Edwinstowe at the time of closure on 2 January 1956, although holiday excursion traffic continued.

As the railway gave connections to five major collieries, concentration sidings were laid north of Mansfield, which at their fullest extent could cope with 1,750 wagons daily. Traffic from Thoresby, Ollerton and Welbeck collieries was also handled there. The line has now been lifted south of Mansfield Colliery.

Mansfield belatedly benefitted from the railways which were intended to open up its adjacent coalfield. However, as it was not on a main passenger line, its train services were increasingly uncompetitive in the age of the bus and car, taking forty to fifty minutes for the sixteen to seventeen mile journey to Nottingham, although parcels traffic with the hosiery trade remained brisk. Passengers must travel eight miles to the reopened (1973) Alfreton & Mansfield Parkway station for Southbound expresses; since the 1950s they have tended to go to Chesterfield for the North.

LANGWITH JUNCTION AND THE DUKERIES

The first railway through the small Derbyshire town of Shirebrook—on its eastern side—was the Midland's Worksop branch in 1875; the station became known as Shirebrook (West) in 1951. The LD & ECR came next, on the northern side of the town. At Langwith Junction station—Shirebrook

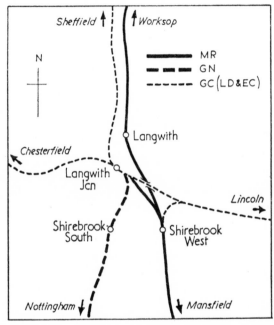

Langwith Junction. Competition for coal traffic brought three railway companies into this area. Unification under BR, and decline in coal consumption inevitably led to route rationalisation

(North) from 1924—the Sheffield branch left the main Chesterfield–Lincoln line. Station, main line, and branch as far as Clowne, were opened on 8 March 1897. The GNR Leen Valley Extension line arrived in 1901. Two important spurs were put in from the Midland to the LD & ECR: the south to east in 1899 and the south to west in 1904. Langwith Junction thus became an important junction, and remains so although in a truncated form and called Shirebrook.

The GNR's Leen Valley Extension was its reply to the

MS & L London Extension; when the latter's Bill failed in 1891 the GNR withdrew its Bill, only to re-enter it successfully in 1892 when the MS & L showed no sign of giving up. The Extension was opened in stages from the MS & L at Kirkby South Junction, having used the latter's Robin Hood's Hills Tunnel to save boring a third. On 9 February 1897 coal traffic began from Silverhill Colliery, Teversall, while 1898 saw coal traffic begin from Pleasley Colliery in March, and passenger traffic to Skegby on 4 April. Shirebrook Colliery was reached on 26 November 1900, and the LD & EC for freight on 29 May 1901. Passenger services ran to the GNR station at Shirebrook (South) from 1 November 1901, but not through to Shirebrook North until 1925. They were withdrawn on 14 September 1931, although reinstated 20 February to 17 September 1956 to serve Sutton-in-Ashfield as compensation for the withdrawal of the Mansfield Railway trains. Football excursions to Nottingham and Sheffield were run weekly. Goods traffic ended in 1968, although a short stretch at Kirkby was reinstated in 1972, with new connections at either end to the Midland's Pye Bridge–Mansfield line, to allow coal traffic to avoid the level crossings on the latter's route.

Although the south-to-east spur only carried passenger traffic to Edwinstowe from 1899 to 1912, it has remained in use for coal. The south-to-west spur was used by Mansfield–Sheffield (Midland) passenger trains until the service was withdrawn on 10 September 1939. These consisted of GCR (LNER) stock hauled by Midland (LMS) locomotives. Before World War I a Saturdays-only St Pancras–Heysham–Isle of Man Boat Express ran this way.

The LD & ECR was primarily a coal line. At Langwith Junction traffic was collected from the two branches before moving eastwards to Immingham, through the old Dukeries towns of Edwinstowe and Ollerton. These two became mining centres, but having one large mine rather than several smaller pits as in the old coalfield. Ollerton became the junction for the Mid-Notts Joint Railway, a joint LMS–LNER line authorised in 1926 from Hucknall to Checker House on the GCR Worksop line. Building began in 1929 on the central section from Farnsfield to Ollerton, which opened in 1930, but depression and war curbed further development of the coalfield here and Bevercoates colliery was not opened until

1965. In LD & ECR days coal trains were worked through to Immingham by its own tank engines, necessitating water stops at Pyewipe Junction and Market Rasen. During operations at the former the locomotive crew would make smartly for the inn for refreshment, while at Market Rasen the fireman fetched fish and chips, always going to the head of the queue.

Running through Sherwood Forest, the LD & ECR tried to exploit the tourist potential by advertising itself as 'The Dukeries Route'. This name was carried everywhere, even on dog tickets. Edwinstowe station was correspondingly spacious to accommodate the traffic, and Dukeries Junction station was built as an interchange where the LD & ECR crossed the GNR. Although initially popular, traffic never really developed.

BEIGHTON AND KILLAMARSH TO RETFORD

The earliest railways here linked local coal pits with the Chesterfield Canal at Eckington, and ironstone and coal mines with Renishaw ironworks. The main railways were the NMR opened in 1840, and the Sheffield & Lincolnshire Junction Railway to Worksop, Retford and Gainsborough, which crossed the NMR at Beighton, where a connection was made. Opposition from the Chesterfield Canal was overcome and the S & LJR was authorised in 1846, immediately becoming part of the MS & L. The Sheffield to Beighton line was opened on 12 February 1849, when MS & L trains ran through to Eckington. (These were withdrawn on the opening of the MS & L Beighton–Staveley line in 1892.) To complete the picture at Beighton, the Waleswood curve was opened between the two MS & L lines in 1893, and the LD & EC junction with the Midland on 21 May 1900. (The Clowne–Killamarsh section opened on 1 October 1898.) The LD & ECR was joined to the GCR at Killamarsh when that company took it over in 1907, thereby allowing through traffic to Sheffield Victoria, although the local passenger trains still ran to Midland.

The line from Woodhouse Junction to Worksop, Retford and Gainsborough was opened quietly on 16 July 1849, becoming the main line of the MS & L. Worksop did well out of the line, taking over from Retford as an important malting centre. Retford, notorious as a parliamentary pocket borough until 1867, stagnated throughout the nineteenth

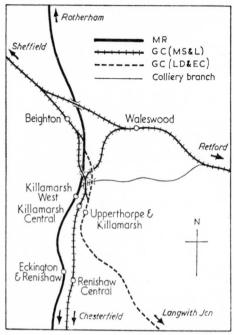

Beighton and Killamarsh. Railway competition, chiefly for coal traffic, made this a complex junction in the 1890s, with the southward expansion of the MS & L and the arrival of the LD & ECR.

century and did not develop as an industrial centre until the twentieth, despite its favourable site on two main lines.

Retford was also notorious for its level crossing dating from 1852 when the Towns Route was opened, which hindered both fast East Coast expresses and vital west–east coal traffic. In the early 1960s the CEGB began a programme of building coal-fired power stations along the Trent. Those at West Burton and Cottam, east of Retford, would require about ten million tons of coal annually from Nottinghamshire pits, coming via the MS & L line. To prevent intolerable delays at Retford to all traffic, a new flyunder was built costing over £1 million, and opened in 1965. Associated works included a 2½ mile diversion of the MS & L, and a new low-level station, so that MS & L trains no longer use the GNR station via the Whisker Hill curve, opened in 1859. And unlike the other lines in this chapter, most of the original stations on this GCR line are still open.

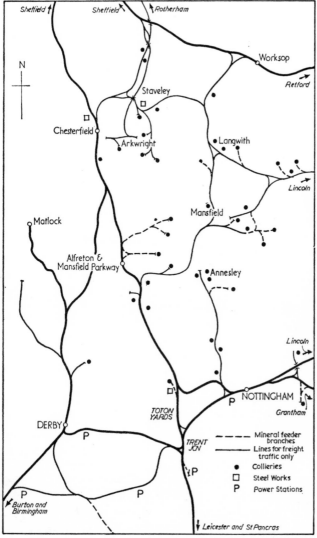

The Coalfield's railways in 1974. It is mainly ex-Midland lines that still serve this productive coalfield, the main exceptions being the LD & ECR east of Langwith Junction and GCR to Arkwright and through Worksop. The results of excessive Victorian competition became a liability to a British economy weakened by two world wars and recurring trade recessions

CHAPTER IX

Derbyshire

DERBY

Derby is well-known for its fine porcelain, football club, Rolls-Royce and railway engines. It was the centre of the Midland Railway, but unlike Crewe, Derby was not originally a railway town. During its long history, it was the chief market for locally-produced lead and iron, and during the eighteenth century it was an important and progressive hosiery town, rivalling Manchester in cottons until canal building benefitted Manchester twenty years before Derby. It also had the advantage of being the crossroads on the Manchester—London and Leeds–Birmingham roads. Although its trade was temporarily slack, Derby was a flourishing town of over 30,000 people, a natural target for railways.

The railways promptly revived trade in Derby, and encouraged the establishment of fishmongers, for they would only open shops when fresh sea fish was available daily. Local industry found new stimulus, in addition to the establishment of the railway works, which was of great importance. William Bemrose, a local stationer, won a contract to supply the Midland Railway with its stationery and to print its time-tables, thus enabling him to build up a business which still supplies British Rail. Similarly, Andrew Handyside, who had established his Britannia Iron Works in Derby in 1818 to turn out high-grade castings, was soon supplying Derby Works, ultimately providing ironwork for stations and bridges throughout the world.

New industries were also attracted, with many factories being alongside the railway, although for the firms which moved in from other towns, like Rolls-Royce in 1906, railway communications were only one influencing factor. So although the railways have always been a major employer in Derby, with a labour force of over 12,000 by 1900, they have not monopolised labour. Indeed, by 1972 Rolls-Royce employed nearly three times as many people as British Rail.

Derby did not escape the trade depression of the mid-1840s, when Chartism made a powerful appeal to the town's working classes. To counter this influence, the Midland Railway put its weight behind the Conservative candidates in the 1848 election, although unsuccessfully. Radical candidates denounced this 'railway influence' in elections, which persisted until further parliamentary reform rendered it impossible. However the Midland Railway led the way in Derby in providing amenities for its employees, such as the orphanage (1887), sports clubs, leisure societies and the Institute where there were reading, club and lecture rooms, and a library.

Not everyone welcomed the new freedom to travel. A local clergyman, a prolific pamphleteer, vigorously attacked children's excursions to manufacturing towns, where 'far from the eye of their parents, they may acquire a taste for the vices of the town'. He saw such an excursion reach Derby in 1844 and was shocked to see its youthful patrons, of both sexes, thronging the public houses and spirit shops; many were drunk.

It is evident then that the various railways serving Derby played a major part in developing the prosperity of the town. Its population had doubled by the 1870s and trebled by the 1890s. It has nearly doubled again in the present century, to level off at 215,000 today. Although most people live and work in Derby, an increasing number commute from the northern villages. As the main centres of industry are south of the town, road congestion is increasing so that the local Junior Chamber of Commerce is hoping to see better bus services between Midland Station and industrial estates enabling commuter traffic to be more effectively developed on the Matlock line (see page 247).

DERBY STATION

Within seven weeks in the summer of 1836, three major railways were authorised to serve Derby. From the south came the Birmingham & Derby Junction Railway (19 May); from the east the Midland Counties Railway (21 June) and from the north the North Midland Railway (4 July). Various plans had been maturing since 1832, and when the B & DJR was announced in October 1835 to link the London & Birmingham Railway with the NMR, the *Derby Mercury* commented that it would 'make Derby a centre of communication, and must, we imagine, increase the trade and importance of the town.'

Initially the MCR planned a station in Derwent Street and the NMR one near Nottingham Road. The B & DJR decided to bridge the River Derwent to use the NMR station, a plan endorsed by a public meeting in the Town Hall in December 1835. Two months later the council suggested that a joint station for all three railways would be preferable. After protracted haggling over the proposed site on the Holmes, as it was prone to flooding, and on the adjacent Castle Fields, plans were available by March 1839 for a large joint station, together with separate locomotive workshops and sheds. Wishaw described the new station as 'a building of good proportions but not so pleasing to the eye as the buildings of the intermediate stations.' He was enthusiastic over the impressive trainshed behind with:

> . . . admirably contrived and elegant roofs; the spacious platforms;
> . . . all unite in rendering it the most complete structure of the kind in the United Kingdom, or, perhaps, in the world.

Behind the 1,050ft façade was a single long platform, with a short bay at either end to accommodate MCR and B & DJR trains.

Additions over the next forty years included a shareholders' meeting room (1856), boardroom, covered porch and booking hall (1872) and additional platforms, footbridge and waiting rooms (1881) to cater for the extra traffic generated by the holding of the Royal Agricultural Show that year in Derby. In the 1850s experiments in the use of steel rails took place at the north end of Derby station, where certain iron rails needed replacing every six months. A replacement steel casting lasted sixteen years.

On 15 January 1941 the station was bombed, when 100 yards of the trainshed roof was demolished and six people were killed. As a result a £200,000 modernisation plan was instituted (1952–4) involving the complete replacement of the iron trainshed with individual reinforced concrete roofs over each platform. The station is now light and clean, although rather bleak in appearance. However the façade was kept and is well-maintained, with the Midland's wyvern insignia proudly rivalling BR's double-arrow motif above the porch.

THE LOCOMOTIVE SHEDS AND RAILWAY WORKS

All three companies built locomotive sheds and workshops near the station. The B & DJR's small establishment only lasted for thirty years, but the MCR's engine shed still stands near the north end of Derby station. It was used for several years for shareholders' meetings until someone was killed by a train while crossing the lines to a meeting.

The NMR's shed and workshops became the real nucleus of Derby Works. The No 1 roundhouse is still standing, although long since incorporated into the works. Number 2 roundhouse was added in 1847 but ultimately it too was taken over by the works. Number 3 roundhouse came in 1852 and was badly damaged in a Zeppelin raid in 1916. Johnson built No 4 shed in 1890 as the need for covered locomotive accommodation was serious. Two turntables each served twenty-two roads, while a third, opened in 1900, served another sixteen roads. This shed was demolished in 1969, replaced by the new Etches Park diesel depot.

At first, major repairs to locomotives and rolling stock were done by the original outside builders. As this caused unnecessary delays and expense, Matthew Kirtley, the Superintendent of the Locomotive and Carriage Departments of the newly-formed Midland Railway at the handsome annual salary of £250, embarked on a five-year plan of expansion. By 1851 Kirtley was ready to build locomotives. Expansion continued over the next fifteen years so that the works area quadrupled. The final expansion of the works came between 1872 and 1876 when Kirtley put the Carriage & Wagon Works on a new site at Etches Park, with Thomas Clayton in charge. This released vital space for the increased locomotive work. By 1891 the average annual turnover of locomotives was twenty to thirty built, 120 rebuilt with new boilers, and 750–800 undergoing heavy repairs.

In LMS days, Derby remained important while Sir Henry Fowler was Chief Mechanical Engineer, as he had occupied the same post on the Midland prior to grouping. However, when Sir William Stanier took over that post in 1932, Crewe

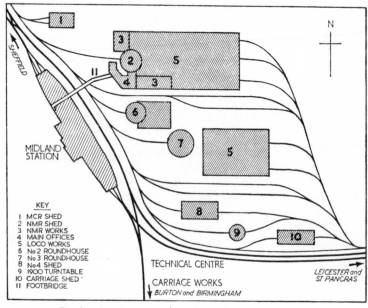

Derby Station, Locomotive Works and Sheds

emerged as the major locomotive works of the LMS and Derby built few of the express locomotives. Nevertheless Derby did make a major contribution to the LMS and BR locomotive stock with large numbers of 2-6-4 tank engines which were built between 1927 and 1955. Another major contribution was in the field of diesel traction. The first experimental diesel shunter was built in 1932, with regular production beginning in 1939. Main line diesel locomotive building began with the pioneer LMS No 10000 in 1947, continuing after 1958 with large numbers of 'Peaks' (classes 44, 45, 46) and Type 2s (classes 24 and 25). Altogether 2,941 steam locomotives, 1,010 diesels and one battery-electric locomotive have been built at Derby.

Both World Wars saw the Works engaged on munitions production, and employing women. During World War II the carriage works specialised in aeroplane wings and fuselages, while gun parts, bailey bridges, and shell cases were made in the locomotive works.

Under BR, Derby has been an important design centre, even when most of the locomotive building was done elsewhere. This had been reinforced by the establishment of the Technical Centre in 1964 where, amongst other tasks, considerable research has been done on the High Speed Train and Advanced Passenger Train.

The Works has always been a major employer. By 1862, over two thousand men were employed, rising to nearly four thousand by 1891. All Derby knew when work began and ended each day, and when the meal breaks were, for 'Loco Bull', a stentorian steam whistle, echoed over the town. It was always accurate, except once in 1881 when its elderly operator opened it at noon instead of one o'clock. Great was the consternation in the Works and neighbourhood as cooks and housewives surveyed half-cooked lunches and hungry men! The operator was pensioned-off, and he soon died of a broken heart.

There were three large messrooms, for the men who were unable to return home for meals. Here cooks prepared the men's own food to their own liking, and rarely made a mistake. The smoking room held 700, the non-smoking one 500, and the third 300. Here services were held during meals, and places were at a premium, being treated like a family pew in church or chapel. Many preachers, including bishops, who visited Derby on Sunday were constrained to address the railway engineers on Monday, speaking above the clatter of cutlery and dishes. While many mastered this, others faltered in this unaccustomed atmosphere and were lost as the clatter increased.

Most of the railway workers lived in Litchurch, which in 1801 was a hamlet of thirty-five inhabitants. Expansion of the silk and lace industries increased its population over fifty years to 1,720 but the next decade saw it rise to 6,560 as the Works enlarged. There was no school, and only one pew available in the town church. However the local vicar held popular services for the railway families and determined to provide Litchurch with its own church and Sunday schools. The Midland gave financial help, and St Andrew's Church was consecrated in 1866. The Sunday schools opened in 1863, with the buildings used as day schools from 1864. Adult education followed, and the vicar opened clubs to rival the local public houses. He even began a nursery for the children of working mothers (1858). St Andrew's was a railway church, and it was a Works' privilege to join its bellringers, long headed by Sir Henry Fowler.

The decline in the building of locomotives, the greater availability of diesels, and the reduction in rolling stock on BR has led to a drop in the Works' labour force in recent years. From 20,000 in 1920, it now numbers about 7,000. This includes the Carriage & Wagon Works, which in 1956 was still providing an average of 300 coaches and 5,000 wagons annually, while repairing a further 3,500 coaches and 10,000 wagons. At its peak between the wars, reorganisation in the saw mills enabled 200 standard 12 ton wooden-frame goods wagons to be produced weekly.

THE MIDLAND COUNTIES RAILWAY

Of the three initial railways at Derby, the first to be opened was the MCR to Nottingham on 4 June 1839. Immediately revenue was good, with an average of 590 passengers, mostly second class, being carried daily. Receipts up to the end of 1839 were £8,569 13s 8d (£8,569·68) from passengers and a mere £707 4s 11½d (£707·25) from goods.

The line left Derby to the north before curving south-east past Chaddesden to Spondon. While the Midland remained a provincial railway this route did not matter, but with the London Extension (opened 1868) and the completion of the Peak Forest line (1867) came the prospect of through Midland trains from London to Manchester. Reversal at Derby would be inconvenient so a connecting line was opened from Spondon to the B & DJR at the south end of Derby station on 27 June 1867.

Afterwards only a few regular passenger services used the Chaddesden line, the main ones being fast Manchester expresses including the diesel-electric 'Midland Pullman' between 1960 and 1966 and the Tamworth–Lincoln night mail. Lincoln–Derby trains also ran that way until dieselised, to avoid reversal in Derby station. Otherwise it became a goods line, with an important general freight marshalling yard developing at Chaddesden. By the 1890s it was handling a train on average every seven minutes throughout the twenty-four hours, with six shunting engines and between fifty and a hundred horses available. Its eight reception roads, seven departure and thirty-one sidings handled up to 2,500 wagons daily in 1960.

Plate 25 A handsome GCR locomotive heads a rake of less distinguished coaches on a Grimsby train amid the baronial splendour of Lincoln (Central) Station in August 1899. [LCGB, Ken Nunn collection.]

Plates 26 and 27 At the seaside:
The GNR gave 'The Jolly
Fisherman' *(left)* to Skegness,
where it built *(below)* a
substantial station for dealing
with the holiday crowds.
[Skegness District Council;
S. W. A. Newton collection,
Leicester Museum.]

THE BIRMINGHAM & DERBY JUNCTION RAILWAY

This major trunk line was authorised unopposed in 1836, and with no difficulties in construction, the easily-graded line was opened on 12 August 1839 between Derby and Hampton-in-Arden, on the L & BR. This company took B & DJR trains on to Birmingham until the latter's direct line from Whitacre was opened in 1842.

The B & DJR's promoters knew that there was little local population to be served en route with Burton-on-Trent (7,000 inhabitants) as the only important town. However they saw the line's potential as part of a NE–SW route which by 1842 was complete between York and Gloucester. It also offered an alternative route between Derby and London to that of the MCR, being only nine miles and fifteen minutes longer. Moreover, it could supply Birmingham's smithies with the Derbyshire coal which they liked.

Burton was the principal intermediate station, and in 1955 enjoyed a total of sixty-five weekday departures on the B & DJR, North Staffordshire, and Midland (Coalville) lines. By 1973 these had fallen to twenty-six, and only along the B & DJR, for the NSR shuttle service to Tutbury was withdrawn on 13 June 1960, the Coalville line trains on 7 September 1964, and the remaining main line local services on 4 March 1968.

Until the widespread use of long-distance road haulage in the 1960s, Burton's most important rail traffic was its beer. Brewing began in local monasteries, and by the seventeenth century Burton beer was being drunk in London. Its beer became internationally famous in the next century, being drunk as far afield as Russia. William Bass opened his brewery in Burton in 1777, producing 2,000 barrels annually. Good inland transport was as vital for the Burton brewers in their exploitation of wider markets as it was for the Eastwood coal-owners. They therefore took full advantage of the railway system, and most of the twenty breweries and malthouses were linked to the main line by a complex system of branches, spurs and sidings, developed after 1859, and worked by distinctive saddle tanks with combined brass domes and safety-valves. These lines brought congestion to road traffic, because of the many level-crossings, which handled over a thousand wagons daily. Now most of the system has gone, as only six breweries remain through amalgamations and increased production methods. Although beer production has reached three million barrels annually, and many hundred firms exist supplying malt, yeast, machinery and kegs, the industry's reliance on the railway has decreased, and the fast beer trains reaching in all directions from Burton have disappeared. In 1900 there were three daily trains to London alone, with more during the October brewings; the casks were stored in the purpose-built vaults under St Pancras station.

From an early date Burton was attractive to other railway schemes, and in 1846 the NSR line from Stoke to Burton was authorised, with an important spur from Marston Junction to Willington Junction to allow through running to Derby. Opening into Burton (from the NSR's temporary terminus at Uttoxeter) came on 11 September 1848, with the Willington spur following on 13 July 1849. The NSR used the Midland's stations in Derby and Burton. From 1868 it entered the LNWR Horninglow Street goods depot, via a new line from Stretton Junction.

The arrival in 1890 of LNWR trains in Burton over the LNWR–Midland Joint line from Nuneaton opened-up the prospect of long through workings on to the NSR. Beginning with a Nuneaton–Ashbourne service, a through Rugby–Macclesfield train was soon provided via Burton and Uttoxeter, and in 1899 a through coach was provided between Euston and Buxton, being slipped at Nuneaton and working via Burton and Ashbourne.

The NSR regarded its main line as running to Derby, with the five trains each way in 1896 connecting at Tutbury into the Burton shuttle service. The opening of the GNR to Egginton Junction from Nottinghamshire in 1878 increased the potential of the NSR route, and the latter was quick to gain running powers over the GNR, although it only used them for excursion trains to Nottingham and goods traffic to Colwick. The NSR's excursion traffic, especially to Llandudno, emanated from both the Midland and GNR lines at Derby and Nottingham. Both the latter companies had running powers to Stoke, but only the GNR exercised them.

Burton generated sufficient freight traffic to warrant the NSR having three goods agents there, more than at any other NSR town. As well as beer, traffic consisted of timber plaster slabs, engineering and chemical products. A brisk traffic left Derby, Burton or the GNR for Liverpool and Manchester via the NSR. Similarly, LNWR goods from Liverpool to Nottingham ran via Egginton Junction. Also there was a regular NSR mineral service from Alsager to Wellingborough via Burton, Swadlincote and Coalville.

It was hoped that the dieselising of the NSR main line in 1957 would have generated more traffic over the Burton branch, but this was not to be and passenger trains ceased running in 1960. Goods traffic between Burton and Marston Junction was cut back in stages between 1966 and 1968. This included the GNR curve to Egginton Junction which had lost its passenger trains to Derby in 1939. The NSR locomotive shed at Burton was badly bombed in 1916. The main line, however, is still an important link between the East Midlands and the Potteries and North West. In 1973 it carried an hourly service between Derby and Crewe.

THE SOUTH DERBYSHIRE BRANCHES

West of Trent the country is better suited for dairy farming than industry, so railway construction was limited but important in stimulating milk production for the London market. The branch from Trent to Weston-on-Trent was authorised in 1865, but even as this was being built, an extension was authorised to Stenson Junction on the B & DJR, thus making a useful Derby avoiding line. The Weston branch opened on 6 December 1869, and the extension on 3 November 1873. Almost immediately the NSR ran a through Liverpool–Nottingham coach over the line, and although it could not maintain a local passenger service beyond 22 September 1930, it remained useful for excursion traffic, while many Manchester–Stoke–London expresses were diverted this way during the electrification of the West Coast line after 1959. It is also an important freight route, especially in Erewash Valley coal to Castle Donnington and Willington power stations, and to Birmingham.

Another branch was authorised in 1864–5 to link Derby with Ashby-de-la-Zouch. The first section, from Pear Tree (on the outskirts of Derby) to Melbourne was opened on 1 September 1868, and on to Worthington on 10 October 1869. The section thence to Ashby, which involved rebuilding part of the Ticknall Tramway, was not opened until 1 January 1874.

Passenger traffic through Melbourne was as sparse as on the Weston line, and services on both ended on the same day. During World War II, the southern part of the line was taken over by the army as the Melbourne Military Railway, as an alternative to the Longmoor Military Railway in Hampshire, and the army maintained the small local goods traffic. The LMS regained possession in 1945, but cut back services, a process completed by BR in 1980 (page 247).

The meadows of the Trent and Derwent valleys produced good milk, which was popular in London because of its keeping properties—an important consideration in the days before household refrigeration. In the 1880s London consumed some 15,000 gallons of Derbyshire milk daily, while more went to Nottingham. Early morning and afternoon local trains brought milk churns to Derby for forwarding to London by the next express.

THE NORTH MIDLAND RAILWAY

The NMR was both the last of Derby's three original lines to be authorised in 1836, and the last to be opened, without ceremony, on 11 May 1840, though from Derby to Masborough only; full opening came to Leeds seven weeks later. As George Stephenson was its surveyor, gradients were kept below 1 in 330 (except around Leeds) and earthworks were correspondingly heavy, including the crossing of the watershed between Ambergate and Clay Cross. Although opposition from landed interests needed buying off, the line was seen as having many advantages. Both coal and limestone areas would be opened-up and good north-south access would at last be provided, for there was no competing canal, and the Derby–Leeds coach road had a reputation among drivers for being one of the worst in England. The potential of the line as a trunk route was the same as the B & DJR's.

The NMR came in for some mixed comments from Wishaw in 1842, when he wrote that the stations gave the architect ample scope to demonstrate his talents, but:

. . . we cannot but deplore the growing evil of expending large sums of money on railway appendages. Instead of cottage buildings, which, for the traffic of most of the intermediate stopping places on this line, would have been amply sufficient, we find the railway literally ornamented with so many beautiful villas.

This perhaps is an unfair denigration of such architectural gems as Francis Thompson's Wingfield station. Perhaps a more immediate defect of these establishments concerned the doorways into the 'gents', which were:

> so exposed...as naturally to shock the female portion of travellers, who, while the trains are stopping, cannot fail to observe the constant bustle about these buildings, and more especially when the bell rings for the departure of the train.

He recommended an entrance lobby.

At Ambergate George Stephenson and his business partners built a limeworks of twenty kilns, whose annual output soon rose to 25,000 tons. The stone came from his quarries at Crich, two miles away, and already in use for a century. Originally the lime had been burned there before being taken by packhorses, each carrying two hundredweight, to the Cromford Canal. In 1837 Stephenson replaced the packhorses with a 3ft 3in gauge tramway, which considerably increased output, although steam locomotives were not used until 1897.

As Stephenson lived by the NMR outside Chesterfield, he was a frequent traveller over the line, and the NMR gave him a free first class pass, although he would just as readily take a makeshift seat in an empty coal truck if no passenger train were due. Once at Derby he was waiting for a train when a locomotive stopped opposite him, at dead centre. The driver was unable to move it, so Stephenson immediately hopped on to the footplate to sort it out, beaming with pleasure.

THE GNR IN DERBYSHIRE

The Midland Railway thought it had given much to Derby. It therefore felt very aggrieved when municipal magnates supported the *entrée* of the GNR. As discussed in Chapter VIII, the GNR planned its 'Derbyshire lines' in 1872 in order to tap the coalfields with outlets to both east and west. Eastwards the lines would link up with the main GNR system. The western outlets would be at Stafford and Burton-on-Trent. Here the GNR would meet both the North Staffordshire Railway and the LNWR, as well as the Midland. A double junction with the NSR was necessary at Egginton to cross the main Stoke–Derby line, before the GNR joined the Stoke–Burton line at Dove Junction. Opening came in 1878, to goods in January, and to passengers on 1 April.

Through running to Stafford was also possible from that date, as from its opening on 23 December 1867 the GNR had worked the impecunious Stafford & Uttoxeter Railway, although through passenger workings did not begin until the GNR bought the line in 1881. The NSR gave running powers to the GNR between Egginton and Bromshall Junctions, and also on to Stoke for goods traffic, for the GNR hoped to sell Derbyshire coal in the Potteries.

GNR westbound trains ran in to Derby Friargate station over a locally-made ornate cast-iron bridge, now subject to a preservation order. The station boasted four platforms but only a small wooden office block. It was nearer to the town centre than the Midland station, and still offered a competitive service of twelve trains to Nottingham in 1955. Services in 1910 were more lavish, comprising eighteen to Nottingham, nine to Burton and six to Stafford (including one from Boston), with four more terminating at Uttoxeter, and one at Stoke. The NSR only provided seven trains from Derby to Uttoxeter and beyond, using the Midland line.

The Burton and Stafford services ended on 4 December 1939, but holiday trains and excursions ran west of Derby until 1964. East of Derby passenger trains continued to run until 7 September 1964, although Breadsall station, unusual in having a lady stationmaster, closed in 1953. The section between Egginton and Mickleover is used by BR for research connected with the Advanced Passenger Train.

RAILS THROUGH THE PEAK: (1) FROM AMBERGATE

As the 'capital' of the thriving Lancashire cotton industry, Manchester attracted many railway schemes from more distant parts of England, including the East Midlands and Sheffield. The latter, as they affected Derbyshire, are dealt with in the next section; here the connection from the East Midlands is discussed.

In the plethora of railways produced by the Mania which would allow communications, albeit indirect, between the

East Midlands and Lancashire, one stands out as having considerable potential. This was the Manchester, Buxton, Matlock & Midlands Junction Railway (1845) which would join the NMR at Ambergate. It offered a direct route between these two regions by boldly proposing to cross the Peak District, whose wild moors and hills, cut by steep-sided meandering dales, had long hindered communications. The route, surveyed by George Stephenson, would pass up the Derwent Valley to Rowsley, then up the Wye Valley to Miller's Dale and Buxton. Here it would pass under Combs Edge in a $2\frac{1}{4}$ mile tunnel to Whaley Bridge and Stockport. From Ambergate, an associated trunk line, the Ambergate, Nottingham & Boston & Eastern Junction Railway, would complete the link into the heart of the East Midlands.

However, the very boldness of the MBM & MJR was its temporary undoing, for although authorised in 1846, its necessarily heavy earthworks would be expensive, and after the Mania, money for such schemes was not forthcoming. Deviations were authorised in 1847; one avoided Combs Edge Tunnel by using a route similar to the Cromford & High Peak Railway from Whaley Bridge, while another continued the railway up the Derwent Valley from Rowsley towards Chatsworth before cutting into the Wye Valley at Hassop. But in spite of these, the only portion of the MBM & MJR to be built was from Ambergate to Rowsley, opened on 4 June 1849. Similarly, the AN & B & EJR only appeared as a branch line from Grantham towards Nottingham.

From 1852 the MBM & MJR was leased by the LNWR and Midland. By then the Midland was stronger financially after Hudson's crash in 1849 and consequently able to revive the MBM & MJR's Manchester dreams. This was bound to upset the LNWR which considered the southern access to Manchester as its preserve. It promptly heavily backed a local project, the Stockport, Disley & Whaley Bridge Railway (authorised in 1854) to block Midland access to Manchester, and as the Midland had no lines there, it was unable to object.

The LNWR overreached itself with an SD & WB extension to Buxton, authorised in 1856, for this upset the Manchester, Sheffield & Lincolnshire Railway which, as owners of the Peak Forest Tramway, considered the Buxton area as its territory. The Midland proposed to the LNWR that the

MBM & MJR be revived from Rowsley to Buxton to join the SD & WB extension, with Midland running powers thence in to Manchester. As the LNWR opposed this, the Midland looked to the MS & L for support. In 1860 the Midland was authorised to build the Rowsley–Buxton line, and in 1862 an extension from Miller's Dale, over Peak Forest, to New Mills, where it would join an MS & L-backed line into Manchester, with full running powers.

Saturday, 30 May 1863 was an important day for Buxton, for both the Midland and the SD & WB staged their opening ceremonies, although the latter's line was not quite ready. The Duke of Devonshire, whose family had long helped to develop Buxton as a spa, had supported both lines, despite the threat to his turnpike road to the south. He attended only the Midland's dinner at 2.00pm; Sir Joseph Paxton however, who also had interests in both lines did well for himself by attending both the Midland's dinner and the SD & WB's dinner an hour later. Once the celebrations were over, the Midland began running passenger trains on 1 June, but the LNWR not until 15 June. (The SD & WB had begun public traffic to Whaley Bridge on 9 June 1857. The LNWR absorbed it in 1866.)

Work on the Midland's Peak Forest line proceeded well until a disastrous landslip occurred at Bugsworth in the wet autumn of 1866, its impact effectively straightening a curved masonry viaduct! Goods traffic had already been operating for a month, but had to be suspended until a deviation and new timber viaduct were hastily constructed. Midland passenger services to Manchester began on 1 February 1867.

In 1871 the lease of the MBM & MJR expired. To counter any possible LNWR obstruction, the Midland had opened the Wirksworth branch up the parallel Ecclesbourne Valley on 1 October 1867. It would have been expensive, but not impossible, to have built an independent line through the hills into the Derwent Valley and up the opposite bank to Rowsley. However the LNWR gave in to this Midland threat, which would have left it with a useless branch, and concentrated on developing the C & HPR, leaving the Midland to take over the MBM & MJR.

The opening of the Buxton line involved new stations at Ambergate and Rowsley. The imposing edifice at Ambergate remained in use as offices until the early 1970s when it was

finally demolished, nearly a century after it had been super-
seded by the famous triangular station of 1876. Although
all the inner platform faces were joined, services on the
north side, on the curve opened in 1863 to allow through
Sheffield–Buxton trains, declined after the opening of the
Hope Valley line in 1894. NMR line locals used a new spur
serving the station, while expresses used the original line. At
Rowsley, the Buxton line diverged short of the terminus,
which became a goods depot. The new station was suitably
appointed to serve the Duke of Devonshire's Chatsworth
House, facilities including a 'Gentlemen's Room First Class.'
His fellow peer, the Duke of Rutland, of Haddon Hall, where
at his insistence the railway was covered in for 1,058yd, used
Bakewell station.

The gradients were heavy, being 1 in 100 from Rowsley
and 1 in 90 for the final stretch from Miller's Dale up to
Peak Forest. This meant that heavy goods trains needed
banking from the yards at Rowsley where Lancashire traffic
was collected.

The scenery however was magnificent, invoking the nick-
name 'Little Switzerland' which was used in advertising from
an early date. To some people though the line was an assault
on this lonely beauty. Inevitably the attack was led by John
Ruskin, who had long denounced the commercialisation of
the Industrial Revolution for its lack of concern for the
environment. Ruskin loved Monsal Dale and hated the
intrusion of the Buxton railway:

> Into the very heart and depth of this
> and mercilessly bending with the bends of it
> your railway brings its close-clinging damnation.

Although a landmark at 72ft high, the Midland's five-arch
stone viaduct ultimately blended into the landscape of Monsal
Dale. Perhaps it was fortunate that Ruskin was dead when
the Lancashire, Derbyshire & East Coast Railway proposed
to erect one there some 272ft high. Ruskin certainly would
have been justified in making comments on the limestone
quarrying which the railway promoted. Stone has always been
quarried in Derbyshire, either for building or for burning as
lime, and was responsible for the two early railways in the
Peak District: the Peak Forest Tramway and the Cromford
& High Peak Railway.

The Peak Forest Tramway, another of Outram's plateways, was opened in 1797 to bring stone down from Dove Holes at Peak Forest to the terminus of the Peak Forest Canal at Bugsworth, six miles away. Trains of about twenty full wagons would descend by gravity, being pulled up again by horses. The line lasted until 1920 when more efficient methods of transporting stone in bulk were needed, but in its heyday over 600 tons of stone were carried daily. The MS & L took control of the canal and tramway in 1846.

The C & HPR, which is fully discussed in the companion volume on the West Midlands, was the outcome of a scheme to link the Peak Forest and Cromford Canals, once it had been decided that a canal across the High Peak was impractical. Although designed as a through route, and contemplated as such until into the present century, its real importance lay in generating local traffic, including stone. It was opened throughout in 1831, but remained independent of other railways until links were put in at Cromford in 1853 and at Whaley Bridge in 1857 when the SD & WB was opened. Six thousand tons of limestone a month were leaving Whaley Bridge by 1860.

The Midland's activities around Buxton caused the LNWR to view the possibilities of the C & HP, which it had leased in 1861, as part of a through route from Buxton to London. In 1874 it was authorised to build a line from Buxton to Hindlow, to avoid the incline and meandering route from Whaley Bridge to Hindlow. The powers were revived in 1887, including those to absorb the C & HP, and by 1892 goods traffic was using the new line, which involved two substantial viaducts in Buxton. The section on to Parsley Hay was doubled, and passenger services from Buxton began on 1 June 1894. Finally on 4 August 1899 the new line to the NSR at Ashbourne was opened, and until World War I a through service was maintained from Euston to Buxton.

The line was unnecessary for through traffic, and with gradients of 1 in 60 up from Buxton, unsuitable for expresses. It lost its passenger services on 1 November 1954. However, it did give easier access to the quarries at Hindlow and Dowlow, south of Buxton, which still send out over 40 per cent of their annual tonnage by rail; in 1972 two new 990 ton trains of lime were operating regularly between Dowlow and Teesside.

One of the main quarries between Miller's Dale and Buxton is ICI's Tunstead Quarry near Peak Forest, at which about 6 million tons of stone a year is quarried, a substantial proportion of which is burned to lime on the site. From this Works about 60 per cent of the final product is despatched by rail. Since 1937 ICI has used special bogie hopper wagons for transporting crushed limestone from Tunstead to its chemical plants in Cheshire in trainloads of about 800 tons. These ICI wagons are vacuum-braked, but not all stone trains have been, and workings over the ex-LNWR line have to be cautious. In 1957, one loaded train ran out of control down the 1 in 58/60 which persists from Dove Holes (where the LNWR loops over the Midland) to Whaley Bridge. The driver heroically stayed on board trying to bring his train under control, but at Chapel-en-le-Frith South Station his train, whistling frantically, ploughed into another freight train, killing him, and the other guard, and demolishing much of the station. The driver was posthumously awarded the George Cross.

Buxton undoubtedly benefitted from the railways. Its hot springs had tempted both the Romans and Mary Queen of Scots, but despite the efforts of the Dukes of Devonshire from the eighteenth century, its height (at 1,000ft above sea level, the highest market town in England) and isolation, kept patronage down. Its population grew only slowly before the railway (1,877 in 1861), but then more than trebled over the next forty years. Its fame as a spa continues, although the use of spas has altered considerably, and the 1908 guide book listed bath chairs as among public conveyances available, at 1s 3d (6p) an hour.

By influencing the design of the two stations, adjacent across a wide road, Sir Joseph Paxton ensured that they were an ornament to the town, but the very fact that there were two stations meant that Buxton had lost out badly in its railway position. The original MBM & MJR would have put Buxton on a main line to Manchester, but thanks to early railway politics, and especially the obstructionist tactics of the LNWR, the town finished up with being on two branch lines. This mattered less during the railway age, when through trains ran to Buxton, but in more recent years, a shuttle service connecting with main line expresses has been no adequate substitute for a main line service, and under the

1963 Beeching Plan, Buxton was threatened with complete withdrawal of passenger services.

In 1910 Bradshaw listed over thirty-five routes to Buxton, from places as diverse as Folkestone and Edinburgh. World War II ended the through services, and only one return London coach was restored in 1953. In addition one train ran through to Derby and three to Manchester via the Midland Route. Otherwise every train on the main line connected at Miller's Dale with the Buxton push-and-pull trains. Miller's Dale consequently boasted a five-platform station although the community was so small that its post office was in the station booking hall.

During the electrification of the West Coast main line the Midland route to Manchester carried a heavy express passenger service, but once electrification was complete in 1966, two routes from London to Manchester were unnecessary, and East Midlands traffic could easily be diverted via the Hope Valley line. The change was initiated on 1 July 1968. Local passenger services between Matlock and Chinley including the Buxton branch, were withdrawn on 6 March 1967. Strenuous opposition, especially from commuters, has kept at bay the closure proposals for the ex-LNWR line from Buxton, which in 1973 carried twenty-four Manchester trains daily.

Nearer Derby, Matlock had also benefitted from the railway, both in raising production from the old-established Cawdor quarry, and in developing the town as a spa. Commuter and tourist traffic down to Derby was sufficient to keep this portion of the old MBM & MJR open after 1967, while an increase in traffic justified the reopening of Matlock Bath station in 1972, when the line enjoyed ten trains daily to Derby.

RAILS THROUGH THE PEAK: (2) THE HOPE VALLEY

Railways between Manchester and Sheffield, across the Pennines, of which the Peak District is the southern part, were discussed from the 1820s, and in 1830 the Sheffield & Manchester Railway issued its prospectus as a continuation of the newly-completed Liverpool & Manchester Railway.

The arguments in favour of a railway were sound enough, for horses and carts were the only existing means of transport.

They were slow, taking two days to do the return journey, limited in capacity, carrying only 130,000 tons annually, and expensive, charging £1 14s od (£1·70p) a ton for merchandise over the single journey. There was also the limestone to win, and a connection would be made at Whaley Bridge with the C & HPR.

The engineering works needed in North Derbyshire were tremendous, and George Stephenson's proposals to deal with them totally inadequate. The summit of the $43\frac{1}{4}$ mile line, in Rushup Dale, would have been a thousand feet above either terminus. To reach this, four inclined planes were envisaged, totalling over $4\frac{1}{2}$ miles, with two miles in tunnel! In addition a three-mile tunnel north of the present Totley tunnel would have been needed. In 1833 the shareholders were given their money back.

A rival scheme, the Sheffield, Ashton-under-Lyne & Manchester Railway (later the MS & L) was a far more practical scheme, despite its Woodhead Tunnel, and this provided the main route between the two cities until the 1890s.

In 1884, however, the Dore & Chinley Railway was authorised as an independent concern to provide an alternative route. The Midland was obviously interested as the line linked its routes at either end, and when the engineering obstacles proved too much for the original company, the Midland took over in 1888, using engineers experienced from building its Settle & Carlisle line. Although the steepest gradient was no more than 1 in 100 over five miles, it was at the expense of two of the longest railway tunnels in Britain. Totley Tunnel at the Sheffield end, 3m 950yd, was the longest on the Midland and the second longest on BR; Cowburn Tunnel, at the Chinley end, at 2m 182yd was the ninth longest on BR.

Inevitably, Ruskin and his followers attacked the scheme for its intrusion into the isolated Edale, but in vain, and in fact the railway checked the population drift out of Edale, by enabling residential development to take place, as well as developing the tourist and industrial potential of the Dale; there is an important cement works at Hope. Goods traffic began on 6 November 1893, excursion trains to Lancashire on 15 May and regular passenger traffic on 1 June 1894.

The rationalisation of trans-Pennine routes following the electrification of the ex-LNWR London–Manchester route ended speculation over the future of the Hope Valley line.

As the electrified Woodhead route was already well-used by freight trains, it was decided to concentrate passenger traffic on to the Hope Valley and close the Miller's Dale route. Passenger traffic over Woodhead ended in January 1970. In 1972 the Hope Valley line carried each way nineteen through trains a day including two through to St Pancras using the Dore south curve, as well as nine stopping trains. The Woodhead route was closed amid controversy in 1981, resulting in more freight traffic using the Hope Valley; the east to south curve at Chinley had already been reinstated. Passenger traffic has also increased, the 1983 timetable showing nineteen daily long-distance and eight local trains going east, and eighteen and nine respectively going west.

DERBY

CHAPTER X

Lincolnshire

Lincolnshire has been described as 'one of England's most highly industrialised counties—the industry being agriculture.' The absence of heavy industry made Lincolnshire less attractive to early railway promoters as a source of new lines, although from an early date they were planning to cross it with trunk routes linking London and Yorkshire. Lincolnshire, indeed, has only four towns over 30,000 population; of these, Grimsby, Cleethorpes and Scunthorpe belong to Humberside, and are considered in the next chapter. Otherwise only Lincoln (population 76,660) has developed as a major industrial centre, at the focal point of the county's railway system.

There are some seven smaller towns in the 10,000 to 30,000 range, towns such as the small port of Boston; or Grantham and Spalding, but these still function essentially as local markets though railways have played a considerable part in their modest history. Skegness and Mablethorpe also owe their belated development as popular seaside resorts to the railways. On the whole, those old market towns on the through routes, such as Louth, have prospered more than those on branches, like Horncastle, while Caistor, which missed the railway by three miles, has decayed into insignificance. Similarly Stamford stagnated as the London & York Railway avoided it in favour of Peterborough, which then grew rapidly.

Although other companies served Lincoln, it was the GNR which came to dominate southern Lincolnshire. The company had a reputation for speed and smartness, but also for not providing refreshment rooms. Ackworth complained of travelling for twelve hours through Lincolnshire one hot summer's day existing only on buns. In fact the GNR tied up as little capital as possible in non-train-working enterprises, for as Sir Frederick Banbury, its chairman, once remarked, 'There is no money in stations.' The more attractive village stations like Firsby were built by the original companies and the contrast is strikingly seen in the much better buildings of the Manchester, Sheffield & Lincolnshire Railway in northern Lincolnshire.

THE GREAT NORTHERN EMERGES

Although the Rennie's proposal for a London & York Railway in 1827 was premature, after 1833 there was considerable rivalry over lines to connect these cities, many involving Lincolnshire. The issue was further complicated by the bitter opposition from established interests jealous of their monopoly. Opposition from George Hudson was especially protracted because any proposal for an East Coast route to York would compete with the original route through the Midlands opened in 1840, which he largely controlled.

At a public meeting (chaired by the Mayor) in Lincoln in October 1834, it was resolved that railways were important and useful to the community. A committee was established to examine proposals, reporting in March 1835, with the comment that:

> Railway transit appears destined to restore to the Eastern side of the island some of the advantages which it lost, when the discovery of America and other causes turned the current of commerce to the Western shores of Great Britain.

It had to consider also a deputation at the October 1834 meeting from 'a Midland Counties railway' which saw a line into Lincolnshire as a feeder for its growing schemes. While not rejecting this prospect of a 36 mile branch to lines already authorised, the committee considered that the 180 mile direct line from London to York recently proposed by Lincolnshire's MP gave advantages to Lincolnshire's farmers by allowing quick and cheap transport of their grain, manure and cattle to London. Traffic in perishables was bound to grow with the great reduction in journey times. Even if this traffic, as important as merchandise, were ignored, they thought that there would be sufficient pull for Yorkshire goods from the London market to make a line worthwhile. Moreover, the

Plates 28 and 29 On Lincolnshire byways in LNER days: *(above)* a train of elderly stock leaves Sutton on Sea for Firsby; *(below)* a breezy wait beside the Humber at Immingham for this New Holland local. [T. G. Hepburn; T. E. Rounthwaite.]

Plates 30 and 31 From Grimsby to Immingham: *(above)* a tram traverses a Grimsby street in 1955 en route for Immingham Docks, where the coal drops are prominent *(below)*. [Ian L. Wright; Grimsby Evening Telegraph.]

flat fenlands of eastern England would make construction
easy and cheap at £8,000 a mile. They also warned that the
power of money must not be underestimated in influencing
the course of a line; events over the next decade were to
demonstrate the accuracy of this.

In 1836 Parliament rejected two East Coast schemes while
authorising the chain of smaller companies (Midland Counties
Railway, North Midland Railway and York & North Midland
Railway) which linked the London & Birmingham Railway
at Rugby with York. The influence of Hudson at York, and
George Stephenson in the Midlands was decisive, and on 1
July 1840, Hudson, now Lord Mayor of York, saw off the
first passengers from his city to travel to London by rail,
via Derby.

Meanwhile, the idea of a trunk route to Scotland was being
canvassed, so the Board of Trade ordered a commission to
determine the merits of the East and West Coast Routes, and
also of routes to York via Derby and Lincoln. The commission
preferred the Lincoln route as a trunk line but maintained
that such a development would be premature: the Derby
route was not yet working to capacity and the expenditure
of £4 million was felt unnecessary merely to shorten the
journey to York. However, there was a need for railways in
Lincolnshire and probably they would be built by local
companies. On the other hand, the *Railway Times* ridiculed
the idea of a Scottish link, and spoke for many people in 1841
when it maintained that the railway system was already
adequate.

By 1843, one of the great assets brought by the railways
to central and northern England was the ready availability of
cheap fuel; Lincolnshire demanded this too. The need was
pressing, as bad inland transport prevented Midlands' coal
from entering Lincolnshire, while South Yorkshire and
Durham coal, even on canal routes, cost forty or fifty shillings
a ton. Moreover, the City financiers, were suddenly interested,
as railways were paying high dividends, and foreign securities
were unattractive because of events in South America. The
result was several schemes presented to the Lincolnshire
public early in 1844, some running east to Lincoln, others
running north-south as trunk routes through Lincoln.

Of the east-west schemes, the Wakefield & Lincoln was the
most popular, being supported by the Lincoln city council.

Its route to Lincoln lay along the ancient Fossdyke canal, with an extension to Boston along the Witham Navigation. These waterways had been important in rebuilding Lincoln's prosperity in the early nineteenth century; by guaranteeing shareholders a permanent six per cent dividend the WL & BR gained their support and the necessary land. In a broadsheet war with its rivals in Lincoln, the WL & BR supporters extolled Wakefield and blasted Barnsley and Manchester as markets for Lincolnshire malt, flour and wool, and as sources of coal, lime, linen, cotton and woollen goods. In September 1844 it amalgamated with the London & York.

By the end of May 1844 there were three major trunk routes affecting Lincolnshire, aiming to link York with London. The Direct Northern Railway via Peterborough, Lincoln and Gainsborough was backed by Sir John Rennie. The London & York Railway, backed by Yorkshire interests led by Edmund Denison MP, envisaged a line via Peterborough, Grantham, Newark, Gainsborough and Doncaster. Finally, the Eastern Counties Railway was instructing Robert Stephenson to extend his survey of a line from Wisbech to Lincoln through to Doncaster. Of these, the London & York was the most promising, and as such constituted a direct challenge to Hudson's monopoly of the route to the North, for in 1844 the Midland Counties and North Midland lines amalgamated as constituents of the new Midland Railway under Hudson's control.

Yet Hudson could not ignore the public demand for an East Coast route. He therefore determined to control as much of it as possible using branch lines, and thus kill the London & York by making it unnecessary. He had already proposed a Midland Railway branch from Nottingham to Lincoln, reviving a project of 1834; this was to be extended to March via Boston and Spalding. Doncaster would be reached by a Y & NMR branch, and Peterborough by another Midland branch from Leicester. The Eastern Counties Railway would co-operate by diverting its authorised Peterborough branch via March to meet the extended Midland branch, and thus make possible a through line from London to York via Cambridge, March, Lincoln and Doncaster. The London & Birmingham Railway was already building its Peterborough branch; its support was bought by Hudson's support for its Bedford branch. The ECR, which also aimed at Bedford, was

ought off by an offer of a half share of traffic to York and
eyond in return for curtailing this branch at Hertford. This
widespread bargaining was applauded by the *Railway Times*
as a 'great and valuable alliance'.

The Board of Trade's railways examining committee then
backed Hudson by reporting in favour of his schemes. This
caused uproar. The London & York promptly defied it by
announcing that it would continue, which aroused the fury
of the *Railway Times*. In Lincoln, a meeting said to be
attended by 6,000 ended in a free fight when the Mayor
declared passed the resolution in favour of the London &
York. Hudson's supporters maintained that labourers had
been hired at 2s od (10p) each to vote for the Mayor.

Joseph Locke was briefly the engineer to the London &
York and chose as its main line the 'Towns' route from
Peterborough to Doncaster via Grantham, with branches to
Newark, Lincoln and Sheffield. Lincolnshire feelings were
mollified by a branch to Boston to join the Wakefield's exten-
sion as the 'Fens' line loop. Lincoln, Grantham, Newark and
Retford voiced their approval.

The committee stage of the London & York's Bill was
crucial, and was dragged out by Hudson interests to an
unprecedented seventy days. Support came from various MPs
including W. E. Gladstone, member for Newark. Brunel,
and Betts (the contractor), gave supporting engineering
evidence, while the estimate that Yorkshire coal could be sold
in London for £1 1s od (£1·05) a ton, saving 8s od (40p), was
overwhelming, despite Robert Stephenson's comment that
his was unprofitable. The Bill ultimately passed the Commons
in 1845 but Hudson had ensured that it would not complete
its passage through the Lords that session, while his lines to
Peterborough and Lincoln were passed entirely. Both the
Direct Northern, and the ECR's Lincoln line Bills failed on
engineering errors. The DNR joined the London & York,
which was finally authorised in June 1846 as the Great
Northern Railway. Although shorn of its Wakefield and
Sheffield branches, this 272 mile project costing some £6½
million was the largest railway authorised by that date.

At the same time were authorised the Sheffield & Lincolnshire Junction (via Retford to Gainsborough) and Sheffield
& Lincolnshire Extension Railways (Clarborough Junction
to Lincoln, to join the Great Grimsby and Sheffield Junction

branch from Market Rasen); also the amalgamation o
these and other companies into the Manchester, Sheffiel
& Lincolnshire Railway. As the S & LER was to follow th
GNR Gainsborough–Lincoln route from Sykes Junction
Saxilby, into Lincoln, the GNR was to build the line an
give the MS & L running powers there in return for runnin
powers from Retford to Sheffield. The East Lincolnshir
Railway from Grimsby to Boston was also authorised then

BUILDING TO 1852

By 1846 most of the major lines across Lincolnshire an
through Lincoln had been authorised, but money after th
Railway Mania was tight and Hudson was still harassin
GNR activities. He had boasted that he 'could provid
Lincolnshire with a railway before other people had don
talking about it,' and did so, opening his line from Notting
ham via Newark with great festivities on 3 August 1846
barely a year after its authorisation. Then on 2 October 184
the Stamford to Peterborough section of the Syston line wa
opened.

To counter Hudson's renewed projects in Lincolnshire th
GNR took control of the ELR. It also needed authority t
divert its route at Peterborough alongside the Midland line
to make economies in construction. In return for this, an
Midland assistance in carrying materials, the GNR promise
not to build stations at Walton and Helpston. Delays over th
diversion, and the easier nature of the Fens loop cause
construction on that to begin first, as it was necessary to brin
in revenue. Opening was scheduled for 1848, along with th
ELR which had running powers over the MS & L to Ne
Holland for the Hull ferry. Diversion of the loop north o
Gainsborough from Bawtry to Rossington was successfull
opposed by powerful local hunting interests, forcing th
GNR to rely on the MS & L Retford route.

The GNR first ran trains, from Louth to Grimsby and o
to New Holland, on 1 March 1848, with five return service
Further openings that year were Louth to Firsby on
September, Firsby to Boston on 1 October, Peterborough t
Boston and Lincoln on 17 October, and Lincoln to Marke
Rasen on 18 December. In spite of offering a through rout
to Hull, the circuitous route south of Peterborough mad
these Lincolnshire lines still essentially local, and up to 3

June 1849 goods only brought in £13,168 revenue compared with passengers £40,184, plus £4 in fines for smoking in passenger coaches. During 1849, the Lincoln–Gainsborough section was opened on 9 April, followed by the Sykes Junction–Retford (MS & L)–Doncaster (GNR) lines on 4 September. Finally on 7 August 1850 the London to Peterborough section was opened; ten days later Hudson, fallen from power, travelled the line from London to Leeds.

Immediately the LNWR and Midland companies, resenting the threat to their traffic monopoly, carried on Hudson's work by forming the Euston Square Confederacy to block GNR traffic. The Confederacy brought together the LNWR, Midland, Lancashire & Yorkshire and MS & L companies into an uneasy alliance to further primarily the interests of Captain Huish of the LNWR in protecting traffic to the north. The Confederacy was very effective, especially through the adherence of the MS & L who cut off water for GNR locomotives at Retford, and placed blocks over the rails at Grimsby to prevent through running to New Holland. When the GNR obtained Chancery injunctions against this, the MS & L retaliated by simply running its last ferry before the GNR train arrived.

The building of the Towns Route over the limestone ridge around Grantham was delayed by labourers going off to help with the harvest, and by heavy rain. It was at last opened for goods traffic on 15 July 1852, and for passengers on 1 August. Expresses immediately cut an hour off the journey to York and the North, and the Midland route faded out for London traffic, although under the notorious Octuple Agreement forced on the GNR by the Confederacy, it still got a proportion of the receipts.

MINOR LINES

With the trunk routes completed by 1852, the way was left open for the promotion of cross-country lines and feeder branches over the next two decades. From July 1850 an independent railway had run from Grantham to Nottingham. The GNR leased this from 1855, and the line became part of a through route from Nottingham to Boston, involving the Boston, Sleaford & Midland Counties Railway. This was opened from Barkston, near Grantham, to Sleaford on 16 June 1857, and on to Boston on 13 April 1859. The GNR worked the line from the beginning, absorbing it in 1864. The Honington to Lincoln line was opened on 15 April 1867, providing a more direct route from London to Lincoln. It also opened up small iron ore deposits, which were sent to Derbyshire or Scunthorpe until World War I. It was closed to passengers on 1 November 1965 when Lincoln trains were diverted via Newark. The cut-off from Sedgebrook to Barkston, enabling through coal trains from Nottinghamshire to gain direct access to Lincolnshire, was opened in 1875.

As the GER was trying hard to get access through Lincolnshire to the Yorkshire coalfield, the GNR proposed a line from Sleaford to Bourne, and to absorb the independent Essendine & Bourne (opened 16 June 1860, closed 18 June 1951). GER proposals for a new line from Cambridge, through Bourne and Sleaford to Lincoln and Doncaster were refused by Parliament in 1864, but the GNR ones were authorised in 1865. Opening from Bourne to Sleaford came on 2 January 1872 and closure to passengers on 22 September 1930.

The Spalding & Bourne Railway was authorised in 1862 and opened on 1 August 1866. It became part of the Midland & Eastern Railway which wanted to extend westwards to the Midland at Saxby. The GNR opposed this, but instead gave running powers between Bourne and Stamford. In 1893 the line became part of the Midland & Great Northern Railway, which then opened its direct Bourne–Saxby line to passengers on 1 May 1894, controlling it to Little Bytham Junction. It was a useful cross-country route from the Midlands into East Anglia, avoiding Peterborough, and in 1955 it still boasted four through trains each way, with seven extras on summer Saturdays. It succumbed to rationalisation on 2 March 1959.

Near Little Bytham the M & GN's Saxby line ran over part of the route of the erstwhile Edenham & Little Bytham Railway. This was, even by 1857 standards, a rather primitive private railway built by Lord Willoughby de Eresby. As it was intended to carry passengers, a Board of Trade inspection was necessary, but it took three such inspections before the line was declared fit to carry passengers; even then there was a speed restriction of 8mph on curves and downhill, and the GNR refused to operate it. Opening was on 8 December 1857, and nearly 3,000 passengers were carried over the four-mile line in the next six months, but their fares only amounted to £63. Goods traffic, in farm produce, coal, fireclay and stone was more profitable but insufficient to prevent the line running at a loss. With passenger traffic running at under 1,000 a year the service was withdrawn on 17 October 1871. Anyway, the locomotives were worn out so horses were substituted for the goods traffic, which petered out in the early 1880s.

The GNR finally completed the Lincoln loop on 15 July 1867 when the Sykes Junction–Gainsborough line was reopened (it had closed in 1864) and the new Gainsborough–Doncaster link was opened. The huntsmen had again had this line thrown out by Parliament in 1863 but in 1864 the GNR succeeded although the MS & L was awarded £25,450 as compensation for loss of traffic on its Retford line, plus a toll equal to one mile's receipts on all trains using its Trent Bridge at Gainsborough.

In the Wolds, the Horncastle Railway was authorised in 1854 and opened on 11 August 1855, being worked by the GNR from the beginning, although retaining its independence until 1923. The directors hoped to see Horncastle develop as a local market, but being off the main line, it never grew like its Fenland neighbours. Its six daily trains in 1910 were supplemented on market days. They were withdrawn on 13 September 1954. Woodhall Spa, the intermediate town, failed in its pretensions to become a spa. Further east the single-track Spilsby branch was authorised in 1865 and opened on 1 May 1868. In 1910, although half the size of Horncastle, it could support eight daily trains but these were withdrawn on 11 September 1939 and never reinstated.

The Louth & Lincoln Railway, authorised in 1866, had great pretensions as a through route from the Midlands to Grimsby, already ably covered by the MS & L Market Rasen line. Its sole utility would have been to give eastern Lincolnshire direct access to Lincoln and thence the Midlands or North, without going via Boston, which could be advantageous to the farmers around Louth. The promoters were confident of inexhaustible supplies of ironstone around Apley and Donnington, equal to those near Caistor which were sending out 70,000 tons annually to Yorkshire furnaces. Using coal from Derbyshire, furnaces could be erected on these beds, sending their products out via Grimsby, thus rivalling the growing Northamptonshire industry.

Reality was more sober. The junction at Five Mile Bottom, facing Lincoln, was abandoned for one at Bardney, facing Boston. The line was single, and heavily graded, and needed extra capital before it was opened on 1 December 1876. Although iron ore was extensively mined over the Wolds at Greetwell, near Lincoln, and Nettleton Top, near Holton-le-Moor, output was taken away to Scunthorpe by the MS & L line, and furnaces never appeared on the L & L. Maintaining four return trains daily for most of its life, it closed to passengers on 5 November 1951; goods trains were progressively cut back, ending in 1956.

THE GN & GE JOINT RAILWAY

The GER, although virtually monopolising East Anglia, was very dependent on agriculture for its freight traffic. It desperately wanted access to Doncaster for the far more remunerative coal traffic from South Yorkshire, to carry it both to London and into its own territory. At first, the GNR was jealous of its coal traffic, still feeling vulnerable financially after the effects of the Confederacy and Octuple Agreement. By the later 1860s it was feeling more co-operative towards the GER, to the extent of joining in a proposed direct line from Spalding to Lincoln. The GNR already had a line from Spalding to March, on the GER, opened on 1 April 1867. Successive palace revolutions within the GER over finance kept the scheme dormant until 1876 when, a proposal for amalgamation with the GNR having failed, the GER resurrected the joint line plan, plus joint ownership of lines to Doncaster. The GNR wanted more joint ownership in East Anglia which the GER rejected, proposing instead its own line from March, via Sleaford and Lincoln, to Askern, beyond Doncaster, where it would join the Lancashire & Yorkshire and tap coal supplies. Finally the GNR proposed a joint line from Spalding to Lincoln via Sleaford, with joint ownership throughout from Huntingdon to Doncaster via March and Gainsborough. Although the GER was not happy, the necessary Bill was approved by Parliament in 1879.

The joint line was opened from Spalding to Ruskington, beyond Sleaford, on 6 March 1882, and on to Pyewipe Junction, Lincoln, on 1 August 1882, when the joint committee took over. At Sleaford and Lincoln, the main line avoided the stations, which were connected by spurs. Until the 1970s this was an important main through freight line, especially after 1928 when Whitemoor marshalling yard, March, was developed. Local freight was in agriculture between the main market towns, with the potato and beet fields at Nocton providing useful traffic. Here in 1926 some twenty-six miles of 2ft 0in gauge railway were laid, serving the fields and glasshouses. The system was closed in 1960.

Passenger services have never been heavy, but have included long-distance cross-country trains. GER trains from Liverpool Street ran through to Doncaster immediately, and from 1892 on to York. Boat expresses ran from Harwich to Liverpool, Manchester or York until 1973 when the remaining Manchester service was diverted via Peterborough, leaving summer Saturday extras as the longest trains. Otherwise, most trains ran from March or Sleaford to Doncaster or Sheffield.

RAILWAYS AT LINCOLN AND STAMFORD

As Lincoln commands the gap through the Lincoln Edge, it was inevitable that most east-west lines went through the city. The result has been a mass of junctions in a small area, complicated by the many level crossings. The Midland crossed the High Street first, assuring the Council that there would be no danger. Two years later the GNR did likewise one hundred yards away. The Council asked why the two railways could not share the crossings, but were assured that no problems would arise. For years they have caused congestion in the High Street. Pressure was such on summer Saturdays that the LNER's High Street signalman was relieved of the obligation of making-up his train register. Immediately east of the Central (LNER) Station, Pelham Street level crossing crossed the junctions. Congestion to rail and road traffic was relieved after thirty-five years' planning by the opening of the Pelham Street flyover in 1958. In 1984, a new spur at Boultham will divert trains from St Marks into Central. St Marks, the ex-MR station, built in a severe classical style, has only two platforms but became in 1970 the principal station, handling the four daily London–Cleethorpes expresses, as well as the Nottingham locals. The baronial style ex-GNR Central Station has eight platforms, but deals mainly with short DMUs on cross-country services.

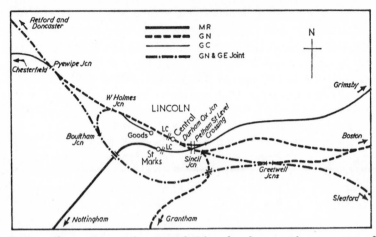

Four railway companies served Lincoln, but at the expense of too many level crossings, which have been a nuisance for over a century

By the early nineteenth century Lincoln handled thirty London coaches weekly, but without coal it could not compete for industry with Midlands towns. Local enclosure developed barley and oats production, making Lincoln an important market, aided from 1826 by steam packets on the River Witham. Agricultural industries like tanning and malting followed, and by 1841 the population had doubled to 14,000 since 1801. By 1871 it had doubled again, for the railways brought engineering. Nathaniel Clayton, the local packet-boat owner, and Joseph Shuttleworth, a shipwright, foresaw that railways would end river traffic, so they set up in partnership as ironfounders in 1842. Six years later, by introducing a fourth class fare of ½d a mile, the GNR drove the packets off the river. By 1850 Clayton & Shuttleworth was building agricultural steam engines, and other engineering firms soon followed, including Rustons. So Lincoln prospered from the railways and engineering, blossoming to a 66,000 population in 1921, but dependence on one industry made the city vulnerable to slumps, and stagnation.

Stamford, however, missed the main line and such prosperity, for which the Second Marquis of Exeter must be blamed. He held virtually all the land in Stamford, restricting house building and factory development, so preventing the town from benefitting fully from the Midland Railway. Stamford lay on various schemes for trunk lines to the north and until mid-1846 Lord Exeter had supported the GNR, not being antagonistic to railways, as was once thought. However, early in 1847 he hotly opposed the GNR's deviation along the Midland, and all prospect of routing the GNR via Stamford vanished, to the consternation of the local shopkeepers who feared the consequences when the opening of the GNR killed their Great North Road coaching trade. Exeter's opposition was partly because the Midland was already in Stamford, and he had opposed the GNR, making respectable his political opposition. The repeal of the Corn Laws, on the same day that the GNR was authorised, split the Tory Party, and it was essential for anti-repeal Tories, like Lord Exeter to maintain their political hold. This could well be difficult if Stamford, like Peterborough, boomed into an industrial town, through being on a main railway route. The GNR was a major local issue in the 1847 election.

By 1855 the Marquis had regretted his stand and was building a branch to the GNR at Essendine. This was opened on 1 November 1856, with four trains each way, worked by the GNR. A southern extension to Wansford on the LNWR was proposed in 1859 and opened on 9 August 1867. Once a small GNR tank engine fell into the River Welland, ever afterwards being nicknamed the 'Welland Diver'. In 1914 a driver was so enthralled by watching a balloon over Stamford, that his train ran into the buffers, doing considerable damage to the line's rolling stock. By then the Essendine line carried fifteen return trains daily, the Wansford line eight.

The Wansford line largely duplicated the LNWR main line from Seaton, and was closed on 1 July 1929. Essendine trains ceased to use Stamford East Station, built in the style of Lord Exeter's Burghley House, on 4 March 1957, running from Stamford Town until withdrawal on 15 June 1959.

THE SEASIDE LINES

Although sea bathing was popularised by George III, it remained a preserve of the leisured classes until well into the nineteenth century. Gradually the middle classes took up the habit, but not until after 1850 could the working classes join in, using Bank Holidays and the Saturday half-day. So

although the fishing villages of Skegness and, to a lesser
extent, Mablethorpe, had a reputation as watering-places
they were not considered significant enough to be included
on the ELR.

The ELR, like the canals, was out to exploit the market
potential of the rich agricultural land below the Wolds and
the intervening towns, not the good sandy beaches five miles
away. Boston had developed as a major corn market and
port, sending out potatoes to London, and importing coal,
timber and fertilizers. Louth was not only a haunt of absentee
socialising clergy, but an inland port rivalling Grimsby, until
the docks at the latter place were improved. Louth is still
an important agricultural centre, and the huge maltings,
dwarfing the Elizabethan-style station, supplied the bulk of
the truncated line's traffic until final closure in 1980.

The first branch to the coastal settlements was the Firsby &
Wainfleet Railway, Wainfleet being a decayed port and
stagnating market town of 1,355 inhabitants when the branch
was opened in November 1871. Before this line was opened,
an extension was planned to Skegness, a medieval port until
the sea washed it away, and then a fishing village of 349
inhabitants. Opening was on 28 July 1873, the GNR operating
the line, and laying-on excursion trains into the specially
large station. The branch was doubled in 1900, as was
the south curve at Firsby installed in 1881 to permit through
running from Boston.

Skegness never looked back; while Wainfleet stagnated,
Skegness equalled its population in ten years, thereafter
expanding gradually, with big jumps after each war, but even
now its resident population of 14,452 is still dependent on
the holiday trade. Unlike the MS & L at Cleethorpes, the
GNR never invested in developing the town. This was left to
the ninth Earl of Scarborough in 1878, who laid out the new
town, to the urban district council in the 1920s, and to Sir
Billy Butlin who established his first holiday camp there in
1937.

August Bank Holiday 1882 brought in 22,000 day trippers,
and more would have come had there been more stock
available. They cleaned the shops of food, and by evening
crammed the station waiting to go home. The last train got
away at 02.30, still leaving hundreds behind but, commented
the GNR Chairman, 'It was a beautiful day and no doubt

they all enjoyed themselves very much.' The 1890 guide book described Skegness as 'one of the most crowded and popular seaside resorts in England . . . but not much to be recommended for quieter visitors.' Indeed, outside the station were stalls selling cockles, rock, and beer from tin baths replenished from buckets. Tankards were refilled by simply scooping them in.

From 1904 the GNR ran regular Sunday excursions, to the indignation of the Council and hoteliers who complained to the railway that they catered for a good class of visitor, who would be driven away by these trippers. The evangelical churches loudly declaimed the desecration of Sunday and protested to the railway that it was shocking to sell trippers tickets for half the price that God-fearing folk had to pay on Monday! The railway was unsympathetic; far from sacrificing business to set a moral example the company wanted to encourage it. The excursions continued: in conjunction with one for 3s od (15p) from London at Easter 1908, the GNR issued the famous jolly fisherman poster proclaiming 'Skegness is SO bracing.'

In 1884 the Lincoln & Skegness Railway was proposed to give direct access to the seaside from Yorkshire, over the Wolds, but this scheme failed and Yorkshire folk have still tended to patronise Cleethorpes, leaving Skegness to the Midlanders. A link line was opened on 1 July 1913 below the Wolds via Midville (the Kirkstead & Little Steeping line) to provide a cut-off from Lincoln, but it was closed between 1915 and 1923 as a coal economy measure. Although it was well used by summer excursions, local traffic was always slight, never carrying more than four trains each way from Lincoln to Skegness. Tumby was an important railhead for despatching potatoes.

The LNER enlarged the facilities at Skegness, for the branch needed to handle over one hundred trains a day in summer. On summer Saturdays in 1955 there were thirty-eight departures, mostly expresses, to London and the Midlands, compared with nineteen in 1973, including one to London, two to Sheffield and three to the Midlands. Ordinary daily connections at Grantham for Nottingham could be better.

Further north, Mablethorpe and Sutton-on-Sea (formerly Sutton-le-Marsh) have never developed to the same extent as Skegness, and in 1973 had only 5,500 inhabitants, although serving the same catchment area, even in the car era. The Louth & East Coast Railway, with GNR backing, was authorised in 1872 from Louth to Mablethorpe via Saltfleetby, whence a branch was planned to go north to Saltfleet Haven, and ultimately to Cleethorpes. Originally this was an agricultural line, but this traffic proved less lucrative than seaside excursions, opening being on 17 October 1877. A meandering branch from Alford was rejected by Parliament as unnecessary, but Sutton, too, wanted a railway, hence the authorising of the 2ft 6in gauge Alford & Sutton Tramway, opened on 2 April 1884 along public roads. A standard gauge tramway was also authorised from Alford to Skegness but had no funds for building.

The A & ST was killed by the Sutton & Willoughby Railway authorised in 1884, which would connect the ELR to the docks recently authorised at Sutton. These extensive dock plans remained extant until killed by the development of Immingham Docks by the GCR from 1906. Meanwhile, the GNR was not keen to work the line, as the L & ECR saw it as a threat to Mablethorpe traffic. The GNR told the S & WR that it would not work the line until the docks were built, to which the latter replied that it could not build the docks until the line were open. An extension to the L & ECR at Mablethorpe, forming a loop off the ELR, changed matters. This was authorised in July 1886, the S & WR was opened on 4 October 1886, and the extension on 14 July 1888, after financial embarrassment had delayed commencement of construction. Traffic on the A & ST flourished until 1886 when it immediately collapsed, although the line struggled on until December 1889.

The Mablethorpe extension was a great success, with 3,000 people travelling it between 14 July and 25 September 1888. The following year between July and December, 40,328 passengers including excursionists were carried to Sutton, and 38,600 (19,300 excursionists) to Mablethorpe, although facilities were never as extensive as at Skegness, and the S & W was never a success financially, especially after the collapse of the LD & ECR line and dock scheme, thus allowing the GNR to buy it up in 1902, followed by the L & EC in 1908.

The Lancashire, Derbyshire & East Coast Railway was

an ambitious proposal for an east-west line linking Sutton and Lancashire via the Nottinghamshire coalfield. It was authorised in 1891, taking over the Sutton Docks scheme which was to be developed in preference to Boston, as land was available and Trinity House said that Sutton was the best site for a port of refuge on that coast. The LD & EC's middle section from Chesterfield to Lincoln was opened on 8 March 1897 but financial difficulties prevented further work, and when the GCR bought up the LD & ECR in 1907, the Sutton Docks scheme was forgotten.

CLOSURES

Apart from those already mentioned, major closures were few before 1963. The remaining LD & EC passenger services were withdrawn on 19 September 1955, the S & LER over Torksey Bridge on 2 November 1959 and the L & EC on 5 December 1960, leaving Mablethorpe at the end of a single-track branch from Willoughby. The provision of diesel trains from 1955 had helped reduce overheads; this had been fore-shadowed by the trials of a GWR diesel car from Boston in October 1952.

The Beeching Report of 1963 proposed to cut out all rail-ways in east Lincolnshire, leaving Boston and Grimsby as railheads, plus the Midland line from Newark. Closure was proposed for 1964, but the local councils strongly opposed it. Lindsey County Council declared that population decline would increase in the rural and coastal areas, for agricultural employment was declining with no industry to replace it. Adequate transport was needed for shopping, health and education in Lincoln, Boston and Grimsby, yet the roads were poor. A third of Butlin's campers and Skegness caravanners still came by rail, while at Mablethorpe, of 402,000 passengers in 1962, 110,000 were day trippers and 190,000 were holiday-makers. Most might well holiday elsewhere. Louth RDC strongly stressed that the economy of the area was precarious, and Mablethorpe would be badly hit.

Closure, except for the Woodhall–Boston line on 17 June 1963 was stayed, and paytrains introduced in October 1968. Then in December 1969 closure was authorised between Spalding and Boston, Lincoln and Firsby, Firsby and Grimsby, and Willoughby and Mablethorpe, the Skegness branch being retained as the southern railhead. The Ministry of Transport said that most passengers using the Midville line went on to Skegness, and so could travel via Sleaford, and those going to Coningsby could go by bus with little hardship. On the main (ELR) line, one-fifth of the passengers came through Peterborough and so could travel on an augmented service via Newark, the Midland line being raised to a trunk route and Market Rasen becoming the distant railhead for Alford and Louth. The Mablethorpe branch carried little winter traffic, and although the railway was valuable in the summer, the season was short, coaches were available for many places, and as it had been decided to close the main line, there was insufficient traffic to justify a branch from Firsby. Closure came on 5 October 1970, except for goods north of Louth, despite continued opposition from local councils.

CHAPTER XI

South Humberside

A torrential thunderstorm over the Humber on the morning of 12 July 1906 nearly wrecked the ceremonial sod-cutting which began the construction of Immingham Docks. As it was, the only casualties were the stewards' top hats which they had placed under the tables in the lunch marquee; they were filled with rain and water. Otherwise, the waiters successfully relaid the tables for nearly seven hundred guests, and Lady Henderson, the Railway Chairman's wife, in brilliant sunshine, cut the first sod of the Great Central Railway's most important dock and ultimately one of the major ports in the country.

Immingham Dock was the logical extension of the development of nearby Grimsby over the previous sixty years as a port and major fishing centre by the Manchester, Sheffield & Lincolnshire Railway. Its importance further increased in 1973 when the British Steel Corporation announced plans to increase imports of iron ore through Immingham for its plant at Scunthorpe, twenty miles inland, which was to be developed as one of six major steel-producing centres.

Of these centres, Grimsby, Immingham and Scunthorpe, together with the seaside resort of Cleethorpes, only the first-named was of any significance before the railways came. Their importance and dependence on the Humber was recognised in 1974 when local government reorganisation separated them from Lincolnshire into the new Humberside authority. They have little in common with the rest of Lincolnshire; Lincolnshire is agricultural, Humberside industrial; only Lincoln can compare in industry or size (76,000 population) with Scunthorpe (66,000) or Grimsby-Cleethorpes (128,000).

The area looks west to industrial Yorkshire, or like Grimsby's fish to the country as a whole, rather than to its immediate hinterland. Only in education, recreation and shopping is Grimsby, like Lincoln, a major centre for its part of Lincolnshire, and even so Hull, once reached by the railway ferry at New Holland, now by the Humber Bridge, is a larger magnet.

The railways emphasise this. Grimsby and New Holland were the eastern terminals of the MS & L's main line, while only on a branch of the London-orientated Great Northern Railway. The implementation of the Beeching Report has shown this clearly, for the main lines out of Grimsby run west and south-west, to Doncaster, Retford and Newark, ie towards industrial Britain: the southbound line (GNR) was closed in 1970.

PLANNING AND BUILDING TO 1850

The *Stamford Mercury* for 6 May 1831 reported that in the previous week engineers were surveying the country between Gainsborough and Grimsby for a railway planned between Manchester and the East Coast, via Sheffield and Gainsborough. Hull was to be the destination, but as the ground between Gainsborough and Hull was difficult, Grimsby was chosen instead, reaching Hull via a ferry over the Humber. Branches included one to Lincoln.

Eighteen years later this line, by then known as the Manchester, Sheffield & Lincolnshire Railway, was fully opened. In its origins, the MS & L approximates more to the Midland than to the L & BR or the GNR. Not only were both provincial railways, but both built up their main lines through promotion by local companies and subsequent amalgamation, therefore avoiding the widespread opposition and consequent delays endured by the great trunk route proposals of the L & BR and GNR. The MS & L was created in 1846 by the Act which almagamated the Sheffield, Ashton-under-Lyne & Manchester, Sheffield & Lincolnshire Junction, Sheffield & Lincolnshire Extension, and Great Grimsby & Sheffield Junction Railway Companies, plus the Grimsby Docks Company.

The SA & M was first in the field, joining Sheffield and Manchester via the Woodhead Tunnel. This was opened in stages, the last being the Woodhead Tunnel section late in

1845. Before then, it was looking for outlets eastwards, having met the provisional Committee of the S & LJ in August 1844. The S & LJ proposed a line from Sheffield (joining the SA & M) to the important port of Gainsborough, on the Trent. A month later the S & LJ was surveying the route on to Grimsby and influenced the promoting of the GG & SJ in October 1844. By the end of the year the Grimsby Haven Company was joining in. Sheffield men were the main promoters of these railways, but the public meeting in Caistor on 28 October which launched the GG & SJ in October was well attended by North Lincolnshire landowners, with Lord Yarborough in the chair.

Unlike that of the S & LJ, the route of the GG & SJ was less clear-cut. At a meeting in Grimsby on 6 November, John Fowler, the engineer, suggested three routes between Gainsborough and Grimsby. The shortest ran via Caistor, but involved a long tunnel and gradients of 1 in 100; the longest ran via Market Rasen and also involved similar gradients. The easiest route ran via the small market town of Brigg. To some extent this meeting was merely a public relations exercise, for although it unanimously endorsed the Brigg route, the railway wanted that one despite the sparse population, for it allowed a convenient junction for the projected New Holland Ferry branch. Market Rasen was to have a branch from Brigg.

Supported by the Grimsby Haven Company, the GG & SJ obtained its Act in 1845 with little opposition. It then helped to get the Grimsby Dock Company authorised, superseding the GHC. The S & LJ's Bill had failed because Parliament ran out of time. Nevertheless, it was active both in opposing two Mania schemes, the Lincoln & Grimsby Direct and the Boston, Newark & Grimsby, and in producing its own counter scheme, the Sheffield & Lincolnshire Extension Railway, which was essentially a Lincoln branch where it would meet the GG & SJ's extended Market Rasen branch, proposed at the same time.

Initially the S & LJ was only seriously opposed by the river interests in Gainsborough, being well supported by the Councils and populace of Retford, Worksop and Gainsborough. By 1846 the Chesterfield Canal shareholders, whose canal joined the Trent north of Gainsborough, were demonstrating their opposition by promoting the Manchester &

Lincoln Union Railway along a similar route. By offering to amalgamate, the S & LJ obtained its Act in 1846, while the newly vested MS & L took over the M & LU scheme and the canal in 1847. On the same day in 1846 the S & LE was authorised from Clarborough Junction, east of Retford, to Lincoln. However, as it would follow the GNR's authorised Lincoln–Gainsborough branch between Lincoln and Sykes Junction, Saxilby, the GNR was to build that part of the line and allow the S & LE running powers into Lincoln, in return for running powers over the S & LE and S & LJ to Retford and Sheffield.

Before the end of 1845, the GG & SJ was aiming to extend its influence, not only by extending its Market Rasen branch to Lincoln, but with branches from Grimsby to Cleethorpes, North Kelsey to Caistor, Gainsborough to Newark, Lincoln to Horncastle and New Holland to Barton-on-Humber. The New Holland, Barrow and Goxhill Ferries were bought by some GG & SJ directors for £10,300 in response to Hudson's sudden interests there. Although the directors were supposed to be acting on their company's behalf, actually they bought the ferries themselves, forming the Humber Ferries Co, which then sold the ferries to the GG & SJ nine months later for £21,000. This financial sharp practice was heavily censured in 1849 by the MS & L shareholders, the offending directors subsequently repaying their exorbitant profit.

In 1846 the Lincoln, Barton, Newark and Caistor lines were authorised, as were GG & SJ steam ferries over the Humber. The Market Rasen branch was authorised to leave the main line nearer Barnetby, the junction facing north, thus allowing through running from Lincoln to New Holland. The Horncastle project faded out, to be revived in 1855 as an independent concern. The Newark and Caistor lines were quietly forgotten, so that the old hilltop market town of Caistor was bypassed by the new lines of communication and gently decayed. Finally that year much GG & SJ energy was devoted to securing the East Lincolnshire Railway, a newly-authorised independent railway linking Grimsby with Boston and the south, via Louth and Alford. The GG & SJ wanted both to develop the East Lincolnshire hinterland and protect Grimsby from invasion from the south, but despite protracted negotiations and the same engineer in the person of John

Fowler, the lease of the ELR was secured by the GNR in 1847.

As money was in short supply after the Mania, it was essential for the new MS & L to get some return on its capital outlay as soon as possible. Work during 1847 was therefore concentrated on the easier Lincolnshire lines, and, especially on the Lincoln line, leaving some lesser stations to be completed later. As the ELR's line to Louth was also nearing completion, a joint opening from New Holland to Grimsby and Louth was arranged for 1 March 1848, the directors inspecting the lines and celebrating the previous day.

At New Holland a wooden pier 1,500ft long, and three acres of docks for cattle and general merchandise had been built on the creek where smugglers were notorious. The station was extended the length of the pier, and a floating landing stage erected to enable trains to meet the ferries which could sail at all states of the tide. Two second-hand ships were bought to improve the service. A large community of MS & L employees grew up, the Company paying the resident schoolmaster and maintaining the library there from fines paid by errant railwaymen east of Retford.

The next openings were on 1 November 1848 from Ulceby to Brigg and the Market Rasen branch from Barnetby, followed on 18 December by the Lincoln extension. Although no official celebrations marked this latter occasion, the Barrow brass band accompanied the first train from New Holland to Lincoln, while on the corresponding down train ninety Lincoln schoolboys, including twenty musicians, supplemented a Lincoln band, which 'contributed no little to the hilarity of the day'.

Then on 1 March 1849 the Barton branch opened from a triangular junction at New Holland, the intermediate halt at Barrow Haven coming into use on 8 April 1850. This was followed on 2 April by the Brigg–Gainsborough section, the day being declared a public holiday in Gainsborough, and finally, quietly on 16 July, from Gainsborough to Woodhouse Junction, between Retford and Sheffield. The main line of the MS & L, from Manchester to New Holland, was complete. The Grimsby line was then considered a branch, passengers changing at Ulceby. The loop through Lincoln was opened from Clarborough Junction on 7 August 1850 with temporary

intermediate stations opening in December. They were
replaced with permanent buildings in 1853. The GNR
Lincoln–Saxilby–Gainsborough line had been opened on 9
April 1849.

GRIMSBY—EARLY DOCK DEVELOPMENT

Grimsby was an important port in medieval times, based on
fishing and coastal and overseas trade. However, silting of the
harbour became a serious problem in the sixteenth century,
and as the government then favoured Hull, Grimsby declined
seriously. Attempts made to arrest this decay with a new
harbour only became effective with the establishment of the
Grimsby Haven Company in 1796, supported by the local
gentry. Sir John Rennie was engineer.

The dock, later known as Old Dock, was opened in 1801
and immediately Grimsby began to develop, almost doubling
its population to 2,700 by 1811, but the dock was soon too
small for modern needs, retarding further growth. Louth was
still more important as a port, until the discovery of new
fishing grounds on the Dogger Bank gave renewed impetus
for dock construction in Grimsby. In 1845 the Haven Company
was dissolved and the Dock Company incorporated, closely
allied with the GG & SJ, with Lord Yarborough as chairman
of both boards.

Work began on reclaiming marshland, and in 1849 Prince
Albert laid the foundation stone on a magnificent occasion,
whose expense partly precluded official junketings on the
opening of various lines that year. This Royal Dock, covering
twenty-five acres, had two entrance locks, worked by hydraulic
power in the distinctive 300ft brick tower, now a local landmark. Another sumptuous banquet, lasting well over four
hours and including fifteen toasts, marked its opening in
1852, first traffic being handled on 27 May. The rail link from
the Town to the Docks and Pier Stations, and associated dock
lines, were opened on 1 August 1853.

The new docks were an immediate success, ships totalling
134,334 tons being handled in 1853. Ten years later shipping
tonnage had increased by nearly 150 per cent; 170,000 tons of
coal were exported and 121,604 tons of timber imported, as
well as general merchandise. Weekly steamer services to
Hamburg and Rotterdam were begun in 1852, and were soon

increased to serve other North European ports. Then in 1855 the MS & L joined the South Yorkshire Railway and French interests to promote the Anglo-French Steamship Company, mainly to export coal to France. Ten years later the MS & L bought out its partners.

THE FISH DOCKS

The fishing industry was also promoted. This was non-existent in 1800, so the borough corporation tried to encourage the landing of sprats for manure. The opening of the railway throughout in 1849 allowed fish to be quickly transported to the London market. In 1851 50,000 Norwegian lobsters were landed and railed to the capital, but the real impetus came when the MS & L opened the Fish Dock in 1856. As a joint venture between the MS & L, the GNR and the Midland, fishermen, especially from Brixham, were invited to settle by being offered low landing dues, while in 1858 the MS & L and GNR built fifty fishermen's houses. To gain practical experience the three companies formed the Deep Sea Fishing Company, originally with nine vessels. Again, success was immediate, for whereas only 500 tons of fish had been sent out by rail in 1852, some 10,360 tons were thus despatched in 1863, while three hundred fishing smacks used the dock.

By the end of the 1850s the MS & L had made Grimsby an important fishing and general port. The population had risen accordingly, to 11,000 in 1861, although conditions in the town were poor as the council did not appreciate the problems of an expanding town; sanitary reforms were criticised, and in 1858 the entire police force was dismissed as unnecessary. But these were not railway problems, although in 1896 the MS & L tried to avoid paying rates for the borough police, or alternatively to transfer the obligation of policing its docks to the borough. Neither Parliament nor the Council were sympathetic to this attempt to avoid normal responsibilities.

Both fish and general traffic using Grimsby Docks increased steadily during the later nineteenth century, causing the MS & L to make constant additions to its port facilities. As early as 1859 the smack owners had petitioned the railway to enlarge the dock to handle 500 smacks, to extend the jetty, to install cranes, build a marketing shed and bring up the sidings to facilitate despatch. This was done in 1860 when the dock was doubled in size, to twelve acres, and marketing began on the quayside, free passes being offered to fish merchants travelling on business from Grimsby.

No 2 Fish Dock was opened in 1877, and during the next decade fish tonnages landed increased from 45,000 in 1880 to 70,000 in 1890, when about 800 trawlers regularly fished from Grimsby. By the end of the century large steam trawlers were fishing off Iceland and bringing back increased catches, the 1900 tonnage being 135,000. This had increased to 175,000 tons by 1909, and has since levelled out at about 200,000 tons. Further dock area was required, No 3 Fish Dock being authorised in 1912. World War I delayed the building of this, and it was not opened until 1934. This brought the water area up to sixty-three acres, and created a market one mile long, including 314,750 sq ft under cover.

Before World War I over ninety per cent of fish landings were despatched by rail, bringing £293,030 in revenue in 1911. Up to three dozen fish vans might be attached to the Cleethorpes–Leicester express. The trawlers also needed a million tons of coal annually, while subsidiary trades additionally generated substantial rail traffic. Although the Wednesday before Good Friday 1929 (the busiest day of the year) saw 1,348 tons of fish despatched in 346 vans, between the wars road haulage was beginning to take over, a process accelerated after World War II as the large wholesalers built up fleets of lorries to carry fish from their ships to inland distribution centres, leaving their uneconomic small loads to the railways. Although eight express fish trains left Grimsby daily in 1957 for Banbury, Leicester, Leeds, London (three), Manchester and Nottingham, and odd vans were still attached to local passenger trains, thus serving 4,000 stations, the traffic was uneconomic as many vans were seriously underloaded. This led senior Eastern Region officials to declare that the Fish Docks were a grave financial liability to the British Tranport Commission, and that railway services must be better patronised if they were to survive. From the early 1960s road haulage reigned supreme, and fish traffic by rail became negligible, with large numbers of insulated fish vans converted to express parcels vans.

OTHER DOCK DEVELOPMENT

The MS & L was constantly occupied in expanding its port facilities at Grimsby, and by the 1870s was contemplating a new dock. Liddell, their consulting engineer, favoured an upstream site at Killingholme where land was better and cheaper, but the MS & L bought 105 acres of West Marshes in 1873, to build a link between the Old and Royal Docks and a new basin at right angles to them, this and the Old

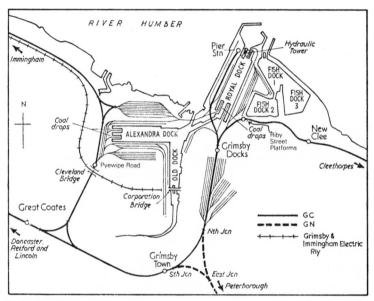

Grimsby Docks. The GNR never succeeded in penetrating these important docks, developed by the MS & LR

Dock to be served by a branch from Great Coates. The connecting dock was opened by the Prince and Princess of Wales on 22 July 1879, hence the name Alexandra Dock for the new docks, together with the original Old Dock. The new dock was completed in 1880 and the Great Coates branch opened on 27 March 1879. This quickly carried all Grimsby's coal exports.

During this period the Pier Station went out of use and was converted into a hostel for emigrants. There was a lively traffic in North Europeans en route for America, and the

MS & L obliged by running regular boat trains from Grimsby to Liverpool; up to 30,000 were carried annually.

From 1888 the great importance of Grimsby at last over-shadowed the New Holland Ferry, and from April the MS & L regarded Grimsby Town as its eastern main line terminal. All New Holland passengers on expresses changed at Brocklesby, where the station was suitably enlarged.

By 1900 Grimsby Docks were again overcrowded, but instead of expanding on the existing estate, Liddell's plan was revived and new docks were built six miles upstream at Immingham. However, this expansion was not continued into the inter-war years. Coal exports slumped, world trade was depressed, North Sea catches declined through over-fishing, and only deep-sea fishing off Iceland flourished, bring-ing No 3 Fish Dock into commission in 1934. As Grimsby had suffered during the depression years being basically a one-industry town, the Council after World War II determined to broaden the range of industry on South Humberside while maintaining Grimsby as 'the world's premier fishing port'. As a result, Courtalds and Dunlop established large factories, the chemicals industry has expanded around Immingham, and the area is the largest world centre for manufacturing titanium oxide. Grimsby has also become a major European food-processing centre, especially in frozen foods, although little of this is carried by rail.

Since 1967 the docks have developed the roll-on/roll-off technique, which is particularly suited to containerised traffic such as the large, old-established traffic in dairy imports from Denmark. Again, little of this traffic—over 100,000 tons annually of bacon alone—is railborne. Other traffics include the import of timber to Dixon's paper mills nearby, and the export of motor vehicles, in place of coal. To quote BR: 'Grimsby as a port has become overshadowed by Immingham . . . As a result, Grimsby has little rail traffic but Immingham is very busy . . .'

Grouping in 1923 put Grimsby entirely in LNER hands, and as part of its post-World War II reconstruction plans, the LNER planned a new station between Town and Docks stations, replacing both. Not only would this allow Peter-borough (and London) trains to run through to Cleethorpes without reversing, but Town station was notoriously cramped by level crossings at each end. Trains of more than seven coaches hang over the platforms, fouling crossovers, and often the crossings too. The plans were shelved and Grimsby still has its fine awkward original station. The Peterborough trains, which in 1955 included two through London expresses, were withdrawn on 5 October 1970. London trains, increased to four, were diverted via Newark, taking twenty minutes less for the twenty-five mile longer journey (see page 246).

(see page 246)

IMMINGHAM

By 1900, dock users were urging the GCR to extend Grimsby Docks, resulting in the Humber Commercial Railway & Dock Act 1901, backed by the GCR. Possibility of silting made an upstream site preferable, at Immingham, where the deep water channel comes close to the southern shore. At first Grimsby was hostile, although detailed investigations by the council brought a change of heart. Then the Board of Trade raised difficulties over Humber navigation which prompted the GCR to threaten abandonment of the scheme, thus arousing anger against the Board in Grimsby; the Board backed down, and a new Dock Act was passed in 1904, providing for the GCR to lease the Docks for 999 years.

Three light railways were needed to connect the docks with Grimsby, the main line and New Holland. The first was the Grimsby District Light Railway, authorised in January 1906 and operating in time for the sod-cutting ceremony in May. Thereafter it was used as a contractors' line, and finally as a route for commuting dockers. Public services began on 3 January 1910 with a steam railcar operating four return services. Connections were to be made into the Great Coates branch and Grimsby Tramways.

Meanwhile in 1909 work had begun on an electric tramway parallel to the GDLR on the West. Ultimately known as the Grimsby & Immingham Electric Railway, it ran from Corporation Bridge (over Alexandra Dock), via Pyewipe depot to Immingham, crossing the Great Coates branch by the Cleveland Bridge. It opened on 15 May 1912 when the steam railcar service on the GDLR was withdrawn. The service was frequent, especially at shift changeovers, when six cars might run in convoy. Extensions were soon promoted into the Dock estate and round to Immingham village. The former, involving reversal, opened on 17 November 1913 to the entrance lock from the Humber. The latter, inspected on 20 July 1915, was never used regularly despite protests from Grimsby RDC, which had pressurised the GCR into completing the branch and providing luggage compartments for milk and produce in some tramcars. Four statutory trains ran annually. There was no connection either with the GDLR or Grimsby Tramways, as the Corporation Bridge was not strong enough for trams until 1928, when the Corporation Tramway system was being phased out. The G & IER was used by up to 2,000 passengers daily until it wore out, closure despite much local opposition coming on 1 July 1961 after major road improvements had been undertaken to accommodate the replacement buses. The Corporation Bridge to Cleveland Bridge section was replaced by buses from 30 June 1956 to reduce traffic congestion.

Access to the Docks from the main line was via the Humber Commercial Railway, which was first used for freight on 29 June 1910. This ran from the New Holland line north of Ulceby, and was completed to the Eastern Jetty, where there was a passenger station, on 15 May 1912 when the docks were first used. Connections were made with the GDLR. This is the main access line to Immingham.

The third line was the Barton & Immingham Light Railway, authorised in 1907 to give Hull direct access to Immingham via New Holland. The original intention was to run from Barton, but this was changed to a junction with the New Holland line at Goxhill, whence the single line ran to a triangular junction with the HCR. Opening between Immingham and Killingholme was on 1 December 1910, and on to Goxhill on 1 May 1911. From 1912 the B & ILR was part of the HCR which was leased to the GCR. Patronage was never as heavy as on the G & IER, four return trains sufficing during the 1950s. It closed on 17 June 1963.

Immingham Dock was formally opened by George V on 22 July 1912 with excitement reminiscent of earlier railway openings. Lunch was served to 1,418 guests, two small locomotives providing boiling water, and the King ended the ceremonies by knighting Sam Fay, the GCR's energetic general manager. Although to be called the King's Dock, the name never stuck. More important was the fact that any ship able to use the Suez Canal could use the Dock, for jetties extend into the Humber.

The Dock estate covered over a thousand acres, of which forty-five were water. The river frontage extended for 1½ miles, and inside were a timber pond, quays for iron and steel traffic, general merchandise sheds, a grain elevator and seven coal hoists, all served by 170 miles of track. The GCR invested £2·6 million in the docks, and they have become a national asset, handling especially bulk cargoes. This has encouraged the development of oil refineries and chemical works up to Killingholme, and in the ten-year plan announced in 1973, the British Steel Corporation envisage substantial increases of bulk iron ore imports bound for Scunthorpe to enable production there to increase by over fifty per cent. In 1969 the total volume of imports and exports handled at Immingham and Grimsby—both docks are under the Grimsby Port Master—was over fifteen million tons, dominated by imports of oil, chemicals and iron ore, and exports of hydrocarbons, steel, coal and chemicals.

CLEETHORPES

Thanks to the railway, Grimsby and Cleethorpes have long been contiguous, although separately governed. Situated where the Humber mud gives way to sand, Cleethorpes originated as a watering place for the genteel, but the growth of Grimsby and its accessibility after 1863 by rail from industrial Yorkshire gradually turned it into a popular resort for the lower classes, genteel patronage going elsewhere.

The Cleethorpes branch was long awaited, but was delayed by opposition from landowners and intervening building. Authorised in 1861, it was finally opened as a single-track branch from Grimsby Docks Station on 6 April 1863. Increased traffic caused the line to be doubled in 1874. The sharp curves by the fish docks are due to extensions there in 1896.

Although the 1,200ft pier opened in 1872, real development came in the twenty years after 1880, when the MS & L spent over £100,000 in creating modern Cleethorpes. In 1880 the MS & L wanted to enlarge the station. The local authority asked the railway to preserve the cliffs for recreation, although they were liable to severe erosion. Under powers granted from 1881, the MS & L bought the land, extended the sea wall, laid out gardens, lit up the promenade, and erected swimming baths, a restaurant, a colonnade, a grotto, stalls and a pier pavilion. It leased the pier company in 1884, buying it out in 1904, and even licensed the beach donkeys. Up to 30,000 trippers a day patronised these delights, so convenient to the station, which by 1909 was inadequate. The original single-platform and runround were increased to six platforms.

BR modernised the station sympathetically in 1961–2 and it has taken Grimsby Town's place as the main line terminus. Normal services were thirty-one booked trains each way daily in 1973, with three extra on summer Saturdays, plus up to six charter trains; a far cry from the halcyon pre-war days, but still performing a useful service, especially for industrial Yorkshire.

NEW HOLLAND AND THE HUMBER BRIDGE

Ferries across the Humber have existed in this area since antiquity, Barton developing as a town in consequence. The opening of the New Holland line in 1848 and associated main lines in 1849 confirmed this as the direct route from London to Hull, although subsequently railway building in Yorkshire offered a better route. The ferry is still important as the first road bridge is at Goole, and Hull acts as a magnet for North Lindsey as a shopping, business and educational centre. As the road system is poorly equipped to deal with commuting traffic, the branch has been important, carrying over 11,500 passengers a week to the Ferry in 1963. The ferries also carry cars, which were lifted on board by a vast crane up to 1936. Long 'trains' of parcels trolleys have trundled along the extended platform from New Holland Town, the drivers acting both as porters and seamen, changing into jerseys en route. In earlier days livestock, including a whole travelling circus, was carried along with the passengers.

The New Holland and Barton lines were scheduled for closure under the Beeching Plan. Lindsey County Council was very opposed to this, claiming that the lines' presence was vital for the industrial development of the area, which was still under-exploited. The future of Barton depended on attracting new industry and its continued access to Hull and Grimsby. At this time the prospect of a Humber Bridge was remote.

Ten years later, however, the bridge had been begun at Barton and the branches wore a decrepit air. The Barton branch was just a long siding from New Holland, and graced only by a bus shelter. The driver of the lunchtime diesel train which waited there for well over an hour often dared not stop his engines in case he could not restart them. But it did not close as a train–bus link from Grimsby to Hull crossed the bridge when it opened (1981). Pier and ferry closed, the *Farringford* having taken over from the last coal-fired paddle steamer, *Lincoln Castle* (page 247).

RAILWAYS AROUND SCUNTHORPE

The rich agricultural marshland and iron ore deposits of north-west Lindsey were only developed later in the nineteenth century. Ironstone was discovered at Frodingham in 1858, midway between the rivers Trent and Ancholme, and eight miles from the MS & L at Brigg, although the South Yorkshire Railway was approaching completion to Keadby on the Trent. Rowland Winn, son of a local landowner, having already considered the desirability of a railway linking the two rivers, was now convinced of its need, and began to acquire the necessary land. Winn also brought in George Dawes to exploit the ironstone. Dawes planned a furnace on the Ancholme, which would be fed by railway from the pits, but then changed his mind to favouring a Trent-side site because of its superior transport facilities. The railway would need extending westwards from Frodingham, as well as completing the original eastwards line, which was done during July 1860.

Before the end of 1860 both the SYR and the MS & L were interested in this private ironstone line. The South Yorkshire Railway & River Dun Company was the culmination of earlier projects for a coal railway to Doncaster, opened in 1849. On 1 July 1856 passenger trains began running on an extension eastwards along the banks of the Keadby Canal to Thorne, where everything was transhipped on to the canal for the journey to Keadby to connect with the Gainsborough–Hull packets. The railway reached Keadby on 10 September 1859. The MS & L decided to meet Winn's line with a branch from Barnetby, and extend it over the Trent to Keadby. Although the SYR was not happy with these proposals, it joined the MS & L in promoting the Trent, Ancholme & Grimsby Railway, which was authorised in 1861.

In a separate act the SYR was authorised to bridge the

Trent south of Keadby at Althorpe. This aroused much opposition from the river interests, but their opposition was unco-ordinated and unsuccessful, in spite of the way local bargees were hindered by the scaffolding in their efforts to obtain passage through the workings. Incorporated in the 484ft long structure was a swing bridge of 160ft span. Both the bridge and the new TA & GR lines were ready by 1864, but the Board of Trade inspector would not pass them until certain improvements had been made, including completing the doubling of the track. Opening was delayed until 1866, goods on 1 May and passengers on 1 October, with two trains each way.

The line fulfilled its potential; by 1910 a new bridge was needed as the original needed heavy repairs. A diversion was planned to a new bridge $\frac{3}{4}$ mile downstream, but this was abandoned in favour of a single Scherzer lifting span of 160ft, 66yd north. This King George V Bridge, which included two fixed spans of 135ft and incorporated a road, was finished in 1914, but the deviation railway and new station were not opened until 21 May 1916. It ceased to 'lift' during 1959.

Further east the TA & G approached the iron ore ridge on the 1,020yd Scotter Road viaduct, which was partly filled-in during 1911. The five settlements there which make up modern Scunthorpe totalled 1,423 inhabitants when the TA & GR was opened. Iron had been worked there in Roman times, and from 1859 the ore was taken into Yorkshire. In 1864 Dawes, having abandoned the Trent site, erected his ironworks east of Scunthorpe. Four other companies followed, erecting ten furnaces within the next thirteen years. By 1881 the population had risen to 4,300, and in 1887 a larger station, Frodingham & Scunthorpe, was opened.

By 1898 nearly eight million tons of ore were raised locally to feed twenty furnaces which produced 300,000 tons of iron. Population was approaching 10,000. Ore reserves further north were exploited by the North Lindsey Light Railway, promoted in 1900 with encouragement from the GCR, which hoped that this would keep the ambitious Lancashire & Yorkshire Railway out of Lindsey. The L & YR was already in Axholme and contemplating an extension of their Fockerby branch under the Trent to Barton.

The first stage of the NLLR was opened on 3 September 1906 from the GCR near Frodingham to West Halton. Extensions were soon in hand to Winteringham, with a branch to Winteringham Haven, opened on 15 July 1907. Further branches from Winteringham were planned to Barton, and to Whitton, Alkborough and Burton-on-Stather. These proposals squashed L & YR proposals, although only the Whitton line was built, opening on 1 December 1910; the Barton line plan was revived in 1913 but killed by World War I. Passenger traffic to these Humberside villages was sparse, but freight traffic over the southern section was augmented by two blast furnaces at Normanby Park. This section is now used by the British Steel Corporation for its iron ore traffic.

Development at Scunthorpe has been continuous. In 1919 the five settlements became the Urban District of Scunthorpe & Frodingham, although the name Scunthorpe was not finally settled on until it became a borough in 1936 when the population was over 37,000. New steelworks were erected in 1921, and a pleasant new station in 1928 which is unusual in being virtually run by women, as the men are working in the steelworks. By 1939 Scunthorpe was producing ten per cent of the UK's total steel output, drawing ore from Northamptonshire and abroad via Immingham. These trends continued so that by 1967, with a population of 70,000, over three million tons of steel were produced (eleven per cent of UK total), which BSC want to increase by over fifty per cent by 1983. Railway investment has kept pace, for in 1958 the Scunthorpe Goods Agent handled 6½ million tons of freight. In 1963 the marshalling yards were mechanised, with further work in 1971 which included more sidings and better signalling. By 1974, 20,000 tons of iron ore were arriving daily from Immingham.

West of the Trent is the Isle of Axholme, isolated but rich agricultural marshland. The Light Railways Act 1896 enabled such areas to be opened up by railways, and two were proposed here: the Goole & Marshland Light Railway and the Isle of Axholme Light Railway. The North Eastern Railway was interested in Axholme, while the L & YR dominated Goole Docks. They co-operated in buying these two lines in 1902, when the Axholme Joint Railway was created. By then the G & MLR had opened its Goole–Reedness section on 8 January 1900 and was building the Fockerby branch, while the IALR was progressing from Reedness to Crowle and from Epworth, home of John Wesley, to Haxey Junction on the

GN/GE Joint line. On 10 August 1903 the Crowle and Fockerby sections opened to passengers, but the Crowle swing bridge delayed full opening to Haxey until 2 January 1905. A goods line to Hatfield Moor was opened in 1909, with peat as its main traffic. Passenger traffic was sparse and services were withdrawn on 17 July 1933. Goods services from Goole were progressively cut back until final closure in 1965. The line south of Crowle was retained until about 1972 to serve a proposed power station at Belton which never materialised.

NEW HOLLAND FERRY

CHAPTER XII

Railways for Work and Leisure

Railways originated to meet the needs of industry; industry then demanded specialised forms of railway. In the East Midlands in the heyday of heavy industry a wide variety of industrial railway systems was to be found but many disappeared as industry contracted. Their place has been taken by the phenomenal rise in pleasure railways. Leisure was a growth industry in the 1960s and 1970s, first as prosperity increased disposable incomes, then as recession forced up unemployment. The railways have shared in this growth, not as in pre-war years with burgeoning day excursions—BR's share of this traffic has dropped sharply as Britons have become motorists—but with a plethora of preservation schemes, dependent for survival on voluntary operating labour and free-spending trippers.

Inevitably the extractive industries had the longest private lines, and in this region the most picturesque, for with the exception of coal, much mining has been done in attractive countryside, be it for limestone in Derbyshire's High Peak, granite in Leicestershire's Charnwood Forest, ironstone on the Lincolnshire Wolds, or gravel, sand and clay in the Home Counties pastoral valleys. The last group were the least permanent, often being laid with two foot gauge 'jubilee' track, resembling the old 'Hornby' tinplate, and movable at will. The extensive conveyor belts in the Bedfordshire brick fields, or along the Nene Valley (partly on the bed of the old Northampton–Peterborough line) are a logical progression.

The ironstone tramways had perhaps the greatest variety, if only because there were so many of them; with the closure of the furnaces at Corby, in 1980 their decimation was complete except for limited activity on the northern side of Scunthorpe. Many of the lines were narrow gauge (3ft 0in was preferred), like the photogenic Kettering Furnaces system, the metre-gauge line from Wellingborough up Finedon Hill (the last narrow gauge line in the ironstone field, closing in 1966) and the largest system in the field, the ten mile one centring on Islip, outside Thrapston, which finally closed in 1952, its mining and iron production having been taken over by Corby. Standard gauge systems began to predominate after World War I and some later systems were built to main line standards, as at Harlaxton near Grantham in 1941. These modern systems, which at Buckminster (near Grantham), Exton Park (near Oakham) and Corby extended to over ten miles of main line, were victims of international competition from better ores and high transportation costs. They lasted into the 1970s, some latterly using fleets of ex-BR class 14 0–6–0 diesels.

Despite the thinning of the ranks as old pits are closed—the West Leicestershire coalfield has a limited lifespan—the National Coal Board, together with the Derbyshire limestone quarries and Leicestershire granite quarries, remain in the 1980s as the major private railway operators. On the manufacturing side, town gasworks and electricity generating stations have largely gone, while too many factories have severed their rail connections in the last decade, leaving BSC as the major operator. The ending of steel making at Corby drastically reduced its internal system there, so that the Appleby–Frodingham complex at Scunthorpe was left as the largest private railway, with some impressive workings. Smaller ones remain at the other steelworks in Derbyshire.

Not all industrial railways were conventional. Aerial ropeways existed in both the ironstone and brickfields, and one remains in use at Eye, near Peterborough. There were rope-worked inclines in the ironstone industry, the best known—and last—being at Eastwell down the scarp into the Vale of Belvoir, closed in 1960. A variation of these were the continuous cable haulage systems in the brickfields at Fletton and Ridgemont, the latter closing with the works in the mid-1970s.

While few industrial steam locomotives were built in the East Midlands, there were two major internal combustion locomotive builders, Motor Rail at Bedford and Ruston Hornsby at Lincoln. Early Motor Rail 'Simplex' petrol locomotives saw service in France in World War I; later they spread to every conceivable type of line needing sturdy light locomotives, with 2ft 0in gauge being most popular. Ruston Hornsby entered the same market and from 1932 developed flameproof diesel locomotives for use in mines. Examples from both builders can still be found at work.

A rectory garden is at first sight an unlikely location for a collection of preserved industrial locomotives, but in the early 1960s the incumbent at Cadeby, in remote West Leicestershire, gave a home to a diminutive 2ft 0in gauge 0–4–0ST from Cranford quarries in Northamptonshire. The Cadeby Light Railway developed round the Rev E. R. Boston's garden as his collection of steam and internal combustion engines grew. The public have regularly been admitted to ride the trains, usually once a month.

However, most of the British narrow gauge lines currently operating passenger services had industrial origins. As described in Chapter II the 2ft 0in gauge Leighton Buzzard Narrow Gauge Railway began life carrying sand into Leighton Buzzard, but closure of the western end came in 1969. Two years before, a local group of enthusiasts, wanting to establish an American-style narrow gauge line, tried to buy redundant materials from the line. The outcome was the establishment of the 'Iron Horse Railroad' at Pages Park, Leighton Buzzard, in 1968 with running facilities over the entire main line. The pseudo-American image was quickly dropped and from 1969 the LBNGR concentrated on restoring the track to acceptable passenger-carrying standards over nearly $1\frac{1}{4}$ miles. Over the next decade a further $1\frac{1}{2}$ miles of route was commissioned and the whole undertaking consolidated. Among the small stud of steam locomotives are a vertical-boilered veteran from a Caernarvonshire slate quarry and typical light contractors' engines. The larger diesel stud comprises units which could be seen on any quarrying or contracting under-taking in post-war years, with several being built locally by Motor Rail of Bedford.

The Whipsnade & Umfolozi Railway was built purely as a pleasure railway to take visitors at Whipsnade Zoo on Dunstable Downs safely into the broad expanses of the rhino paddock. These huge beasts tend to sit immovable on the line and ignore the trains thus providing passengers with an unforgettable ex-perience. It opened in 1970 using redundant locomotives and rolling stock from Bowaters' paper mill railway in Kent, the carriages being built on former pulp-carrying flat wagons. Although at 2ft 6in the gauge is only six inches more than that of the LBNGR, the locomotives have an altogether more massive appearance. The line was extended into a $1\frac{1}{2}$ mile circuit in 1973.

The other narrow gauge passenger railway in the region was actually built for public service; the Lincolnshire Coast Light Railway links bus terminus, holiday camps and beach on the outskirts of Cleethorpes. Even so there was an underlying 'preservation' theme as some enthusiasts looked for a site where they could run interesting steam locomotives. Much of the equipment was ex-industrial, especially from the extensive 2ft 0in gauge potato farm railways at Nocton, although some coaches came from the much earlier Ashover and Sand Hutton Light Railways. The first line opened in 1960 but in 1966 it was moved across the road and doubled in length, to almost one mile. The intensive service, mainly in charge of 'Simplex' diesels, carried some 70,000 passengers in 1967 during the four month summer season, working a thirteen hour day, seven days a week. Ageing equipment and shoe-string budgets akin to the erstwhile 'Colonel

AMBERGATE TUNNEL

Stevens Railways' gave the line, in the words of the 1970 guide-book, 'some of the raffish charm of those endearing railway byways', and it resembled the Rye & Camber Tramway. Unfortunately, nemesis caught up with it in 1980 and the Railway Inspectorate had some unkind comments to make after a youth fell out of a train and was injured. Instead of abandoning the line, the directors began a complete refurbishment, including fitting continuous brakes to engines and coaches, relaying the track and improving the signalling, ready for 1981. The next year the twenty minute daily diesel service was supplemented on Saturdays by steam trains.

In obvious contrast to the narrow gauge railways just considered, the four privately-owned standard gauge passenger lines are definitely products of the 'preservation era', which began with the reopening of the Bluebell Railway in Sussex in 1960. Early in the field was the Midland Railway Society in 1969 looking for a home for its elderly industrial well-tank. Eventually the Society moved to Shackerstone station, on the LNWR/MR Joint line from Nuneaton to Ashby. As the Shackerstone Railway Society it began assembling a collection of industrial locomotives, mainly from the Midlands, ready for running trains south to Market Bosworth and then to Shenton. Here the station lies adjacent to Leicestershire County Council's recreation centre, based on the site of the Battle of Bosworth Field (1485), and the railway's development has taken place in conjunction with the council. Although members' trains began running in 1973 over a short length of track, it was not until 1978 that public services over $2\frac{3}{4}$ miles to Market Bosworth began, while an appeal in 1982 hoped to raise enough funds for restoration of the $1\frac{1}{2}$ miles on to Shenton by 1985 in time for 500th anniversary celebrations of the battle.

Simultaneously a more glamorous and certainly more ambitious scheme was hatching nearby at Loughborough: nothing less than running large steam locomotives over a lengthy section of the Great Central route at express speeds. Steam operation had been superceded on BR and in many eyes the operation of express locomotives at low speeds over meandering branch lines was both anachronistic—for they never saw service there—and like keeping tigers in small zoo cages. It was a grand dream, especially for photographers, but reality has been more sober, not least when some of the Main Line Steam Trust's trains have been hauled by ubiquitous ex-industrial tank engines. In any case, BR relaxed their ban on steam locomotives on their tracks in 1971.

The MLST had emerged in 1968. By 1970 it was firmly based in Loughborough and had made a six figure bid for the Loughborough to Abbey Lane, Leicester, section of the former GCR, plus an option on the Loughborough to Ruddington portion, nineteen miles in all. Its first main line locomotive, *Boscastle*, arrived in 1973 for restoration; ten years later the job was only nearly completed. Meanwhile, however, other engines arrived, open days began and from the end of September 1973 it was running trains as far as Quorn & Woodhouse, using a Black Five. Unfortunately, the MLST did not own the track yet so problems arose with BR who insisted on one of their staff being on every footplate trip. The ceremonial reopening to Rothley came in September 1975, although public trains did not begin until January 1976, only for a locomotive to suffer a serious blow-back in service, injuring three on the footplate. By then BR were tired of waiting to sell the track and early that summer delivered an ultimatum that track lifting would commence within weeks. An immediate attempt to raise £350,000 capital to buy the entire line from Loughborough to Birstall succeeded in raising enough in the stipulated time to allow the single line from Loughborough to Quorn to be bought, with the Rothley section, vital for the viability of the whole enterprise, coming later, a far cry from the 1970 ambitions. Matters were not helped when, in peak season, with running already temporarily cut back to Quorn, BR lifted not just the line from Birstall but the second track from Quorn into Loughborough, obliging the MLST to suspend running entirely for three weeks. Since then, the respectability of the MLST, and of its associated company the Great Central Railway Co (1976) Ltd, has been demonstrated by the increasing number of important locomotives which it hosts, including appropriately the National Collection's ex-GCR *Butler Henderson*.

By contrast, the Nene Valley Railway has a more straightforward history, beginning again in 1968, with the acquisition of a BR Standard class 5 locomotive by a local vicar, and leading ultimately to the creation of the Peterborough Railway Society. With the locomotive stored in the British Sugar Corporation's sidings at Woodston, open days began in 1971 and the next year negotiation began with the Peterborough Development Corporation over the acquisition of part of the old line to Northampton.

MONSAL DALE

As this fitted in with the PDC's concept of a linear park and major recreational feature westwards along the Nene Valley, in 1973 the PDC bought the 6½ miles of railway track from Longville Junction to Wansford tunnel (west portal) for £61,000, and formally authorised the PRS to operate the Nene Valley Railway. Since 1974 Wansford has been the line's operational base and gradually the necessities of railway operation have been installed. While the line was being brought up to standard, from 1975 public passenger trains were allowed westwards through the tunnel towards the site of Yarwell Junction.

In order to move their stock from the British Sugar Corporation site in 1974, the PRS civil engineers had to reinstate the connection with BR at Woodston sidings, thus effectively reopening the Fletton Junction–Longville Junction line. This through connection to BR at Peterborough was used commercially early in 1976 when a freight train left Nassington (two miles beyond Yarwell Junction on a BR-owned stub) with an export order, the first of several freight operations which have made the NVR unique in standard gauge preservation circles. Since 1981 it has been used for through excursions on to the NVR, and BR DMU shuttle trains from Peterborough.

Following inquiries it was decided that the reconstruction of the line would be to the more generous Berne loading gauge in order to accommodate Continental locomotives and rolling stock. It is a treat to dine in an Italian-built Wagon-Lits restaurant car, behind a Swedish 4–6–0 while rolling through the lush English countryside on a fine summer's evening. Opening came as planned in June 1977 between Wansford and a new station at Orton Mere, just short of Longville Junction, with an intermediate station in 1978 at Ferry Meadows to serve the expanding Nene Park. Plans are being formulated to extend services back to Yarwell Junction (bought in 1977) and on the original route nearer to Peterborough.

The difficulties which some preservation schemes, especially the MLST, were experiencing in getting financially established might have deterred other ambitious schemes in the mid-1970s. Nevertheless in 1975 the Peak Railway Society was born to gauge public support for reopening the twenty mile route from Matlock to Buxton. Despite some misgivings locally and nationally the scheme readily found local backers, including industries with generous offers of materials, as the intention was to operate a daily local passenger service, with steam-hauled tourist trains in season, and a freight service as an alternative to the congested Peak District roads. Connections would be maintained with BR at either end, so a presence was quickly established in redundant station buildings at Matlock, followed by a lease of the former Midland Railway site at Buxton, and locomotives began to arrive from Barry scrapyard for restoration. In 1978 Peak Rail (Operations) Ltd was formed as the operating share company and to contol the organisation of the railway. Its first issue of £200,000 loan stock, in 1981, had encouraging initial results. The previous year, the Peak Park Planning Board, which had bought much of the trackbed passing through its area, had indicated its willingness to lease back to the Society enough land for a single track line, and during 1981 planning permission was finalised throughout the route. Reopening of a limited section was proposed after two years and throughout after five. Meanwhile from 1979 the Society had chartered regular DMU specials between Derby and Matlock on summer Sundays, and it publicly announced that it would be interested in taking over the branch should BR be obliged to close it for economic reasons.

The Steam Centre is an open-air railway museum, where the public can browse among railway relics in various stages of restoration, watch asthmatic steam locomotives trundling sedately up and down a siding and perhaps ride behind one in an elderly coach or open wagon. It is as old as the preserved branch line, but in some ways more specialist, although in practice the differences between the two can be blurred, for at some locations like Loughborough there are accumulations of rolling stock away from the running lines to wander around, and at Buxton the running lines have yet to be restored, while at Butterley the museum project envisages some three miles of operational railway.

As the BR Modernisation Plan of 1955 began to take effect, far-sighted enthusiasts realised that all interesting engines and rolling stock could not be preserved by the state museums, so the Railway Preservation Society came into being in 1958 to acquire privately items which would otherwise be lost. It split into regional groups including one for London, which ultimately in 1969 was able to settle at Quainton Road where in 1971 it became the Quainton Railway Society Ltd. The site itself is interesting as the junction of the Metropolitan and Great Central Railways and for the Brill branch (see Chapter II). Stock from BR, London Transport and industry soon filled the yards, for the QRS is also host to a multitude of individuals and sub-groups with their own items undergoing restoration.

Whereas the Quainton Railway Centre has a general appeal, the Midland Railway Centre is, as its name suggests, specific. For twenty years after the war Derby's main exhibit about the Midland Railway was the magnificent model railway in the City Museum, but in 1969 its then curator put forward a plan for a working museum illustrating the development of the Midland Railway and its successors. A group, now known as the Midland Railway Trust Ltd, was formed to oversee this tremendous project backed by Derbyshire County Council and their choice of location fell on the section of the Amergate–Pye Bridge line around Butterley. The western half to Swanwick Junction had recently closed (23 December 1968) while the eastern half was a private siding for the Butterley Company's works; there was land at Swanwick Junction for an industrial museum complex; and the whole scheme fitted in with the local planning authority's

leisure developments. Although BR had stripped the whole line
this did give the MRT unlimited scope to reconstruct as it
wished, with work commencing at Butterley late in 1973.
Progress enabled steam open days to begin in 1975 and passenger
traffic over the section from Hammersmith, through Butterley
to Swanwick Junction, in 1981; running throughout to Ironville
began the next year, when through trains from BR were also
possible. The stock list is impressive and ranges from the Kirtley
2–4–0 of 1866 to an early Peak class diesel, and includes some
magnificently restored coaches, as well as some pioneer Pullman
car bodies. 'Butterley' station actually came from Whitwell and
the first signal box from Ais Gill. As this is a long term project,
progress should be evident for many years yet, especially at the
museum complex at Swanwick Junction.

Equally specialist is the Tramway Museum at Crich, near
Cromford. As tramways began to disappear much earlier than
railways, the Tramway Museum Society is older (1955) than
the railway societies. Since 1959 its activities have centred on
the Cliff Quarry where over fifty tramcars have been assembled
from Britain and overseas, and the street tramway scene
recreated. Horse-drawn rides began in 1963, and electric

MILLER'S DALE VIADUCT

operations in 1964, over some 1,000yd of track which was extended in 1978 to one mile.

The other two railway museums in the region are much smaller concerns and both have leanings towards the once-extensive iron ore quarrying. In 1973 a group of enthusiasts in Rushden were wanting to gather, restore and operate some locally used industrial locomotives. As the Northamptonshire Ironstone Railway Trust they settled on the overgrown trackbed of the Hunsbury Hill ironworks tramway, last used in 1921 and lifted in 1940. Backing came from the Northampton Development Corporation, which was developing Hunsbury Hill as a leisure area, and Northamptonshire County Council. The first locomotive ran in 1976, with the public admitted from 1977. Track of three gauges was necessary, standard, 2ft 0in (the gauge of local quarry lines) and metre (specifically for the three locomotives from Wellingborough). An industrial museum is also to be developed.

The closure of Harlaxton quarries in 1974 brought to an end a century of ironstone mining in that area of East Leicestershire, Rutland and South West Lincolnshire, but prompted consideration of a local industrial museum. In 1979 the Market Overton Industrial Railway Association revived the idea, based on the quarry complex at Cottesmore, near Oakham, and moved stock there. As the Rutland Railway Museum it held its first open day in 1981.

Railway preservation can take unexpected forms. Retention of the Cromford & High Peak Railway, and its associated line to Ashbourne, was obviously impractical, even on a limited scale, but as the two routes had considerable historical significance and above all passed through magnificent scenery, the Peak National Park and Derbyshire County Council bought long sections of them for conversion into trails suitable for walkers, cyclists and horseriders. The 'Tissington Trail' opened first, in 1971, between Hartington and the northern edge of Ashbourne and with access also at the three intermediate stations. At the same time as the PNP had bought the High Peak Junction to Parsley Hay route from BR for £1, the two authorities were planning to open the Cromford & High Peak line as the High Peak Trail towards Buxton and Whaley Bridge.

CHAPTER XIII

Accidents

The East Midlands have been relatively free of major railway disasters. It is impractical to detail here every collision and derailment over the past 150 years, so the more significant, either because of unusual circumstances or heavy material destruction or loss of life, have been chosen, and will be described according to type rather than in chronological order.

Boiler failure was an early problem. It was foolish ignorance when an irate labourer at Wolverton works in 1850 screwed down a locomotive safety valve because the noise of escaping steam upset him; a fragment of the exploding boiler sliced off one of his ears. But at Peterborough boiler testing was known to be dangerous and was done when the GNR repair shops were quiet on Saturday afternoons. This was just as well for during the evening of 14 January 1865 the boiler of No 98 blew up, wrecking the shop and killing three men.

Two instances of component failures on goods wagons, almost a century apart, caused nasty accidents but serve also to illustrate how modern rolling stock can withstand collisions and prevent high loss of life. Late at night on 21 June 1870 an up goods train was passing under Clay Lane bridge near Newark when an axle broke on an MS & L wagon which promptly fouled the down line in the path of the returning 9.20pm excursion from London to Yorkshire. The engine, a new Stirling 0–4–2 No 58, struck the wagon, was deflected on to the pier of the bridge, and spun round. The crew and eighteen passengers were killed in the wreckage of the wooden coaches. On the afternoon of 18 April 1967 it was a spring that broke on an empty mineral wagon in a down train on the Northampton Loop near the village of Milton Malsor. Again the wagon fouled the other track, to be struck by the 2.26pm Northampton–Euston train, a new four-car electric multiple unit. Two of the coaches ploughed down the embankment into a field while a wagon finished up on the roof of the fourth, the side of which was also gouged severely. Only three people were detained in hospital out of the twelve admitted. A similar accident occurred barely two miles away in Roade cutting on 31 December 1969. Again the culprit was a broken spring on a mineral wagon and again a four-car EMU hit the wagon; this time the driver was killed.

It was an unfortunate coincidence that both the derailments at Weedon were due to maintenance errors. The loss of a taper pin by the locomotive of an up semi-fast caused the Irish Mail to be wrecked on 14 August 1915 while incorrect fitting of the bogie axleboxes of a Stanier Pacific brought disaster to its express on 21 September 1951.

Driver Brightland was working the 8.45am Birmingham–Euston with 4–4–0 No 1489. While oiling his engine during the Rugby stop he found that the split pin on the offside leading driving wheel crankpin was missing. He asked a fitter, who by chance was on the platform, for a new one. The latter, not wanting to delay the train by trekking over to the stores, knocked one off a nearby shunting engine, but unfortunately, in his haste, did not properly splay out the ends of the new pin and it soon fell out. The securing washer then unscrewed itself—though no one could subsequently explain why it had not done so on the run into Rugby—and the coupling rod came off the crankpin. This flailed about, displacing the down track and spraying ballast the length of the train, breaking every window, before bending double against the tender steps. As Brightland promptly stopped his train, just inside Stow Hill Tunnel, the down Irish Mail thundered past at 70mph drawn by Precedent 2–4–0 No 1189 and Renown class 4–4–0 No 1971. When it hit the displaced track, both locomotives remained upright but the fifteen coaches scattered to left and right with only the last six remaining on the rails. Eight passengers and two postal sorters died and thirty were injured.

As it approached this same spot at 65mph with the 8.20am Liverpool–Euston express the leading bogie of 4–6–2 No 46207, *Princess Arthur of Connaught*, became derailed, but no one noticed as the track was of flat-bottomed rail and the train sped on for $3\frac{1}{4}$ miles, through Stow Hill Tunnel. Then, however, bull-head rails were reached and the derailed bogie began to break up the chairs and track. Before the horrified gaze of some passing

Metropolitan Police officers, 46207 suddenly rolled over, and slid down a low embankment and across a ploughed field on her side. Only the last two coaches stayed on the rails, with the first eight lying smashed and spreadeagled. The immediate death toll was seven passengers and a dining car attendant, but seven more died of injuries. The bogie axleboxes had been packed too tightly in their horn guides, restricting vertical play; it was surprising that 46207 had not derailed much earlier in her journey south.

Excessive speed at the wrong place is the common theme of the next four derailments. The first was at Grantham on the night of 19 September 1906. Most GNR expresses stopped here to change engines, and to expedite working the custom was to set the points on to the Nottingham branch, which gave access to the engine sheds. The 8.45pm East Coast Mail was an exception, changing engines at Peterborough, but it still stopped and the points were still switched to the Nottingham line. The night was dark but clear. There was no customary whistle as the Mail approached the station and it thundered past the South Box at about 60mph, although apparently the brakes were applied as it passed the platform. With its short wheelbase, Ivatt large-boilered Atlantic No 276 rode the reverse curve on to the Nottingham branch, but its long wheelbase tender did not, and plunged down a high embankment, derailing 276 in the process. The first three vehicles piled up against the engine, the next six followed the tender and only the last three remained on the track undamaged. Fire broke out immediately, thanks to hot coals above and escaping gas (from the carriage lighting) below. Eleven passengers, a postal sorter and the locomotive crew died, but why the driver sped through the station, when he had stopped normally the night before, remains a mystery. The setting of the points was also criticised: overrunning stations was not unknown and at least with a straight run the train might have been safely stopped.

Drivers of new Royal Scot class engines often complained about smoke obscuring their vision. This is the probable reason why an experienced driver on the down Sunday Royal Scot on 22 March 1931 took the cross-over from fast to slow lines at the south end of Leighton Buzzard station at 50–60mph instead of the regulation 15mph. The diversion was because of permanent way work and he missed the warning signals. The locomotive, No 6114, turned over and the leading four coaches were wrecked.

The crew, a dining car steward and three passengers all died.

A similar accident occurred at Bourne End, south of Berkhamsted on 30 September 1945. The Royal Scots had been fitted with smoke deflectors by then, but somehow the driver of No 6157 missed two warning signals. He knew that he would be diverted on to the slow lines at Bourne End, because of engineering works in Watford Tunnel, but on a beautifully clear morning he ran on to the cross-over at about 60mph, three times the limit. Only then were the brakes applied but it was too late and 6157 rolled over into a field below the line dragging six coaches with it. Only the last three coaches of the fifteen-vehicle overnight Perth–Euston express were undamaged. In all forty-three people died, then or later, including the crew, making it the worst accident in this book's area, yet one of the least known.

The driver was a conscientious, experienced man, though possibly fatigued. Less so the driver of the 10.35am Manchester–Marylebone express on 7 August 1955 who also took his train into a field. Sunday permanent-way works were again involved with wrong-line running. As a late alteration the up line was to be regained at Barby, just south of Rugby, but the driver failed to see this on the Late Notices, nor did his guard, while the signalman-pilotman failed to give proper instructions. The result was predictable: V2 2–6–2 No 60828 failed to negotiate the 10mph cross-over at 55mph and fell fifteen feet down an embankment followed by six of the ten coaches. However, the difference from Bourne End was that the rolling stock was mainly built of steel and with modern buck-eye couplings, so the casualty list was minimal—a score injured and only the driver killed.

By nature railway accidents are destructive but one in particular stands out; mercifully the four trains involved were all freight or the death toll would have been terrible. At about 11pm on 13 March 1935 the 4.35pm express freight, containing beef, from Canada Dock, Liverpool, to Broad Street was restarting after attention to brakes when it was run into near Kings Langley by the 5.30pm Stafford–Euston milk, headed by a Midland 4–4–0. Milk was cascading down the embankment when the 10.30pm Camden–Holyhead mixed freight, behind Patriot 4–6–0 No 5511, and the 12.25pm Toton–Willesden coal both ran into the wreckage. Only prompt action by the coal train fireman stopped the 10.55pm Euston–Aberdeen sleeper from adding to the pile. The cost of the wreckage reached over

£100,000. The milk train driver was killed while trying to halt the other trains.

Shunting movements were the scene of some accidents. At Sharnbrook in the early morning of 4 February 1909 a down fast goods for Birmingham behind 0–6–0 No 3698 was being diverted from down slow to down fast between the passage of up fast trains. In his haste the signalman pulled the wrong lever and diverted it along the up fast. The driver immediately realised the error but before he could do much his train was violently struck head-on by the Manchester–Somers Town fast goods behind 0–6–0 No 388, travelling down the bank at 60mph. In the destruction the Manchester crew were killed.

At Oakley Junction, some four miles south, a long up empty coaching stock train behind Crab 2–6–0 No 2893 was being shunted on to the Northampton branch on 21 January 1938 when it was rammed head-on by a London–Bradford express behind Jubilee 4–6–0 No 5568. Complex signalling technicalities had diverted the express on to the branch, and although the driver braked heavily his train was still doing 60mph at the impact and the two leading coaches in each train overturned. One man was killed, with seven seriously injured.

More destructive was the collision in Bletchley station on the evening of 13 October 1939. An ex-LNWR 0–8–0 was shunting a van on to the rear of the 7.37pm advanced portion of the Scotch express when it was run into at high speed by the Euston–Stranraer express double headed by Class 5 No 5025 and Royal Scot No 6130. Many passengers were taking refreshments in the buffet when they saw their train begin to move during the shunting. Thinking it was leaving, they rushed out. At that moment the collision occurred and the 0–8–0's tender demolished the buffet, killing its remaining occupant, an airman. The serving girls leapt to safety, although one was scalded by her tea-urn. The last three vans of the Scotch express were demolished, killing a postman, a porter and the shunting engine's driver; the buffet, waiting room and platform awning were wrecked, injuring thirty-two passengers and eight railwaymen. No 5025's driver had missed his signals in the blackout but at his subsequent trial at Aylesbury Assizes the jury dismissed the manslaughter charge without even hearing the defence.

Safety on the railway depends upon the user as well as the staff; momentary carelessness by a postman at Wellingborough brought disaster on 2 September 1898. As he was unlocking a rate his heavy barrow rolled backwards across the platform and tipped on to the track in the path of the down evening Manchester express. While the postman and a stationman frantically tried to push it clear, others grabbed lamps to stop the express but without success. The locomotive—4-4-0 No 1743—demolished the barrow, which derailed the leading bogie while woodwork rained down on the platform. A diamond crossing beyond the station completed the derailment and 1743, its tender and the train all parted company, the former turning round to smash the following coaches. The second vehicle, a packed second class twelve-wheeler, disintegrated against the cutting side and caught fire. Five passengers and 1743's crew died immediately or later.

In conclusion, two accidents occurred along the GNR main line within five months, and affected future junction layouts. On 23 August 1873 an overnight fish train from Scotland overran signals in Retford station because of inadequate braking on the engine. At 10mph it struck the sixth carriage of an MS & L works excursion from Deepcar to Cleethorpes which was on the flat crossing, running under clear signals. The coach was destroyed, as was the signal box, and three passengers were killed. Better GNR signalling and diversion of the MS & L line were recommended; the GNR opted for the former but would not pay for the latter, nor would the MS & L, so the flat crossing stayed until 1965. Then on 10 January 1874 the 6.00pm from Boston overran signals at Barkston where the branch met the main line north of Grantham. The branch train fouled the path of an up Scotch express, the engine of which struck the local's coaches and then grazed the wagons of a passing down goods. The express's driver was scalded when he went to rescue his fireman, who was killed, along with a passenger; nine other passengers and a guard were injured. As a result, the new line being planned from the Nottingham line was diverted to pass under the GNR main line north of Barkston station, before joining the Boston line (see page 126).

CHAPTER XIV

Postscript: A High-Speed Future?

'This is the Age of the Train.' The message has come across repeatedly in an aggressively varied marketing campaign. Behind it is the lure of faster and often more frequent services, typified by the instantly-recognisable HST (or '125'). BR's new image is succeeding; the average passenger who cannot distinguish between a Peak or a Class 47, and frankly does not wish to, can readily identify a High Speed Train and on the whole likes it.

The electrification of the West Coast Main Line to Lancashire in the 1960s demonstrated that fast overall journey times brought a good commercial return. In the intervening decade and a half BR has developed ambitious plans for further electrification including the East Coast Main Line to Leeds and Newcastle, the North East–South West route from Leeds and Sheffield to Birmingham and Bristol, and the former Midland line from London to Derby, Nottingham and Sheffield. However, apathy from the Callaghan government and hostility from the Thatcher administration has left these ambitions as far away as ever. The only tangible results affecting this book's region have been the controversial 'Bedpan' electrification and the compromise solution represented by the introduction of HSTs.

The High Speed Train is ubiquitous in the East Midlands. For over a generation express running on the ECML was synonymous with the Gresley Pacifics. Their place was taken by the Deltic diesels which quickly became as admired, but from May 1978 the HSTs began to displace them, so that by the early 1980s it became rare to see locomotive-hauled passenger trains on regular daytime services. Even after the first two months of operation ER management was crediting HSTs with raising patronage by ten per cent. Their next move was to the 'Heart Line', the brand name given to the lengthy NE–SW services over the old North Midland Railway, from October 1981. Having tasted these services, and seeing its eastern neighbours enjoying faster trains to London, Sheffield wanted them too. Certainly the Peaks, the workhorses of the Midland line since 1960, were feeling their age and no longer represented 'The Age of the Train'. At first BR hesitated, as the curved alignment and switchback nature of the Midland route was not conducive to the full HST potential shown on the straighter, flatter ECML (the ill-fated APT would have been ideally suited). However, the completion of the building programme, relative decline in passenger loadings on the WR, and careful diagramming enabled six sets to be transferred to the Midland in October 1982. More sets arrived in May 1983 to cover virtually all the Inter-City services. Passenger loadings increased dramatically; at Leicester, journeys rose by thirty-eight per cent between January and April 1983 over the same period in 1981.

Commuting from Kettering and Wellingborough was boosted —with serious overcrowding—as journey times at 45–50 minutes compared favourably with those from the more traditional commuter towns like Farnham and Dorking, as did the vastly cheaper houses. Management and passengers alike hoped that the trains would stand up to the necessarily intensive use, for the hot July of 1983 brought a spate of equipment failures.

The smart HST trains stood in stark contrast to the elderly DMUs which rattled their way between St Pancras and Bedford, the more so as the expensive replacement electric trains were still standing idle and rusting on sidings at Nottingham and Cricklewood. The Midland Electrification—or 'Bedpan'— scheme originated in the early 1970s as the poor state of DMUs and the arrears of permanent-way maintenance and simplification meant that the St Pancras to Bedford suburban lines and services had to be renewed, although authorisation did not come until 1976.

The scheme envisaged colour-light signalling over 70 route miles from St Pancras and Moorgate to Sharnbrook (270 track miles) and electrification at 25kV as far as Bedford, 53 route miles (225 track miles) including the sparsely used route to Moorgate which would become the inner suburban terminus. Some twenty-nine manual signal boxes would be replaced by a new power box at West Hampstead. (Subsequently, Irchester South became the fringe box, and in 1983 the next power box, Leicester, was authorised.) As well as track rationalisation, a new platform was added at Luton, Radlett station was rebuilt, and a completely new station was built at Bedford just north of the existing Midland Road one and on a new alignment; it was opened in October 1978 by the BR Chairman, Sir Peter Parker.

Work began in the autumn of 1976 and ran to schedule, with opening planned for 1982. However, a protracted union dispute over single manning of the new trains prevented this (and helped cause a major rail strike in July 1982), so it was not until 28 March 1983 that Sir Peter could welcome the first electric train at St Pancras. Thereafter more of the forty-eight units came into use, including to Moorgate from 11 July, until a full electric timetable could be introduced in the October. The original estimated cost was £78.5 million, and the final cost £153.5 million, which was largely accounted for by the heavy inflation of the period. At 1982 prices, this was roughly broken down as electrification £30.5 million, trackwork £33 million, resignalling £24 million, rolling stock £47 million, the Cricklewood depot and sidings £11 million, the interchange with London Transport at King's Cross £6 million, and other items £1 million. Things had changed since Ellis and Brassey built the Leicester & Hitchin Railway: they had just £1 million; it cost that to build the new Bedford Midland station!

Lincoln and South Humberside also joined the HST system in October 1982 when a return working to London was laid on, leaving Cleethorpes in the early morning and returning in the evening. Lincolnshire and Humberside County Councils had each contributed towards the costs of overnight stabling of the train at Cleethorpes. For the previous twelve months this had been the only through train to London as ER reckoned that a quicker journey was given by running a DMU to Newark to connect into an HST for London. That these arrangements were not well received was shown by the reinstatement of locomotive-hauled trains on the Cleethorpes–Newark service.

By far the most important event on Humberside was the opening of the long-awaited Humber Bridge by HM the Queen on 17 July 1981, linking Barton-on-Humber and Hessle, some five miles west of Hull. Work began in 1971 with an estimated completion date of 1976 and an estimated (1972) cost of £28 million. Both lengthened out, to double the time and treble the cost (£88 million). Additionally, £200 million was freely spent on the road system in the area, which makes an unfavourable comparison with the decade of hesitation over further main line electrification. The debt charges on the bridge are being quietly overlooked in the hope that after sixty years it will have paid for itself. Much has been written about the way the bridge will unite the two banks of the artificial county of Humberside and revive a flagging economy there. It is regrettable that the local railways do not figure prominently here. Indeed, originally it was assumed that the New Holland and Barton branches would close but instead an hourly integrated rail–bus service was provided, the interchange taking place in Barton station yard. The Barton branch closed temporarily to passengers on 1 June 1981 and reopened at lunchtime on 24 June when the New Holland Pier trains were finally diverted to Barton and the Hull bus service began, the bridge admitting its first public traffic at that time. Simultaneously the branch through New ·Holland Town to New Holland Pier was closed (few branches have closed during a day) and a new New Holland station opened nearer the village. The last paddle steamer, *Farringford*, plied her trade for the rest of the day, with many well-wishers, and the pier and ferry service were officially closed and withdrawn on 25 June.

Some other passenger developments must be noted. As foreshadowed on page 167 the proposals for developing commuter traffic on the Matlock to Derby line resulted in extending trains into the Sinfin industrial estate, utilising part of the old Melbourne line. This was still in use serving private sidings at Sinfin, although beyond it had been closed totally on 31 December 1973. Haggling between BR and the local authorities over who met the cost and operating deficit delayed opening until 4 October 1976. Peartree station (closed 4 March 1968) was reopened and two new basic stations were built at Sinfin North and Sinfin Central. Within three months it was realised that the traffic was below expectation and the service of seven southbound and ten northbound trains was drastically reduced in 1978 to two and four respectively. Even that has been reduced to three northbound, and the branch's future is (1983) uncertain.

Equally uncertain is the Bletchley to Bedford branch, despite an energetic Users Association who vigorously promote the services. Bedford St Johns station became a disgrace, without even a seat, but in mid-1983 came the news that at last the trains were to be diverted into Bedford Midland and St Johns closed in May 1984, which should stimulate patronage, especially as Milton Keynes Central Station opened on 17 May 1982 close to the huge shopping complex. Also in mid-1983 came the announcement that in 1984 London Transport was to take over the BR services from Marylebone to Harrow and Aylesbury, transferring them to Baker Street, with Marylebone station being sold for redevelopment. Less fortunate was the GN & GE Joint line from Spalding to March which closed completely on 29 November 1982 after some delays, all remaining traffic being diverted via Peterborough. In Lincoln the avoiding line was due to close in October 1983 to allow construction of a new link between the Nottingham and Doncaster lines west of the city. This would concentrate all traffic on Central station, allowing St Marks and its busy level crossing to be closed in 1984.

On the freight side, the recession from the late 1970s hit hard at the steel and coal industries; the onward march of the lorry—coupled with the cessation of collected and delivered parcels traffic in 1981—has removed further trade, although in places the new 'Speedlink' services are proving competitive; while pipelines are eroding the oil and cement traffic. As an example, Wellingborough was one of the main freight centres on the Midland. The loss of the ironstone traffic has been recorded (page 74); in the five years up to 1982 rail traffic was lost from an oil terminal, two mills and a factory, together with the ferrersand (iron concentrate) traffic (page 77). This had come in the 1970s but was a victim of the recession. The mills found it easier to bring in grain from the EEC and Russia by lorry. No freight originates from Wellingborough now; it used to pay all the wages.

The fortunes of the steel industry have been varied following the reorganisation of BSC in 1973. Part of the BR branch from Belvoir Junction to Denton was briefly reopened in 1976, after two years' disuse, for transporting ironstone from a new face at Harlaxton to Etruria and Shotton, but the recession killed this. That year too, rail services to Grimsby Docks were to be severed but were reprieved thanks to an upsurge in traffic, especially imported steel. From 1980 steel and other traffic was to be handled at a major new Railfreight Terminal at Stallingborough near Immingham. The closure of Corby furnaces meant that steel coil for tube making had to be railed in from Lackenby on Teesside; the 750,000th tonne of this traffic was received at Corby in September 1982 after only eighteen months.

The greater stress on coal rather than oil or nuclear fuels for generating electricity, especially in the strings of power stations along the big rivers flowing towards the Humber, has encouraged the major new development in this region : the exploitation of the Belvoir coalfield of East Leicestershire which will gradually supersede the old West Leicestershire pits. To serve the three projected mines, it would be necessary to rebuild part of the GN & LNWR Joint line from Hose to Bottesford West Junction, put in a connection near Asfordby Tunnel on the Edwalton test track and build a new five mile branch from Saltby to Saxby. Despite a bitter campaign by environmentalists, outline authority has been granted although mining will not begin until the coal is needed later in the decade. Meanwhile more of the big power stations have been adapted to enable merry-go-round unloading.

The block company train has become an important feature of the freight scene, developing from the Freightliner. By 1976 London Brick at Stewartby had dispatched its 1,000th block train to its terminals in London, Manchester and Liverpool. Aggregate traffic has developed strongly; from 1978 Redland were sending block trains from Barrow-upon-Soar (railhead for its Mountsorrel quarries) to various destinations including Radlett; while ARC has developed an important granite terminal at Loughborough. Tarmac have their trains running from Cliffe Hill near Coalville. A new traffic is condensed household rubbish running in custom-built wagons from terminals in London to Stewartby (1,000 tonnes daily from 1978) and Calvert (4,000 tonnes per week from 1981) where it is used to fill old brick pits.

In 1983, as this book was being revised, the Serpell Report on Railway Finances appeared from its government-appointed committee. It discussed six options ranging from cutting the BR network to a supposedly 'profitable' 1,600 miles to maintaining the present system, investing £4,000 million and meeting a claimed annual loss of £803 million, but its general effect was depressing. As the *Railway Magazine* said in an editorial : 'None of the "options" seems to show any consideration for passengers or freight customers.' It has created an atmosphere of uncertainty for the future of the railways, which the result of the June General Election merely compounded. The Beeching cuts two decades earlier have been criticised as misguided in outlook and excessive in scope, but has the lesson been learned? This book is a history, not an almanac; we can but await events.

Bibliography

This bibliography is only a guide to the reader who wishes to delve further into particular aspects of the region's railway history; it cannot be exhaustive.

Among primary sources available in local collections I have found the following useful: railway prospectuses, Acts of Parliament, directors' reports, broadsheets supporting or opposing schemes, newspaper reports of schemes, openings etc, contemporary travellers' companions such as Osborne's *London & Birmingham Railway Guide (1838)*, railway handbills and closure proposals.

The East Midlands has not been well covered by railway literature. The following works are useful.

Victorian histories:

Ackworth, W. M. *Railways of England* (1889)

Grinling, C. H. *History of the Great Northern Railway* (1898, reprinted 1966)

Stretton, C. E. *History of the Midland Railway* (c 1905)

Williams, F. S. *Our Iron Roads* (1884 edn)

—— *The Midland Railway* (1876, reprinted Newton Abbot 1968)

Wishaw, F. *Railways of Great Britain and Ireland* (1842, reprinted Newton Abbot 1970)

Modern histories:

Allen, C. J. *The London & North Eastern Railway* (Shepperton 1966)

Anderson, P. H. *Forgotten Railways: The East Midlands* (Newton Abbot 1973)

Barnes, E. G. *The Rise of the Midland Railway 1844–7* (1966)

—— *The Midland Main line 1875–1922* (1969)

Baxter, B. *Stone Blocks and Iron Rails* (Newton Abbot 1966

Casserley, H. C. & Dorman, C. C. *Railway History i Pictures: The Midlands* (Newton Abbot 1969)

Coleman, T. *The Railway Navvies* (1965)

Dow, G. *Great Central (3 Vols)* (Shepperton 1959–65)

Hadfield, C. *The Canals of the East Midlands* (Newton Abbc 1966)

Perkin, H. *The Age of the Railway* (1970)

Radford, J. B. *Derby Works and Midland Locomotives* (Shep perton 1971)

Robbins, M. *The Railway Age* (1962)

Rolt, L. T. C. *George and Robert Stephenson* (1960)

Simmons, J. *The Railways of Britain* (1961)

The Times. London Midland & Scottish Railway Centenar 1938

Tonks, E. S. *The Ironstone Railways and Tramways of th Midlands* (1959)

Walker, C. *Thomas Brassey, Railway Builder* (1969)

Local and industrial histories:

Abell, E. & Chambers, J. *The Story of Lincoln* (Lincoln 1969

Bell, G. *The Railway as a Factor in the Location of Man facturing Industry in the East Midlands* (University Nottingham unpublished thesis)

Carr, J. & Taplin W. *A History of the British Steel Industr* (Oxford 1962)

Church, R. *Economic and Social Change in a Midland Town Victorian Nottingham 1815–1900* (1966)

Dyer, J., Stygall, F. & Dory, J. *The Story of Luton* (Luto 1964)

Godber, J. *History of Bedfordshire* (Bedford 1969)

Ireson, T. *Northamptonshire* (1950)

Johnson, W. *Hertfordshire* (1970)

Kime, W. *Skeggy! The Story of an East Coast Town* (Skegnes 1969)

Official Guide to Grimsby

Pye, N. (*ed*) *Leicester and its Region* (Leicester 1972)

Palmer, J. & M. *Wellingborough* (Wellingborough 1972)

Rogers, A. *A History of Lincolnshire* (1970)

—— *The Making of Stamford* (Leicester 1965)

Scopes, Sir F. *The Development of Corby Works* (1968)

Victorian County Histories of Derbyshire, Leicestershire, Lincolnshire, Nottinghamshire

Monographs and articles:

The following journals are invaluable as sources of articles and notes: *Modern Railways, Northamptonshire Past and Present, Railway & Canal Historical Society Journal, Railway Magazine, The Railway Observer, Railway World, Stephenson Locomotive Society Journal, Trains Illustrated, Transport History*

Abbot, R. *The Railways of the Leicester Navigation Company* (Leicester 1955)

Birks, J. & Coxon, P. *An Account of Railway Development in The Nottinghamshire Coalfield* (Mansfield 1949)

Cupit, J. & Taylor, W. *The Lancashire, Derbyshire & East Coast Railway* (Lingfield 1966)

Dunn, J. *The Stratford-upon-Avon & Midland Junction Railway* (Lingfield 1952)

Franks, D. *The Stamford & Essendine Railway* (Leeds 1971)

—— *The GN & LNWR Joint Railway* (Leeds 1973)

Hatley, V. A. *Northampton Revindicated. (Northamptonshire Past and Present 1959)*

—— *The Blisworth Hill Railway* (Northampton 1962)

Howe, E. *Coal, Art and the Beaumonts. (History Today* April 1974)

Leleux, S. *The Leighton Buzzard Light Railway* (Lingfield 1969)

Markham, C. *The Iron Roads of Northamptonshire* (Northampton 1904)

Mather, F. *The Railways, the Electric Telegraph and Public Order during the Chartist Period, 1837–48 (History* February 1953)

Pearson, R. *Railways in Relation to Resort Development in East Lincolnshire. (East Midlands Geographer* June 1968)

Ripley, D. *The Little Eaton Gangway* (Lingfield 1973)

Usherwood, S. *Travel Agents Extraordinary. (History Today* September 1972)

Wake, J. *Northampton Vindicated* (Northampton 1935)

Miscellaneous
Bradshaw's 1910 Railway Guide (reprinted Newton Abbot
1968)
Railway Clearing House. *Handbook to Railway Stations 1904*
(reprinted Newton Abbot 1970)
—— *Railway Junction Diagrams 1915* (reprinted Newton
Abbot 1969)

ADDITIONS TO BIBLIOGRAPHY

Baker, S. K. *Rail Atlas of Britain* (Oxford 1980)
British Rail Pre-grouping Atlas and Gazetteer (Shepperton
1976)
Clinker, C. R. *Clinker's Register of Closed Passenger Stations
and Goods Depots in England, Scotland and Wales* 1830–
1977 (Bristol 1978)
Daniels, G. & Dench, L. A. *Passengers No More* (Shepperton
1973)
Hill, N. J. & McDougall, A. O. *A Guide to Closed Railway
Lines in Britain* 1948–1975 (Branch Line Society 1977)

Recent works
Aland, H. *Recollections of Country Station Life* (Blaby 1980)
Cockman, F. G. *The Railway Age in Bedfordshire* (Bedford
1974)
Davies, R. & Grant, M. D. *Forgotten Railways: Chilterns and
Cotswolds* (Newton Abbot, new edn 1984)
Grigg, A. E. *Country Railwayman* (Buckingham 1982)
—— *In Railway Service: The History of Bletchley Branch
of the National Union of Railwaymen* (Bletchley c 1974)
—— *Town of Trains: Bletchley and the Oxbridge Line*
(Buckingham 1980)
Hewlett, H. B. *The Quarries* (reprinted Oakham 1979)
Jordan, A. *The Stratford-upon-Avon and Midland Junction
Railway* (Oxford 1982)
Lambert, A. J. *East Midlands Branch Line Album* (Shepperton 1978)
Riden, P. *The Butterley Company* 1790–1830 (Chesterfield
1973)
Ruddock, J. G. & Pearson, R. E. *The Railway History of
Lincoln* (Lincoln 1974)

Simpson, B. *The Banbury to Verney Junction Branch* (Oxford 1978)

—— *Oxford to Cambridge Railway* (2 *Vols*) (Oxford 1981–3)

Wright, N. R. *The Railways of Boston: their Origins and Development* (Boston 1971)

Acknowledgements

Many people have given me assistance during the preparation of this book. Among them are the staffs of the libraries, museums and record offices at Derby, Grimsby, Leicester, Lincoln, Luton, Northampton and Nottingham; also officers from British Railways, the British Steel Corporation, Central Electricity Generating Board, Fisons and ICI; named or unnamed, I thank them all. I must also thank Geoffrey Webb for his comments on parts of the text, my early typists, Allan Patmore for his most constructive comments while editing each chapter, and above all, Rita, my wife, not just for typing the later chapters, but for putting up with the whole project for so long.

WELLINGBOROUGH,
NORTHAMPTONSHIRE. 1974

Index

Page references in italic face numerals denote illustrations and maps.